Donna Florio

Growing Up Bank Street

A Greenwich Village Memoir

WASHINGTON MEWS BOOKS
An Imprint of New York University Press
New York
www.nyupress.org

Book designed and typeset by Charles B. Hames

References to Internet websites (URLs) were accurate at the time of writing. Neither the author nor New York University Press is responsible for URLs that may have expired or changed since the manuscript was prepared.

Some names have been changed to protect the privacy of individuals.

Cataloging in Publication data is available from the publisher
Cloth ISBN: 9781479803200
Consumer ebook ISBN: 9781479803231
Library ebook ISBN: 9781479803224

New York University Press books are printed on acid-free paper, and their binding materials are chosen for strength and durability. We strive to use environmentally responsible suppliers and materials to the greatest extent possible in publishing our books.

Manufactured in the United States of America

10 9 8 7 6 5 4 3 2 1

Also available as an ebook

This book is dedicated to the neighbors

on every Bank Street in the world

who open their hearts to each other.

Contents

Foreword by Constance Rosenblum VIII

MY BANK STREET

1. Six Blocks of America 3

2. Opera on Bank Street 18

MY BUILDING

3. The Frydels 35

4. Mr.Bendtsen 40

5. Mrs. Swanson and the Browders 45

6. John Lavery 54

7. Grace Bickers 56

8. Lena 61

9. Sabine 70

10. Sid Vicious 80

ARTISTIC BANK STREET

11. John, Yoko, Rex, and Many More 91

12. Al 98

13. John Kemmerer 108

14. George and Gloria 122

STYLISH AND SPLENDID BANK STREET

15. Jack Heineman Jr. 127

16. Jack and Madeline Gilford 134

17. Auntie Mame: Marion Tanner 139

18. Bella Abzug 149

SECRET BANK STREET

19. The Jester, the Bishop, and the Eavesdropper 159

20. Stella Crater 163

21. Yeffe Kimball 170

THE HEART OF BANK STREET

22. Billy Joyce 181

23. Marty, Roz, and Marty's Harem 190

24. The Many Kinds of Friendships 196

Epilogue 203
Acknowledgments 205
Works Consulted 209
Index 213
About the Author 225
Illustrations follow page 123

Foreword

Constance Rosenblum

When we think of the modern American city, at least these days, we typically think of a cold and soulless place, one defined by gleaming towers inhabited by people with unfathomable amounts of money. And these structures can be found not just in the United States. They are quickly transforming the skylines of iconic urban centers such as London and are sprouting like the proverbial weeds throughout Asia—in cities like Dubai, Shanghai, Seoul, and Beijing, home of some of the world's tallest buildings.

Cities defined by these towers are increasingly becoming the norm, both here and around the world. But there once existed a different kind of city, at least in America, one characterized by low or at least not-so-mammoth residential buildings, along with intimate and often idiosyncratic shops and businesses. Perhaps most important, this city was populated by neighbors who weren't necessarily your best friends but were nonetheless people with whom you could exchange a friendly wave or a little chitchat on a doorstep.

This is the city beloved by the sainted urbanist Jane Jacobs. Its contours can still be found in a few places, such as Brooklyn Heights, a landmarked neighborhood of brownstones overlooking the spectacular Lower Manhattan skyline. And one of its most powerful expressions is the exquisite, intimate Bank Street, a six-block strip in Manhattan's Greenwich Village defined by historic townhouses and adorned with trees and cobblestones. Perhaps most important, Bank Street had an intimacy that made it possible to have acquaintances and even friends in nearly every nook and cranny. This is the world that Donna Florio brings to life in this book.

Donna grew up on Bank Street and has lived there for more than half a century. For much of that time she has been amassing memories, in the form of conversations, oral histories, and deep dives into libraries and other places of research, in an effort to chart and capture the heartbeat of this remarkable place.

I first met Donna in 2014, when I interviewed her in connection with an article that was published in the Real Estate section of *The New York Times*. Over the past few years I've watched her book take shape and grow to its present form, an endearing portrait of a singular place, peopled by a captivating and sometimes heartbreaking assortment of characters, nearly all of whom helped Donna become the person she is today.

Even more important, the book is a reminder of the way cities used to be, a reminder of the closeness and camaraderie they used to offer, the spiritual nourishment they used to provide. This is not to romanticize the city of the past. Even the best of them suffered from a depressing assortment of urban ills—crime, poverty, and dysfunction, just to name a few. But despite their limitations there is a reason they have proved so attractive over the centuries: they fulfill basic human needs.

In many respects, *Growing Up Bank Street* is a portrait of a lost world—"my lost city," as F. Scott Fitzgerald described the golden metropolis that existed before the Great Crash of 1929 turned so much to dust. In that respect the book is a moving reminder of what has been lost and can never be found again. At the same time, it's a vivid, often hilarious, sometimes heartbreaking, but always beautifully rendered portrait of an unforgettable place at unforgettable times in its history.

This is not to say that Bank Street has remained untouched by market and social forces over the years. Apartments that when Donna was growing up were affordable even for fledgling writers and artists now can be had only for sky-high sums. At the rate things are going, we won't see its like again. But thanks to Donna's lapidary re-creation, we can lift the curtain that divides us from the past and briefly revisit a memorable place at a memorable moment in its history.

My Bank Street

1 • Six Blocks of America

Mosquitoes and Alexander Hamilton's bank started the whole thing.

A lady scrambles across her muddy lane as wagonloads of panicked colonists from downtown crash by. She glares at the new Bank of New York mansion, an unwanted intruder in the peaceful woods of her sleepy 1798 Greenwich Village. That bank started it, she huffs. They want to escape their yellow fever quarantine, and now we have all the dirty downtowners moving here, bringing the disease to us.

A 1920s scientist strides towards his laboratory near the Hudson River, seeing nothing around him, his mind on his new idea for talking pictures. He passes John Dos Passos, sitting on the steps of his boardinghouse at 11 Bank Street. Dos Passos's new novel, *Manhattan Transfer*, is attracting attention. Young socialite Marion Tanner, decades from stardom as Auntie Mame, hurries to the bootlegger across the street. She needs gin for the salons she holds in her elegant new brownstone.

In the 1930s, everyone broke because of the Great Depression, the poet Langston Hughes climbs the steps to his 23 Bank Street illustrator's studio carrying his latest work. A block down, young John Kemmerer, an aspiring writer from Iowa, admires the pear trees and cityscape from the roof of his new building at 63 Bank Street. Three stories below John, the Swansons practice the tango for their vaudeville act at the Paramount Theater. Above the Swansons, Alice Zecher, newly arrived from California, winks at herself as she applies a bit of rouge for a job interview. Her plan is to be a secretary by day and a Village bohemian by night.

In 1942, a leader of the American Communist Party climbs the steps to his place at 63 Bank as FBI agents eye him from the Swansons' windows.

In the 1950s, Tish Touchette, a female impersonator with a popular nightclub act, hangs his sequined gowns in his new place at 51

Bank and takes his poodle for a walk. He passes the actor Jack Gilford from number 75. Jack, blacklisted by the House Un-American Activities Committee, the government agency that implemented the Red Scare tactics of Senator Joseph McCarthy, is desperate to line up a job—any job.

In the 1970s, when John Lennon and Yoko Ono don't respond to their knocks, FBI agents push deportation orders under the door of their 105 Bank Street home. Photographers shove one other aside seeking shots of the corpse of Sid Vicious, the Sex Pistols bassist, who is being carried away after his overdose at 63 Bank Street.

Today, young transplants from California living in Sid's former apartment pump their fists and high-five as their dream of establishing a taco stand in Chelsea Market comes true. Tish, now an elderly fixture on Bank Street, holds court on his stoop, talking about the 1969 Stonewall Inn uprising on nearby Christopher Street, the night that gay New Yorkers first fought for the right to socialize like anyone else. Down the street, film producer Harvey Weinstein, reputation and career in ruins, pushes through reporters on his townhouse steps.

That's how I see Bank Street, my home in Manhattan's Greenwich Village, and its people. I was born here, arriving from the hospital in 1955 to 63 Bank Street, apartment 2B, next door to Mrs. Swanson, the vaudeville dancer. My small apartment has about 325 square feet. The layout resembles a barbell; bedroom on one end, living room on the other, with a narrow hallway in the middle. The front door opens onto the hall, off of which is a shallow coat closet, a galley kitchen, and a bathroom. The kitchen and bathroom each have a window, both facing the wall of a dark, shallow alley. The apartment doors are solid old wood with raised panels and brass keyhole locks. The living room has three windows, one facing the alley. The other two face Bank Street. One front window opens onto an iron fire escape, which has done duty as a drying rack, an herb garden, a place to set parakeet cages in the sun, and storage for party beer.

Walking back, away from Bank Street, you reach the bedroom. One bedroom window faces the end of the alley. Another looks out at a small carriage house and garden nestled behind the brownstone next door. The bedroom has a walk-in closet with an incongruous, fancy old window of its own. As a baby in a crib, I shared the bedroom with my parents. I threw toys at them when I was ready to be entertained, hastening their decision to give the bedroom to me, like many Village parents of the era, and sleep on a pull-out couch in the living room.

. . .

Elderly neighbors sat with my parents in shabby little Abingdon Square Park around the corner as I toddled in the sandbox. Some, like the journalist who had played chess with Mark Twain, had lived here since the early 1900s. The Bank Street of their youth had cast-iron gaslights and a stately band shell with marble columns. Icemen hawked thick blocks of ice coated in straw. Milk wagons rumbled over the cobblestones at dawn. Peddlers jingled bells as they wheeled hand-carts loaded with fruits and vegetables or offered to buy rags and scrap metal. Horse-drawn trolleys lurched along bustling West Fourth Street. Hand trucks with whetstones clanged, the owners seeking knives and scissors to sharpen. Street musicians performed under windows, hoping for coins tossed down by kind-hearted listeners.

As kids, some of those neighbors watched trees chopped down as 63 Bank, the only building ever to stand on this lot, went up in 1889, providing yet more cheap housing for the immigrants that were flooding turn-of-the-century New York.

Cheap or not, 63 Bank Street, five stories high and with three apartments per floor, had been built with a bit of style. Stubby marble columns rising above lion heads and wrought-iron fencing adorn the entrance while whimsical angels grin beneath the two front windows. Two painted wood doors with panes of beveled glass, flanked by lamps, open to the hallway as a gargoyle glares down from the ceiling. Small, festively patterned red, green, and orange tiles cover the floors. At the end of the front hall, a cast-iron stairwell with smooth wood banisters and gray marble steps leads upstairs, past hall windows that overlook the little garden next door.

A rope-and-pulley dumbwaiter once opened on each hall landing, making it possible to haul coal from the basement for heat braziers and cooking stoves. Rickety wooden steps led down to the basement from the back of the first floor hallway and, on the fifth floor, up to the roof. Cast-iron steps below the stone entrance still lead past the brick coal chute embedded in the sidewalk to the exterior door of the basement, a low-ceilinged maze with cast-iron pipes and wires overhead. In the back of the basement, a heavy metal door leads to a tiny cement backyard and side alley. Fire escapes run down the front and back of the building.

Inside our apartment, in 1889, privacy was nonexistent. Archways led from one dark, narrow room to another, arranged shotgun style. The kitchen, with its heavy cast-iron coal stove, sat at the back end. A privy toilet, off the kitchen, had an incongruously fancy window. Near one front window, a shallow brick alcove held a coal brazier for heat.

The 1920 census for 63 Bank Street reported a mix of Irish, Italian, Puerto Rican, and German tenants. They were shirt pressers, dockworkers, machinists, market workers, saleswomen, bank note printers, mailmen, and factory workers. Virtually everyone over eighteen went to work.

The Italian American family that bought the building in 1925 and still owns it upgraded the place in 1937. Cast-iron steam radiators replaced the coal braziers, and the shallow alcoves that held the braziers were cemented and plastered over. The kitchen of 2B became a bedroom and the privy toilet became the bedroom closet, fancy window and all. A galley kitchen with a gas stove, a ceramic double sink, and a wall of wood cabinets went into the middle of the apartment next to a new private bathroom, complete with "flushometer" and bathtub.

The improvements attracted college-educated John Kemmerer and artists like Mrs. Swanson, who moved in and stayed for the rest of their lives. But number 63 kept some of the old ways. When I was little, the milkman still clanked upstairs at dawn with his wooden basket of glass bottles, leaving ours by the door and taking away the empties. We didn't use coal, but the hallway dumbwaiter was still used to collect the trash we put outside of our doors at night by the super who lived in the basement. It stayed in use until the late 1950s, when we kids played in it once too often.

My childhood neighbors were painters, social activists, writers, longshoremen, actors, postmen, musicians, trust-fund bohemians, and office workers. Some were born here; others came because our street let them live and think as they liked. I listened to debates on socialism, reincarnation, vegetarianism, and politics on stoops and in grocery stores.

I didn't know that our ways had little to do with the rest of America. People lived as they pleased on Bank Street, and I, the offspring of free-spirited artists, thought nothing of it. Katherine Anthony, the elderly biographer at 23 Bank who introduced me to books like *Johnny Tremain*, had openly lived here with her female partner since 1912. They'd both had high-profile careers and raised their adopted children a century before gay marriage was legalized. The mixed-race couple in apartment 1C, whose son was eight when I was born, were just more 63 Bank grownups, frowning as I chained my bike to the hallway radiator. I didn't know that they might well have been jailed or even killed had they lived elsewhere.

. . .

Bank Street is a six-block-long strip south of West Fourteenth Street that starts at Greenwich Avenue and ends at the Hudson River. In the 1950s and '60s, as I looked left to Greenwich Avenue, I saw a gloomy side wall of the Loew's Sheridan movie house, built in the 1920s, its gilded rococo splendors hidden inside. To the right I saw nineteenth-century tenements like my own building, a teacher-training school, a spice warehouse fragrant with aromas, a General Electric factory, and, further down, abandoned elevated railroad tracks crossing high above the street, past a hulking old science laboratory. The street ended at our rotting Hudson River pier.

In those years, as I walked and played from one end of Bank Street to the other, I passed through every social, cultural, and economic layer of American life. Bank Street put its wealthy best foot forward on the first block off Greenwich Avenue. This is where Harvey, a nuclear physicist, and his wife, Yeffe, an artist, lived at 11 Bank Street, in a brownstone with a front garden where Yeffe and I planted bulbs. Their neighbor at number 15 was my friend Jack, scion of a prominent German Jewish family. As I passed other townhouses on that block I saw crystal chandeliers and gleaming silver candlesticks through the windows.

One brownstone owner was Miss Clark, heiress to the Coats & Clark sewing thread fortune. Still others were actors like Alan Arkin and Theodore Bikel. Bikel, who painted his building blue in honor of the state of Israel, founded in 1948, nodded hello in his dressing gown as he collected his *New York Times* from the front steps. TV personality Charles Kuralt, of 34 Bank Street, was on CBS every week with his show *On the Road with Charles Kuralt*. He smiled at me as he passed, looking more like a junior-high-school gym teacher than a celebrated broadcaster.

Around the corner from Bank Street, on Greenwich Avenue, stood a row of small shops, including Heller's Liquors, which had an imposing "Liquor Store" neon sign with a clock above the door. Mr. Heller was particularly proud of that sign because his father had scraped up the money to have it made back in the 1930s. Neatly stacked crates of wine covered the splintered wooden floor in one aisle, with liqueurs in another and hard liquor in a third. The counter was layered with customers' postcards and family photos, including ours.

Next to Heller's was the Casa Di Pre, a small restaurant with candles in Chianti bottles and soft peach walls. When the evening rush died down, the owner joined us for espresso, bringing sesame cookies, to chat about theater and opera. Next to Casa Di Pre, Saul and Min Feldman kept their five-and-dime notions store as they'd bought it from the 1920s owner. Worn wooden bins brimming with envelopes, packets of glitter, straws, bathing caps, shoe polish, sewing kits, and pink rubber Spaldeens filled the middle of the shop. If my parents and I didn't find what we were looking for, Saul or Min rummaged through the drawers below the bins. We seldom left empty-handed.

On one corner of Bank and Greenwich Avenue stood a grocery store with green-and-white-striped awnings and signs advertising freshly butchered meat. I waited outside for my parents, looking anywhere but at the poor skinned lambs hanging on metal hooks in the window. The smell of blood and sawdust inside upset me too. On another corner stood an old pharmacy with marble counters and globes of colored liquids in ornate cast-iron fixtures hanging in the windows. The elderly counterman always put two maraschino cherries on my ice cream, winking at me as he did.

The Waverly Inn, at the corner of Bank and Waverly Place, now a glossy haunt for celebrities, was an inexpensive, casual place back then, with wooden benches, Dutch tiles framing small brick fireplaces, and an open-air garden behind a low stone wall. On summer evenings, my friends and I sometimes tiptoed down the sidewalk with water balloons, counted to three, and threw them into the garden, diving behind parked cars before the cooks ran, swearing, from the kitchen.

Down the street, on the corner of Bank and West Fourth Street, was the Shanvilla Market Grocer. In the early morning, Pat Mulligan, the white-haired Irish owner, put out baskets of lettuce, peppers, apples, and bananas. Chipped freezers with wheezing motors were stocked with eggs, milk, and cheese. Cans and boxes stacked the old wooden shelves, which Pat reached using a pole with a metal claw.

Next to Shanvilla was the venerable Marseilles French Bakery. Wicker baskets lined with waxed paper sat on shelves behind the old glass counters, holding fragrant baguettes, rolls, and thick loaves dotted with salt or sesame seeds, fresh from the ovens in the back. Marie, a thin Frenchwoman with no front teeth who lived down by the river, was usually behind the counter.

Mr. and Mrs. Lee operated their Lee Hand Laundry around the corner, next to a shoe repair shop and Mr. Helping Exterminator. I had a hard time understanding the Lees' broken English, but they were smiling and polite behind their worn Formica counter. Paint peeled from the cracked plaster walls, bare except for photographs of their kids and curling Chinese good-luck signs and calendars. Cast-iron rods filled with shirts and pants on wire hangers stretched along the ceiling. The place smelled like steam and fresh fabric. The dented laundry scale squeaked. One day a kid wrote "No tickee, no shirtee" on a piece of paper and handed it to Mr. Lee, grinning and stretching her eyes to slants. When my father yelled at her, she stuck out her tongue at him and ran off.

• • •

My block, between West Fourth and Bleecker Streets, had a few elegant brownstones, but it had tenements and factories too, making it more of a mix than the block between West Fourth Street and Greenwich Avenue. The stoop at 51 Bank Street, a grayish brick walk-up apartment building on the corner of West Fourth Street, was an informal old men's club. Club regulars included Tom, an elderly Italian who drove a small, battered gray truck with the words "Tom's Ice" written on the sides in big black letters. I sometimes saw Tom, wearing cracked leather gloves, pull out blocks of ice with metal tongs and carry them into Shanvilla's basement or the fish store around the corner. We had an electric refrigerator and so did everyone else I knew. I'd never seen an icebox, the wooden kind that everyone, my parents told me, used when they were kids. Icemen like Tom were becoming things of the past, they said, and I worried that Tom would soon be out of a job.

Tom and other grizzled Bank Street men leaned against number 51's concrete stoop, passing the time. Regulars included Joe, a retired dockworker, and Mr. Hanks, who had been a fireman. They nodded to their neighbor, Tish, the nightclub performer, but rolled their eyes behind his back as he walked away. The commercial space on that corner was a tie-dyed clothing store in the 1960s and later a vegetarian restaurant. The old men disapproved of both businesses. Those dirty hippies do drugs, they fumed to my father. The old men didn't want us bothering them, so they'd shoo us down to play spots like in front of the wallpaper factory at 59 Bank.

Since most Village kids under ten weren't allowed off their block, after-school play groups were arbitrarily defined by address. We got excited when coal trucks pulled up to deliver their wares or when horse-mounted police officers rode by from the stable a few blocks away. We'd pet the horses, and sometimes I'd ask if I could sit on one, but the policeman always said no.

We were careful in front of 60 Bank Street because little Josh lived there. Although Josh was wasting away from an illness that eventually killed him, he usually wanted to join us. His parents looked sad when they had to say no, which was most of the time. We tried to make it up to Josh, making him the referee if he was watching when we played tag or statues. He'd squeak "You're out!" in his tinny voice, perched in his window, pointing to the jail garden below his window.

On his rare good days Josh was allowed out for a little while, his eyes bright with excitement. He was bald and as tiny-boned as a bird. I let him grip my arm, carefully swinging him in circles while his parents smiled anxiously, trying not to hover. Rudy let Josh pummel him to the ground with his little fists. Ginny sat him on her bike and delicately wheeled him to the corner and back. One day a folk singer with a guitar came along and sang with us below Josh's window. The singer had only one leg. He said he'd lost the other one in a place called Vietnam. When Josh died, we sat on his steps. His parents came out and we cried together.

Number 69 Bank Street housed the Bank Street College of Education, located there from 1930 until it moved uptown in 1971. The building had originally been a yeast factory, and its wide sidewalk was the best Double Dutch jump rope spot. Student teachers wearing peasant blouses and dirndl skirts climbed the steps, smiling at us.

Number 68 Bank Street, across the street from my building, was a boarding house. Bill, a burly retired truck driver who lived there, often sat on his stoop reading his *Daily News*. Bill and I watched, smiling, as city workers planted trees up and down Bank Street in 1962. He watered the delicate young honey locust in front of his place every day and grew irritated when people let their dogs pee on it. Finally, out of patience, Bill armed himself with a box of mothballs, and when dogs paused to sniff at the tree's roots, he'd grab a handful and let fly. Dogs yelped and owners cussed, but Bill's tree grew and still presides over the building.

Number 75 Bank Street, on the corner of Bleecker Street, was our block's grandest apartment building, the one with an elevator. Gardens lined the entrance, and a doorman manned the Art Deco lobby. We liked to shimmy up the wrought-iron gate in front of number 75's side alley. It was a daring climb since we had to watch out for Suzy, the live-in super's boxer. If she heard us, she ran up, barking and snapping as we frantically slid down, fingernails scratching the glossy black paint. The alley was an enticing space and we wanted to play in it, but the gate was always locked and we were too afraid of Suzy, although nobody would admit it.

Number 78–80 Bank, the big tenement building on the opposite corner of Bank and Bleecker Streets, was home to tough, older teenagers back in the early 1960s. Girls wearing white or pale pink lipstick sat on the stoop snapping gum and teasing their hair into bouffant towers. Boys with slicked-back hair and black leather jackets nuzzled them, sliding their hands around until the girls slapped their wrists. They lit cigarettes in front of adults, which astounded me, casually flicking butts into the street with a bored flip of the finger. One of the girls bolted to my side when a disheveled man waved an address on a slip of paper and asked me to go into a hallway and help him read it. "Get atta heah, ya dirty creep! Kid, nevah, evah go wit' one of them pervies! He'll do nasty to yah!" I had no idea what she meant.

By 1969 the greasers were gone. I was 13, and I babysat there for a divorced mother who had moved from New Jersey to be a hippie. She was an affectionate mom but rarely cleaned the house. Rolling papers sat on a shelf above the dirty kitchen sink. Even though I searched diligently, I couldn't find her dope stash. One day I couldn't stand the mess anymore and cleaned it myself. The children's dad, who still had a crew cut and wore skinny black ties, beamed when he came to the city to pick them up. "This looks great!" he said. His face fell when I told him that I had done it.

Weekend hippies were obvious; carefully beaded, asking directions to Washington Square Park in the 1960s and '70s. If I was in a nasty mood, I either sent them uptown to Chelsea, then a boring slum unless girl gangs from the projects were chasing me as I ran to and from my junior high school, or down to the rotting Hudson River docks. Maybe, I snipped, they'd try to blend in at the Anvil, a longshoremen's bar by day and a gay, druggy sex club by night: all customers serviced by roving hustlers and prostitutes.

Until the mid-1960s, a hulking spice warehouse sat on the corner of Bank and Bleecker Streets, wafting a delicious orangey aroma through the streets on warm days. A white Greek temple sat by itself in the middle of Hudson Street, opposite the warehouse. I thought the temple was an image from a childhood dream until I saw archival photographs of the city in my twenties. My temple was there, a hexagonal bandstand from the 1880s, its second story framed by fluted marble columns. By the 1940s, an older Villager told me, bums slept in it and kids set fires there. It was demolished in the late 1950s.

A few years later the warehouse was knocked down too, and a new playground went up over both sites. Whoever designed that park either didn't know kids or had it in for them. It had lunacies like a fifteen-foot concrete column with a climbing ladder, topped with a platform, set invitingly next to a sandbox. Luckily I'd just turned ten, a magic age when my parents decided that I was streetwise enough to play in other parts of the Village. I scorned the new kiddie park and met my friends in rowdy Washington Square Park. One kid, still grounded on Bank Street, jumped off the platform and broke his leg. Parents rushed kids to emergency rooms and yelled at politicians. Eventually the column was torn down.

I could also, at ten, walk down the other four blocks of Bank Street to the end, at the Hudson River. There weren't many attractions. The Westinghouse Electric factory that took up an entire block was still open, although after a fire in the 1960s the factory closed and the building became a doorman co-op. Locals snickered at the idea of fancy living in an old factory.

I kept exploring, savoring my independence, passing the factory and walking towards the river, past dilapidated bars, the sour smell of stale beer wafting onto the sidewalk. Our block was tarred, but lumpy Colonial-era cobblestones on those last blocks made for a roller-coaster ride and still do. My father cursed and gripped the wheel as our Plymouth Valiant bumped and lurched.

The block between Greenwich Street and Washington Street was a mix of boxy 1950s brick apartment buildings, 1800s tenements, and small, run-down houses, with a few fine exceptions tossed in. My friend Billy Joyce, a live-in butler for Alwin Nikolais and Murray Louis, the renowned dance couple who owned number 113–115, sunned himself in a beach chair in front of their house and chatted with passersby. Opposite Billy stood HB Acting Studio's three adjoining buildings. Young actors hung around the front, practicing lines, oblivious to the tenement dwellers who lounged in their doorways, drinking beer.

By the time I reached our last block, in 1966, the one that ran to our Hudson River dock, I was in a completely different Bank Street, many social classes removed from the wealthy brownstones at the other end. This block reflected the sad changes that were going on throughout New York City in the mid- to late 1960s. Middle-class families were fleeing to the suburbs. We'd lost the Brooklyn Dodgers. The Brooklyn Navy Yard shut down, taking with it thousands of jobs. A garbage workers' strike left rotting bags, thrashing with rats, on the streets for nine days. Prostitutes and strip joints took over Times Square. The city's crime rate soared.

The traditional longshoreman jobs of the Hudson River piers, once crowded with passenger and cargo ships, were drying up as airplanes took over the transport industry. Those jobs had been the livelihood of many Bank Street families for generations. A hulking cluster of dark, deserted buildings, which had been a famous Bell Telephone research laboratory for a hundred years until it closed in 1966, loomed over one side of our last block. Decayed tenements and boarded-up shops leaned like rotted teeth on the other. One grocery store was all that was left of the small shops that had once flourished by the river. Furtive, hard-faced men lounged against peeling billboards advertising 7 Up and Pall Malls. Heroin addicts swayed slowly in doorways, their limbs twitching.

An abandoned elevated railroad track ran through the Bell Lab building, continuing south on rusty iron pillars along Washington Street. A second derelict elevated track darkened the air along West Street, letting small pockets of dirty dusty sunlight filter down to the sidewalk. Packs of shrill hookers—male, female, and I wasn't sure— swarmed passersby and cars, leading johns to unlocked trucks or the pier. Trolley tracks ran next to the river, but by then there hadn't been any trolleys for decades. Except for the grocery store, the only business still open down there then was a prison. Dad, who spent hours looking for parking spots near our apartment, wouldn't even slow down on that block, let alone park there.

We still had a pier, although it wasn't a smart place to play. Even if I didn't fall through the broken planks or drive a rusty nail through my foot, being there during the week, at any time of day or night, was usually asking for a mugging in the 1960s and '70s. I kicked a junkie who tried to pull my bike from underneath me, but had no answer when one of the watching hookers said to me, "Well, what the hell do you think this is? Central Park? Go play somewhere else." She was right.

By fourteen I'd learned how to handle blocks like this one. I'd walk down the middle of the cobblestones, stepping aside for passing cars, so shifty guys couldn't grab me and drag me into an empty hallway. A nodding heroin junkie was a harmless obstacle to avoid. Roaches ran down the grocery store's walls. I bought my Hostess cupcakes elsewhere.

I needed those new street smarts. My girlfriends and I were hitting puberty, and our young breasts and hips suddenly made us walking targets. Men shouted from cars, licking their lips, or blocked us on the sidewalk. One jazz musician mother, realizing that we'd caught on to her recipe, now boiled chamomile instead of marijuana to make tummy tea for our new ailment, menstrual cramps.

The rotting Bank Street pier changed completely on summer weekends in the late 1960s and '70s. It became a noisy, laughing party, packed with gay men reclining on beach towels, rubbing baby oil on their sculpted bodies. My girlfriends and I quickly learned that the men were safe to be around and far more fun to boot. We joined them, pulling down the shoulder straps of our bikinis and gossiping, playing our transistor radios in peace.

• • •

Bank Street had its share of grumps and jerks, but many others were wonderful. Sabine, the artist who lived in 5C of our building, collected money and furniture for our teenaged black super and his pregnant wife, recent arrivals from rural Mississippi, who were too poor to furnish their basement apartment or pay for prenatal care.

When they moved to a bigger building, we got feisty little Ramiro, a retired merchant marine who could fix any leaky pipe or worn lock and kept the halls hospital clean. As my grandmother in apartment 1A started weakening with what eventually turned out to be brain cancer, Ramiro looked in on her several times a day. When I stayed with Grandma, I did homework with cotton in my ears as the primal therapy group next door in 65 Bank screamed themselves to release. Blocked chakras sometimes kept them howling long after New York's 10 p.m. quiet curfew. Ramiro, obscenely fluent in several languages, reserved some of his best cursing for them.

Charles Kuralt traveled the country doing his *On the Road* TV shows, which profiled Americans from all walks of life with respect and dignity. Marion "Auntie Mame" Tanner broke the locks on her brownstone doors so that anyone who needed shelter could walk in at any time. Lawyer/politician Bella Abzug of 37 Bank Street spent a night hiding from the Ku Klux Klan in a Mississippi bus stop bathroom to plead with the state's governor to spare the life of a black inmate on death row.

In college, I thought about the many artists and social idealists on my street who rejected day jobs. If they'd come from money, or married a worker bee, like Roger, the artist whose wife was a secretary, they got to pursue their passions full time. If not, they scraped by, waiting tables or driving cabs and their older years often brought hard choices between buying food and paying the rent. Their plight was what made me grit my teeth, bypass the writing and philosophy departments I longed to join, and endure boring education courses until I got teaching degrees and grimly took a job in a New York City public school.

I didn't have the self-confidence to chase my artistic dreams like they did. Plodding on, I ignored my doubts and married my high-school sweetheart at a ridiculously immature twenty-four years old because it seemed inevitable. My parents were moving out, and we took their 2B apartment. As teenagers we'd been crazy stupid in love, but we'd already grown apart. Bank Street life together became a jail for some crime we'd unknowingly committed.

When we divorced two years later, I used the teaching degrees and fled, taking a job in a Thai university in the 1980s while a musician friend sublet the apartment. Although I was never going to fall in love again, I eventually did, this time with a Thai-born Dane, a Thai TV celebrity. I spent six magical years as a TV producer expatriate with a teak house, mango trees in the lush garden, and live-in servants. I thought I was done with Bank Street, but the magic died when his hidden alcoholism resurfaced and wrecked our lives. I flew home, crying, to divorce a second time and be a New Yorker again. Teaching again was the fast solution and it worked. I had friends, traveled for months every summer, and even touched some kids' lives. I got an administrative degree. Life on Bank Street was OK.

Still later, on 9/11, when I'd been at work in a small downtown school with devastatingly clear views of the World Trade Center towers, Bank Street became both refuge and mental ward. I fought to regain my sanity, screaming myself awake over and over as the victims I'd seen clawed at my windows, pleading for rescue. Bank Streeters and Village friends saved me with meals, walks to doctors, and soothing words when I panicked, sure every time I heard a siren wail that another attack was underway.

For many years after that I shared the apartment with my late husband Richard, in a wholly unexpected later-life marriage. We met when a mutual friend asked me to help Richard, who had been practicing medicine in Africa, find a New York apartment. We kayaked and grew vegetables at our weekend place and trekked through foreign countries. Children, we agreed, might have been wonderful, but we weren't together when that might have happened and that's OK.

And I still have Bank Street, past, present, and future.

2 • Opera on Bank Street

A squib in *The Villager* for October 1955 bore the headline "Opera Baby Arrives." We were opera people. Like a child of the circus or a farm, I couldn't imagine any other life. New York has had live theater since the 1700s, when a downtown theater entertained General George Washington with Shakespeare's plays, comedies like *The School for Scandal*, and farces with white actors in blackface.

Even if the performers were awful, it was probably a jolly crowd. English immigrants had imported their cheery custom of letting prostitutes ply their trade in the upper balconies of theaters. Policemen pocketed bribes and looked the other way while theater critics warned readers that respectable wives and daughters might be mixed with "the abandoned of the sex."

My parents, Ann and Larry, met during the Metropolitan Opera's 1945 season, both twenty, eyeing each other on the cheap seats line for weeks. Ann and her friend Rose went to every Saturday matinee. Ann was a petite, raven-haired stunner with a dazzling smile who favored short, curled coifs, mascara, black eyeliner, and vivid lipstick. On theater day she wore her one elegant coat and spike heels.

Larry Florio, an aspiring theater director from Hoboken, New Jersey, was there with friends. He'd just left the army, a slim charmer with wavy brown hair, big brown eyes, and an easy laugh. "My goodness, how good-looking your father is, Donna," fluttered Miss Scher, my sixth-grade teacher, after parent-teacher night. "Very handsome indeed." Marie in apartment 5A, my first babysitter, who was a teenager in 1955, still says that he was a dish.

Their 1950 wedding lasted ten hours, because all of the performer-guests were determined to out-sing each other. They'd arranged a dude-ranch honeymoon but realized on their first morning that it was a ridiculous destination for theater people like them. They sneaked around New York that week, going to every show they could afford and avoiding their friends.

My earliest memories are the dusty smells of painted canvas and wood-framed scenery leaning against brick walls at the Amato Opera at 159 Bleecker Street, a former movie theater, where Tony and Sally Amato coached students like Mom through roles like Mimi in *La Bohème*. If it wasn't your turn for the lead role, you sang in the chorus, painted sets, and worked the box office.

The theater was scarcely chic. Winos snored and peed on the sidewalk outside the lobby. Dad bribed them to move away with coffee and doughnuts during shows. It was a place for Dad to learn stagecraft with no budget and on the fly. When he rigged a fountain for one scene, he begged the cast not to use the backstage toilet. Inevitably someone forgot. The audible flush was followed by a drooping spray, while the audience tittered.

The Amatos' idea of nurturing opera singers in the States was radical in the 1940s. Europe, the birthplace of opera, was *the* place that produced singers. Impresarios from American theaters like the Metropolitan Opera wouldn't even audition Americans for lead roles. Aspiring singers, many of them first generation from Europe anyway, joined regional companies in Italy, France, Germany, or Hungary. Suitably exotic stage personas were concocted. With a few years of coaching and leading roles under her belt, a Miss Frances O'Brien of Cleveland might return as Madame Francesca DiBrioni of Rome.

• • •

Ann's parents, immigrants from a village in southern Italy, lost their money in the 1930s Depression. Her home, when my parents met, was a cold-water walk-up in the poor Italian enclave of East Harlem, where only bookies and tough guys had money.

The year before they met, Ann had won a national voice competition. Her prize was two paid years of opera study in Rome. "My sister needed to sing and have a big, exciting life like she needed to breathe," Vicky, her younger sister, told me. Two years earlier, she'd won a scholarship to elite Manhattanville College, a school for moneyed Catholics like the Kennedys, but she'd had to give it up when her father lost his job. "She tried not to let me hear but she cried every night for weeks," Vicky said. "My poor sister had to be an office clerk, the last thing she wanted."

Second chances like Rome didn't often arrive in East Harlem. But Ann's father, usually indulgent of his beautiful daughter, became a raging peasant. "I'll never forget the day that award letter came," Vicky said. "I could hear Pop screaming from the stairs. Your mother was slumped at the kitchen table. She'd been crying so hard her eyes were swollen shut. I'd never seen my father like this, ever. 'You'll leave this house married,' he was screaming, 'or you leave it dead.'"

Larry fell in love with the Village and the arts as an NYU student. Ann wanted out of East Harlem. Two romantics, deeply in love, they had a child to complete the happy picture. But it didn't take long for them to realize that bohemia and a squalling baby were a bad mix. So was a third competitor for center stage, something neither of these charming but insecure and immature people, already shoving each other aside for attention, could handle. Screaming fights rang through apartment 2B at least once a week as I groped the line be-tween smiles and fury, trying to be a good girl and keep them happy with each other and with me. "Your parents shouldn't have had chil-dren," Dad's closest friend, a conductor, told me decades later. "And they should have divorced, forgive me, Donna, for saying so. Singers, especially women, blame anything but themselves if they don't make it. They say, 'If it wasn't for marrying or having kids, I would have been a star.' It's terrible. Their delusions ruin their lives."

It wasn't all bad. When the three of us were laughing and tell-ing each other funny stories, we were happy. Our unconventional lifestyle helped, too. Given our varied theater schedules, we simply weren't together all that much except on Sundays. Grandma, Mom's mother, moving downstairs to apartment 1A in 63 Bank when I was eight, eased things. Visits with Dad's sisters and their husbands and children at my Florio grandparents' rambling old house in Staten Island helped too. But my real haven, where I found the affection and approval our apartment lacked, was on Bank Street with the neighbors who became my allies and surrogate family.

• • •

Ann and Larry were charismatic raconteurs, and my arrival was one of their favorite stories. Sally Amato's younger sister, Annie, and

Annie's husband, John Frydel, both opera singers, were our upstairs neighbors at 63 Bank, and their daughter, Irene, was a year and a half older than me. Irene's first memory is sitting in a lap, watching my pregnant mother sing, alone in the spotlight on a blacked-out stage, in a white ball gown, celebrating her free life in *La Traviata*, her favorite role. In late October, eight months along, Ann planned a cast party for Dad's production of *Carmen*, opening that night. She'd just stopped performing that week and only because her legs swelled. Even heavily pregnant she could still blast full voice, which astounded her coach.

The supermarket cashier eyed her belly and suggested that the groceries be delivered. "Oh, no need," Ann told her. "The baby isn't due for another month." She pulled her heavy cart home and up the steps. As she prepared the food, I announced my own plans: the first of our many disagreements. She lowered herself to a chair and reached for the phone.

As a kid, I learned to keep out of the way before opening nights. Nervous singers wandered around, humming, practicing scenes. They rolled their eyes if I asked them to play. Stagehands hammered, swearing like pirates. Larry yelled at choristers who still weren't hitting their marks on time. "People! The prisoners have to be in place by the downbeat!" Ann knew she was breaking a cardinal rule with that call.

"Who is this?" snarled Tony Amato, score in hand.

"It's Ann. I need Larry. My water has broken."

"Have you lost your mind? It's two hours to curtain! For Christ's sake, Ann, call a plumber!" He banged down the phone.

Ann listened disconsolately to the dial tone. What now? She seasoned the chicken, wondering what to do.

Sally, folding programs, glanced sideways at Dad and sidled out the door. She dodged through the Bleecker Street pushcarts, running hard, and made it to Bank Street in minutes. "We're taking a cab, Ann," Sally announced grandly. A taxi to New York Hospital on the Upper East Side was a huge expense, but Sally's conscience was sore.

Several hours later, in a labor room full of groaning women, as my father finally arrived to pace in the waiting room, Ann was seriously uncomfortable. She called the nurse over, expecting drugs. In the 1950s, American women were typically knocked unconscious and presented with their bundle when they woke up. But her chart had been mismarked "Natural Childbirth." Staying awake and breathing through labor pains was a radical new idea then, and completely unknown to my mother. When the smiling nurse told her that it was certainly "time to do your wonderful breathing exercises," Ann was flattered. Oh, well, of course, they know I'm a singer, she preened. She started blasting the scales, trills, and arpeggios that had wowed her coach.

Meanwhile, on Bank Street, Annie and John Frydel had the keys to our apartment. Everyone was jazzed on opening nights, and no one, happy and hungry, intended to let my arrival cancel the party. The Frydels unlocked our door, and John mixed his lethal Manhattans. None of them could cook, but they sure could party. (Several years later, Annie Frydel would hustle Irene and me out of 4B as party guests laughed hysterically: Larry and John were freeing soused love-makers who'd gotten wedged into the bathtub.)

As Ann sang me to life, the cast lit our rickety stove and attempted dinner. The nurse rushed in as the phone rang in the labor room. "Could we speak with Ann Florio, please?" slurred a voice on the phone. The nurse heard voices in the background saying, "Where does she keep the pepper?" and "Ask her how long the chicken bakes."

The nurse threw up her hands and wheeled Ann's gurney to the phone. "Talk to them, get them off the phone, and then *please* shut up. This place sounds like Bellevue."

The cast got dinner, Ann got drugs, and Larry got a standing ovation when he came home at 4 a.m.

• • •

I toddled around a warm backstage world of Egyptian slaves, French courtesans, and Spanish gypsies. Women in thick white nylon panties and pointy cone bras smiled as they patted on pancake makeup, and then sat me carefully on their costumes, whispering Dr. Seuss and fairy tales as we turned the pages together. "Don't be scared. It's only make-believe," I reassured friends in the audience. I'd learned that lesson out front when Mommy/Madame Butterfly stabbed herself and fell over dead. I screamed myself onto the stage as she scrambled back to life and took her bows with me crying into her kimono.

I made my debut at four, as the love child of Sally's Madame Butterfly. Everyone fussed as they dressed me in a kimono and flip-flops, telling me that I was the most important part of the show. When Butterfly's maid took my hand, we walked onstage to Sally, who beamed and held her arms open. There is nothing for the child to sing, but that didn't matter. Sally, her black wig sparkling with jewels, was a queen, and I was her princess. I felt the hushed attention of the audience as Sally cupped my face and sang her love for me. My parents came onstage, clapping and yelling "Brava!" when I held Sally's hand and took my first bow at the end of the show. They coaxed me into a snowsuit when we left, but I wouldn't relinquish the flip-flops, so Dad carried me home with his scarf wrapped around my feet. Opera folks were special magic people, and now I was enchanted too, a tiny planet circling two blazing stars.

· · ·

Singing in the children's choruses in operas came when I was five. Opera is hard work for kids, although no one thought to mention it. Singers have to memorize every note and perform while moving around on cue and in character, under hot lights, wearing costumes that can weigh fifty pounds. I was allowed to rehearse with a score in hand only for a brief period. I was expected to memorize fast and to make note of the interpretations that each conductor gives to a score. Tony Amato was charming, but if I missed the downbeat a third time, he'd bang on the podium and I'd cower. When Mom and I moved from Amato to the Metropolitan Opera, the stakes were far higher, but the rules were exactly the same. If Leonard Bernstein wanted a *legato* here or a *forte* there, I had to memorize his wishes, and fast.

In addition to the conductor there was the stage director. The director told me how (running, sneaking, marching) and where (stage left, stage right, or in position before curtain) my character entered the scene and what I did as I sang. If my role called for using props, like tearing the *Hansel and Gretel* gingerbread witch into pieces, I had to have the right prop at exactly the right musical moment. If I had to change costumes too fast to reach a dressing room, I had to wriggle out of one and into the next in the wings. And whether I was dancing, fighting, or climbing a ladder, I had to watch the conductor's baton as if it were the eye of God.

La Bohème, a perennial favorite, involved a crowd scene and was relatively easy because chorus ladies usually held us in place and sang with us. *Tosca* was harder. We were altar boys with a priest who had his own music to sing while we skipped around. *Carmen* was the hardest opera for me. I had to spit staccato French lyrics, usually at breakneck tempo, while marching in a crowd. I often stomped on someone's foot or got my own shins kicked. But I had to stay in character and keep going, even if the scenery fell on me. I didn't mind. My parents were right to be theater snobs, I thought. Nothing felt as alive as being onstage.

There is an offstage child shepherd's solo in *Tosca*. A solo is another universe. No hiding behind others if you go off pitch or muff the lyrics. I was deemed ready at seven at the Amato. The shepherd's aria is a soft, plaintive poem to the dawn. It was my own golden moment, just Tony and me, face to face in the tiny orchestra pit. A flute and oboe played quietly, letting my voice glide above them. I remembered Mom's instructions. Breathe deeply. Get onto the first note right away. Hit the descending line just so. Hold the final note until he moves his baton sideways and cuts it off. When the audience applauded and Tony bowed to me from the podium, I felt like a queen. Backstage, my parents hugged me with tears in their eyes.

In addition to working at the Amatos', Dad went on road tours with other companies when I was little. One morning I ran into the living room, thrilled that Dad had come home during the night. A Chatty Cathy doll, my biggest wish, sat in our yellow butterfly chair, and my parents smiled sleepily as I grabbed her and climbed into their sleeper couch. I bragged for days that he'd remembered his special girl on tour until Mom snapped, "Please. I got that doll in Macy's."

• • •

Two huge changes came in 1963, when I was seven: Mom's dad died, and Grandma moved into apartment 1A of 63 Bank Street. Her presence allowed Mom to audition for the Metropolitan Opera chorus, performing their final seasons in their original theater on West Thirty-Ninth Street. The old Met was to be demolished and the company moved to a new theater in Lincoln Center in 1966. They were accepting girls in their children's chorus for the first time that year. I passed an audition, and I too joined the Met. My parents were proud and happy and therefore so was I, although I didn't know that my cozy theater world had just turned upside down.

At first I was scared to death. The old Met had been built in 1898. Backstage looked like a haunted house that went on forever. I was afraid I'd get lost and no one would find me. It was all dusty carved wood and splintered floors, a rabbit warren of lopsided steps with cast-iron banisters leading to dimly lit corridors and strange, hidden rooms. Thick metal pipes ran everywhere: in dressing rooms, through rehearsal halls, and high above audience view onstage. Roman soldiers lumbered by, checking the *Daily News* for the racing results at Belmont.

The chorus women were in a communal dressing room at the top of worn wooden stairs by stage left. Mirrors were ringed with tiny light bulbs in metal cages. Chipped coffee mugs held eyeliners and grease sticks. Wiry old Rosie, one of the ladies' dressers, had been a circus trapeze artist. She coached me through skin-the-cat on a costume bar while the chorus was onstage. The ladies had photos and cards tucked into their mirrors. "See?" Mom pointed to my Kodak picture, missing front teeth and all. "I always have my little girl."

Since I had to wait for Mom to go home, I sat at her cubicle after I'd dressed and studied the mimeographed chorus makeup charts she'd taped to the mirror. Faces were drawn on papers marked "*Faust*—Peasant, Act I" or "*Turandot*—Courtier, Act III." The sketches pointed out correct circle widths under eyes using number 12 brown pancake makeup for the starving Faust peasant and white greasepaint with red lipstick and heavy penciled eyebrows for the Chinese royalty. Powder clouded the air and made me sneeze as ladies flicked matte finishes over their faces with thick brushes and rose like a flock of swans, hurrying to their next entrance.

Rick, the man in charge of the children's chorus, met us at the stage door lobby, signed us in, and marched us upstairs to our dressing room. I was awed the first time I followed him into the wings for an onstage rehearsal. The biggest scenery and black side curtains I'd ever seen towered stories above my head. Stagehands swarmed around us, scrambling up metal side balconies and across high walkways, tying off scenery ropes and positioning floodlights.

In *La Bohème*, my first Met show, I was a Parisian street urchin following a toy vendor, so the costume was easy: ragged pants and a torn jacket. I already knew the music, making the dour chorus master nod approvingly when I jumped in without the score at the first rehearsal. I was supposed to be a boy, so I tucked my hair into a black wool cap and lined up in front of the waiting makeup artists, who swabbed Max Factor pancake and greasepaint dirt streaks on with brisk snaps of the wrist. Rick clapped his hands, calling out "Hurry! Places before curtain!" as we rushed to line up.

When I ran onstage, I tried not to stare at the flashes from necklaces and jeweled gowns in the first rows or up at the golden carved box seats. Huge floodlights, embedded in the wooden stage, sent up waves of heat. The prompter's head peeped out of his little covered box onstage, hidden from the audience. If someone forgot their cue, he'd whisper it. All in all it was a dazzling world: too much to take in all at once.

• • •

I didn't understand until I was much older that Mom had just started a twenty-five-year prison sentence. Movie extras and corps ballerinas rose to stardom, but in the hidebound opera world, choristers were typecast for life. The steady paycheck came with watching stars like Renata Tebaldi and Maria Callas sing roles that she'd studied for years at her parents' kitchen table. This time, saddled with bills and a family, there wasn't going to be another break. When I complained that the chorus master was mean, she told me to work harder and toe the line. I bragged about being a Met singer to my uninterested second-grade classmates at St. Joseph's School, but I had to force myself to forget the warmth and fun of the Amatos.

The easygoing Frydel apartment, 4B, was my second home. Irene and I played with our parakeets and watched *The Man from U.N.C.L.E.*, but we didn't perform together anymore. I rarely saw my father's shows anymore either, even when they were just a subway ride away at the Brooklyn Academy of Music. It felt like we'd left him behind.

Dad was struggling with his theater career too. He was offered the Met stage manager job, Mom told me years later, but the price was having sex with a man on the board of directors. Dad's immigrant parents started businesses and bought real estate, bulldozing their way up the American ladder, fierce and tough, ordering him to become a doctor. Dropping out of NYU pre-med and taking up theater was his one and only act of defiance.

"You ruined my life by being born!" he'd sometimes snap. While I cried, he'd pat my back and bang his fist. "Dammit! How could I say that to my own child? Oh, God, I'm sorry." If he'd been drinking, the cycles of venom and remorse could go on for hours. "Your father needed a mentor," his conductor friend told me. "He needed guidance and he never got any."

My father bowed to financial reality and took a sales job in plastics when I was about ten, although he kept his hand in with operas here and there. One pact Mom and I never broke was our unspoken mutual agreement to be kind about his humiliating exile into the ultimate horror: a non-theatrical life.

• • •

I moved to our new Lincoln Center home with the Met in 1966. The backstage looked like a hospital: dull white concrete walls, red carpeting, and featureless blank rooms. The company wasn't a high-spirited, rushing pack anymore. Soloists, chorus, orchestra, dancers, and stagehands had their own floors and corridors. It was certainly impressive: five underground levels and a stage that could revolve, rise, or drop two stories. But I was used to the bustling old Thirty-Ninth Street house by now and found this one ugly and boring. I had no opinion about the front of house since I was never there.

I took Ann's realistic advice and worked to please the kid chorus master. Newbies kissed up. "Maestro, do we take this measure as a *legato* or continue the *andante*?" I'd snicker, knowing what was next. First, the cold stare. Then, the disembowelment. "You are, unsurprisingly, a musical idiot. Be quiet. You might learn something." Rick loved to remind us that hordes of kids out there hoped we'd drop dead or flunk the yearly re-audition.

The Marx Brothers movie *A Night at the Opera* is cinema verité, down to scenery from other shows dropping onstage. As a little acolyte in *Othello*, I stared adoringly at Montserrat Caballé, the Desdemona, during her aria. When she threw out her hands, her ring caught my thick black wig and twisted it backwards around my head. The audience tittered, but I stayed in place, faceless but firm. Montserrat, still singing, twisted her ring off and gently tugged the wig around, squeezing my shoulder in apology. In *La Gioconda*, we little sailors scrambled up hanging fishnets into position before the act and stayed aloft for the entire act. I missed my grip in the dark and fell sideways, dangling ten feet overhead by one leg but maintaining the director's scene one tableau as the curtain rose.

When a dancer accidentally kicked the prompter's nose, Hungarian curses blistered the air as we sang. One *Tosca* soprano threw herself from the castle parapet and landed on top of a stagehand, snoozing on her offstage mattress. We held hands with a new Gretel and improvised a hopping dance in *Hansel and Gretel*'s final scene after the hot stage lights glued her false eyelashes together. When Larry's *Butterfly* child refused to go onstage, he pushed his wrapped dinner into Suzuki's panicked hands and Butterfly emoted to a meatball hero sandwich. The chorus women chased their own ravishers when the barbarian invaders were cued onstage first by mistake. No one else in junior high had a life like mine.

My parents were too busy scrambling for attention themselves to be stage parents or take my developing tastes into account. When I asked for dance lessons, they said that there was no time in my theater schedule. I offered to leave the kid chorus, but then Dad said no, dancers are too skinny and their careers are too short. I'd fallen in love with Broadway. By nine I knew I'd rather shake my hips and yowl as catlike Anita in *West Side Story* than bellow stupid old *Aida* any day. But my parents didn't take me seriously and they ran my life so that was that.

Several years passed. One day, while the Met kid chorus was on loan to the visiting Royal Ballet, I saw Rudolph Nureyev backstage: a Russian sun god with tousled hair, pouty lips, and of course a rippling, perfect body. He looked through me, but his indifference didn't steady my buckled knees. Neither did knowing that he was gay. Flushed and heated, I watched him glide towards the stage like a panther. Rudy's effect had nothing in common with kissing Neal, another kid chorister, in a stairwell, my entire erotic experience at that point.

The chorus master finally laughed later that year when I sidled in to re-audition, trying to hide my new breasts, and we shook hands. The other kids, waiting their turn in the corridor, looked sympathetic for a moment and then turned away. Like so many others I'd waved goodbye to and forgotten, the curtain dropped on the enchanted opera childhood and I was gone, an outsider.

. . .

The Italian director Franco Zeffirelli was directing *Cavalleria Rusticana* and *Pagliacci*, two short operas often performed together. Zeffirelli loaded scenes with action and non-singing character parts, so Ann suggested that I audition as an actress. The concept of not being at the Met was too strange for me to handle so I agreed.

The other extras fussed and preened before we went to be "auditioned." In my mind, being lumped with them was being flung into mud. Singers were far above extras on the opera hierarchy, and I'd never bothered even chatting with any of them before. And calling this an audition was ridiculous, I snipped to myself. We weren't singing! We were being looked over like pork chops.

As we sat on the steps of the *Cavalleria* set I pushed dental wax onto my new braces so they wouldn't flash in the lights. Franco, a slim man in his forties, with graying blond hair, introduced himself in soft, accented, English. Then he looked us over, making comments to an assistant, who wrote them down. I saw him point to me, mimicking my long hair and nodding. And so, at age twelve, I landed a big role in *Cavalleria Rusticana* as a village virgin—past all doubt the only genuine one in the company.

Directors try to minimize staging complications for kids, but I was an adult now and Franco made me work like one in *Cavalleria*. I waved to a church procession from a balcony, then scrambled back to stage level down two backstage flights of dark, rickety stairs, unbuttoning my heavy floor-length dress as I ran. I had to be in my second outfit and back on stage to flirt by a fountain in eight minutes. Zeffirelli was also adamant that I wear a lace-up corset with painful metal rib that left welts. "You are an eighteenth-century Sicilian girl and you have to move like one," he said when I complained. Between the stair runs, the frantic costume change, and the heat from the lights, I was soaked in sweat by the last scene, when I had to rush up the church steps, yelling that the tenor had been murdered, then collapse with grief as the soprano wailed, my face planted on the dirty painted canvas, until the curtain dropped. It never came down fast enough for me.

Puberty, already bewildering me in the Village, rocked my Met world as well. I had a role in *Pagliacci* too, and a circus fire-eater Zeffirelli had cast in it suggested that we sneak downstairs for a quickie. He choked on his kerosene when I snidely told him my age. I shoved a chorus man's hand off my behind as we walked off stage. Curious, I let a young stagehand kiss me in the blackout curtains as I waited for a cue and he grabbed my breast. I ran on stage, shaking, and never kissed him again. Rick was fired when a chorus kid's parents accused him of molesting their son. He was hardly the only Met predator in those dismally incorrect times, but he had no star power or allies on the board of directors. I tried to focus on homework in the chorus ladies' lounge as a stagehand's wife cried and begged a chorus woman to stop sleeping with her husband and send him home to her and their kids.

On Sundays, glad for a break, my parents and I piled in the car for a day at Jones Beach and then lobsters in Sheepshead Bay, tanned and happy. They had laughing canasta parties with the Frydels, the adults calling Irene and me when the pizzas arrived. We read *The New York Times* over bagels on Sundays and went to museums and Broadway shows. I sent them dancing at the Rainbow Room for their anniversary. We wanted to make each other happy. We just weren't any good at it.

I lived on the right street, though. "How are Sally and Tony?" I asked Annie Frydel in her kitchen. The Amato Opera was marching on, as it did until 2009, when it closed its doors. "Fine, honey," she replied as we peeled carrots. "Come by and say hello to them, anytime. Stay for dinner tonight. You always have the best jokes, you little sparkler." I could go see what Yeffe Kimball, the Native American artist at 11 Bank, was up to, I thought. She had just had an exhibition at the Museum of Modern Art. Or I could check to see if Al, the bon vivant artist in apartment 2A, was home. He'd listen to my adolescent dramas with quiet respect.

Maybe Billy Joyce, the retired dancer at 113–115 Bank, was having another wine and cheese party down at the pier. I could help him carry stuff while we gossiped. And if Marty or Roz Braverman from 75 Bank Street were out with their dog, I could tell them my PSAT scores. They were so proud of me for going to elite Stuyvesant High

School that they'd told the whole block. I had a street full of supporters, young and old.

These Bank Streeters were my family, too. Much more so, in some ways. While there was occasional crabbiness, I hadn't ruined their lives by being born, and so my existence was never thrown in my face. I was fine as I was. If one of them was sick, I ran errands and brought food. Neighbors sometimes found fault with my clothes, my hair, or my behavior, but their comments were gentle. I, in turn, could hear their opinions without throwing up a yelling, sarcastic shield, trying to hurt them into shutting up. Being an opera singer was fun, but the people on Bank Street, caring for and about each other, taught me what it means to be human.

My Building

3 • The Frydels

Tiny Annie Frydel upstairs in 4B sneezed like a bull elephant. We yelled blessings up the alley shaft. And when my father's sneezes shook the walls, Annie, her husband, John, and their daughter, Irene, returned the salute. The Frydels and the Florios have been blessing each other for more than sixty years.

Annie and her sisters, Sally and Margie, were born in 1920s Little Italy. The family moved to upstate New York in the 1930s, and the girls lost their Noo Yawk accents. Mama Bell later brought them back for Sally's singing career, but Pop stayed upstate at his fabric-cutter job for the next fifty years. Mama Bell lived in the Village with her girls until Sally and Tony bought a house in the Bronx and took her along.

In 1948, Sally and Tony started the Amato Opera in a church basement several blocks from Bank Street.

Enter John Frydel in 1949. A handsome, smiling World War II veteran, and complete hayseed, he somehow found his way from rural Maine to opera. The GI Bill paid for his classes. He and Annie made eyes at each other at rehearsals, and a lifelong romance was born. The newlywed Frydels scraped up $40 a month for a walk-up on Commerce Street. The tub was in the kitchen, so drop-in guests waited in the hall if Annie was undressed. This formality was novel for the Village and wore off as the marriage went on. I just threw Annie a towel, looking away, if I'd barged in on her bath. It was years before I understood that not every American neighbor would cheerfully fix me a tuna sandwich in her underwear.

Baby Irene leaped onstage in 1954, arriving with a head of long, wild hair that stretched to her feet. I thought her baby photos were cute, like a baby Bride of Frankenstein, but apparently the effect was electrifying. People just stared, pop-eyed.

Money was always scarce for the Frydels, but the parties went on. When the young parents were close to broke yet again, they splurged on a bottle of gin and tucked it into Irene's carriage for the haul upstairs.

Annie sang at Amato, but by day she kept the books for the realtors that managed 63 Bank Street. When two apartments became available in 1955, Annie took 4B and called her pregnant friend, Amato student Ann Florio. My parents' studio apartment on West Twelfth Street was so small that they slept on a pull-out sofa with their feet under the piano keys. Ann waddled over and grabbed 2B.

The Frydels and the Florios confounded Bank Streeters for years. We had the same apartment two floors apart. Ann Florio and Annie Frydel were both petite, Italian American, brunette singers. Irene and I were one grade apart at St. Joseph's School. Both couples and their kids worked at the Amato Opera for the first seven years of my life.

John Frydel also joined the Metropolitan Opera chorus, and the three of us walked back and forth to the subway together. In the summer, random combinations of adults and daughters trooped to the subway with towels and sand buckets, heading to Rockaway Beach. Either mom would call us in for dinner as we played on the sidewalk. During thunderstorms, I'd run up to 4B to see if Annie or Irene was home. John had to have company or he'd hide in the closet, wringing his hands and praying in Polish.

Once, a neighbor tentatively asked, "Which one, exactly, is *your* father, Donna? Irene's? Or maybe you girls don't know?" She didn't mean to be insulting. It was the Village, after all.

As children's choristers, Irene and I buttoned each other's costumes in Amato Opera's tiny backstage and crouched behind scenery together, waiting for cues to run onstage. Being onstage was fun for us but not exotic. We'd been doing it since we could walk, holding a grown-up's hand as they whispered directions and turned us this way or that.

Number 63 was our personal playground. We rigged a doll elevator between our bedroom windows with coffee cans and string. This evolved to a basket and larger toys. We finally decided it was time to haul ourselves. Annie's mom alarm rang. She ran in as Irene was climbing out of the fourth-floor window.

Privacy was scarce for the poor neighbors with us around. When we were six and seven, Dan, a newly divorced man who lived in 1B, had a beautiful Great Dane. Deane, a single woman, lived in 4C, and they started coming in for drinks holding hands. Irene and I, pining for dogs of our own, were enthusiastic volunteer dog walkers, although we were puzzled when Dan gave us keys to both apartments. Why was the dog in both places? John cleared his throat and changed the subject.

Once, when unlocking 4C, I saw Dan, naked, in Deane's living room. He leaped behind the couch and crouched. Deane wasn't home, but I took baths at Irene's house all the time and figured maybe his shower was broken. No big deal. I yelled hi, took the dog, and left. Another time Irene heard them giggling in 4C. Good, she had Girl Scout cookies to sell. She grabbed her order book and marched over. They took a long time answering that door, but Irene kept knocking. What was the problem? They *loved* Thin Mints.

Dr. K., a Polish psychiatrist who lived in 4A then, enjoyed talking with John in their native language. He was a young bachelor, and that wasn't all he enjoyed. It was rarely the same woman twice. "He's so nice," we said to our parents after passing him on his way upstairs with that night's pick. "Cooking dinner for all these ladies." The men snorted drinks up their noses, and our mothers, trying to keep straight faces, agreed that yes, Dr. K. certainly was hospitable.

Since he had a common wall with the Frydels, Irene and I could hear a lot of goings-on. One activity sounded like galloping back and forth along the length of his apartment, along with slaps and shrieks. Irene and I put our ears to the walls, trying to figure it out. When we asked our parents if he was playing horsie, they got evasive. He started to come home with only one woman, a quiet lady who limped. When she became pregnant, they married and moved to New Jersey.

Irene and I, together in the hidebound world of opera, looked out for each other on Bank Street amid the uproar of the 1960s and '70s Village. She had physical strength but delicate social defenses. I was a runt but had a blasting potty mouth. We dressed dolls, told each other ghost stories during sleepovers, and played Candy Land. We traded Nancy Drew and Hardy Boys books. Sometimes we played in my apartment, but most of the time, usually at Annie Frydel's smil-ing insistence, we stayed in hers.

It was a long time before I understood that Annie worried about me as my parents jabbed at me and each other. I didn't realize that she was listening at her alley window as the yelling in 2B started yet again. Until Irene gently told me, when we were in our forties, I never knew that protecting me was a Frydel family mission, one that Irene had been sworn never to divulge. Annie and John had explained to Irene that my rough mannerisms and tough words were self-protection and that Irene should try to ignore them, and that she shouldn't ever mention the shouting she heard, no matter what. Annie's frequent, well-timed knocks on our door were not just the lucky prison breaks I'd always thought they were.

"Hi, Ann, sorry to bother you, but Irene is bored and driving me crazy. Can Donna come up and play? And I made way too much meatloaf again."

"Run along upstairs, Donna. No, really, it's a favor to *me*. Donna will entertain her."

Growing up in the Village was confusing for us both, but we got through it together. Irene declared (rightfully) that I had the style sense of a goat, and she brought home cashmere sweaters and Ital-ian leather skirts on sale from her high school job at Bloomingdale's while I taught her how to smoke pot. We traded opinions on the lat-est *Star Trek* episode. When I threw our Christmas tree downstairs and it punched a hole in the super's metal steps, Irene flew down-stairs and helped me sneak it away.

Irene stayed in the shelter of parochial schools while I, at ten, left for far hipper public school. It made a huge difference. By the early 1970s, I still sang opera, but I'd started to hang out at the Fillmore East rock club too. Irene dutifully listened to Jefferson Airplane or The Who with me, but she was happy to remain with Amato Opera, in our eccentric, cloistered world.

. . .

During the entire time I lived with my parents, it was safe for me in 4B, even if Irene wasn't home. I could play in her room or watch TV with her parents. No one was angry. John and I traded Met sto-ries and jokes. Annie complimented my help in her kitchen. I felt blessed, even when I hadn't sneezed. I, in turn, have not forgotten Irene's birthday once, ever. When number 63's building management hassled now-elderly Annie and John, I got local politicians to make them stop. If anything were to happen to Irene, I promised to care for John in his last years, in a flash. I sat in Annie's hospice during her brave fight with cancer in 2005. On her last night, I sobbed as I walked home.

I was still crying as I passed an animal rescue group and ended up taking home a frightened and neglected old dog "just to board, until he's adopted." Of course I was in love by the time I'd made him a bed. Corky limped onto Bank Street just as Annie's laughing spirit flew free. With affection and whopping vet bills, Corky recovered and reigned for years, the jaunty prince of 2B. He stayed with Irene when I traveled. Corky was a Frydel blessing. Again.

4 • Mr. Bendtsen

I have a toddler's memory of the door to apartment 1A opening as we passed. An old man who looked like Tweedledum and Tweedledee in my *Alice in Wonderland* book stared out. His head resembled a boiled egg. He had a beach-ball belly and toothpick-skinny bowed legs. When he smiled, putty-colored lips curled over brown gums, like my Grandma when she'd put her dentures in the pink plastic cup by her bed. He said, "Good day, Madam," to Mom in a deep, sibilant voice. She nodded and smiled, but held my hand firmly and kept walking. It took a few more years for me to realize that Mr. Bendtsen was always buck naked, not even wearing boxer shorts, like Daddy wore when he was shaving.

Everyone in the building swapped reads on the first-floor hall radiator back then. There were piles of *Art Forum*, *Horizons*, *Time*, the *Daily News*, and books by Edgar Cayce and Truman Capote. Franz Bendtsen contributed *The New York Times*. He'd bounce down the hall naked, sociably bearing sections as he finished them. He wowed my parents, the Frydels, and the rest of the neighbors with his perfect Sunday *Times* crossword puzzle—in ink—and always finished by early Saturday night. Since the *Times* truck didn't deliver to the grocery store around the corner or to our doorstep until 6 p.m. on Saturday, Mr. Bendtsen obviously solved even the most challenging clues without breaking a sweat. His puzzle was on the radiator by 8 p.m., and somehow it always stayed conspicuously on top of the other sections as he finished them and brought them down the hall. Dad tackled the puzzle on Sunday mornings. He was pretty good, but if he was stuck, he'd sneak downstairs to the radiator for a peek. He wasn't the only one who did that.

Mr. Bendtsen loved to follow world news and was usually excited about some event or another. Rose Moradei in 2C told me that she came home from work one afternoon in 1961, and saw him at the radiator, waving his paper, his eyes dancing.

"Madam! A remarkable day for mankind! Look here!"

Elegant, dignified Rose wasn't quite sure what he meant by "remarkable day for mankind" or where exactly "here" was, so she kept her eyes firmly focused on his face.

To her relief, he held up the newspaper. "The astronaut! The Russians have sent this man, Yuri Gagarin, to outer space! Have you seen?"

Rose looked at the headline, still controlling her eyes. "It really is incredible," she agreed.

He beamed. "We have lived to see this! An amazing day!" As he waddled excitedly down the hall, Rose looked at his sagging buttocks and stifled a laugh. It simply never seemed to occur to Mr. Bendtsen, she said, that his alfresco state altered the discourse. "Keep your eyes up and don't laugh," Mom said when I became old enough to find his nudism funny. "He's a nice old man."

Mr. Bendtsen wasn't our only well-aired neighbor. Elderly Jane Gorham in apartment 3B was a photographer. Her late husband had been a painter, and she'd lived in 63 since the 1930s. Once she invited me, Irene, and my mother into her apartment to look at his paintings and at her photos of their Village group. She'd taken them, she said as she pointed, at the summer place the group rented together on Fire Island through the 1930s and 1940s.

Irene and I traded incredulous looks. Jane's friends, smiling and waving, were all naked. Still mortified by our new pubescence, we couldn't believe that tall, patrician Jane had cavorted al fresco. Jane, serenely misreading our stupefaction as rapt attention, pulled an illustrated Kama Sutra from a shelf. Now she was talking about how she and her circle had freed their creative powers with "mutual libidinal release." Irene and I didn't know what the hell *that* was, but we were electrified by the few of ancient India's acrobatic sexual positions we glimpsed before Mom hurried us to the door.

· · ·

Rose Moradei remembered Mr. Bendtsen telling her that he and his mother had arrived in 1944 or 1945. "Mrs. Bendtsen died around the time I came," she told me. "And I think he kept company with a lady across the hall in 1B until she moved away." Rose was always impressed with his wide knowledge. He shared his opinions about literature, art, science, and politics in his sonorous voice. He charmed her too; few men had his courtly manners, she said.

Rose could never quite put her finger on his slight accent and was hesitant to ask. He'd mentioned being an actor at some point, she recalled, but hadn't said much else. My parents and other neighbors had the same vague memories of a stage career, but it was enough of a clue to get me started on the hunt in the 1990s.

I combed through the archives at the Lincoln Center Library for the Performing Arts, searching their actor biography files. When I found a small manila folder with his name, it felt as if I'd discovered buried treasure. I flipped through the clippings, stifling the urge to cheer. I found you, Mr. Bendtsen! And you got great reviews and never bragged about them to Rose or anyone else. That modesty, in his profession, was remarkable by itself. Actors lived all over the Village, and most of the ones I'd met were wildly in love with themselves. I gave up dating them in my early twenties. All they ever talked about was how fabulous they'd been in some show or about some upcoming audition. If they asked a single question about me, it was a miracle.

Normal clothes probably just bored you, Mr. Bendtsen, by the time you moved into 63 Bank Street, I thought as I read. You'd been in costumes for most of your life.

He'd had a full, steady career, a rarity for an actor in any era. Reviews from 1907 through the 1920s praised him as Launcelot Gobbo in *The Merchant of Venice*, Rodrigo in *Othello*, and the Cobbler in *Julius Caesar*. The accent that puzzled Rose may have been a leftover from his native language or stage training. He was born in Denmark, migrated to the States as a child, and studied at the Chicago Musical College, now the Chicago College of Performing Arts. His first name changed quite a bit in the newspapers. Various reviews called him "Franz," "France," "Franklin," and "Francis," and some got creative with his last name too. Maybe he himself was experimenting with stage names, I thought, or since he was performing around the time of World War I, maybe he was trying to distance himself from any question of German origins.

A 1912 reviewer of *As You Like It* declared that "France Bendtsen played the epicene Le Beau with precisely the required mince and dandeism." The year 1916 was a banner year for him. One newspaper noted that "Francis Bendtsen has had two hits in New York in new plays during the present season, as the German professor in 'Mrs. Boltay's Daughters' and as Dickie Wilkes in 'The Fear Market.'" Another described his day off as follows:

> Lots of folks hide their lights under the proverbial bushel, take it from France Bendtsen of 'The Fear Market' company. For instance, Bendtsen declares that he never realized just how meritorious was the work of the Subway artistic decorators until he chanced to stroll into the Subway at Times Square on Sunday morning. Then, lo and behold! a big four-sheet poster of himself . . . confronted the young actor and Bendtsen was the best customer . . . for the remainder of the day. He rode to the end of the Bronx line, getting off at every station and viewing his likeness on the posters and then began all over again. . . . The Metropolitan Museum of Art may be all right in its feeble way, but for the genuine article—again take it from Mr. Bendtsen—go to the Subway every time!

He must have loved this, I thought.

His career continued to flourish. In 1919 another admiring review declared that Bendtsen "is a young man of whom Broadway should see more . . . he has versatility as well as cleverness."

Bendtsen looked handsome in an ordinary, nondescript way in his publicity photos, with neatly combed straight hair slicked back and pleasant, even features. A bit like F. Scott Fitzgerald, I thought, but hard to recognize as my bowlegged old neighbor with warts and liver spots. I squinted hard, trying to find the cheerful old man who'd called me "Little Miss" and thanked me for sharing my Hershey bars with him by bowing low, hands fluttering in the air by his sides, and elaborately kissing my hand. His dramatic thank-you performance was our special time to giggle together. Plus, we both loved chocolate.

"No wonder he beat all of you at that crossword puzzle," I crowed to my parents and the neighbors, brandishing copies from his file. "And look at these reviews. When did he even sleep?" It was a good question. By 1926 he'd performed in thirty-nine Broadway premieres, thirty revivals, and seventeen Shakespeare plays. He'd acted in works by Molière in French and dramas by Ibsen in Danish. I blew up the photos too, to show the neighbors. "Look at him as a young actor," I said. "Can you believe it? He did movies, radio shows, and musical comedies too." They shook their heads as they looked at the pictures. "I had no idea," Rose said. "This is amazing."

He managed well on his own despite his advanced years until the early 1960s. Then, maybe after a small stroke or advancing dementia, his behavior went downhill. Rose, luckily, was walking up the steps on her way home as he opened the front door, buck naked, about to step onto the stoop and take a walk. "He'd always put clothes on when he left the building before," she said. "He was elegant, in fact, with a silk cravat and a silver-headed walking stick. He was mortified when he looked down and realized what he was doing, the poor man. I felt awful for him."

Mom and the other neighbor ladies brought meals downstairs. Rose made a point of stopping by to check on him on her way home from work. Ramiro, our super, swept his apartment when he cleaned the halls. But our thespian was too fragile to live alone any longer. I was seven or eight. He still thanked me profusely for bars of chocolate as I held them up to him but couldn't manage to bend into his bow.

A tearful group of us waved goodbye from the sidewalk on the day that white-coated attendants carried him down the steps in a wheelchair. He had a box of chocolate-covered cherries tucked at his side, our parting gift. He was dressed up, with a silk scarf draped theatrically around his neck and a plaid blanket over his legs. I reached out and gave him a hug. He swept those fluttering arms out to us, a graceful curtain call at the footlights, and blew kisses. It was a classy, fitting, exit. He moved to the nursing home on Abingdon Square around the corner, where he tarried awhile, then bowed and quietly left the stage for good.

Everyone missed him. We've seen all sorts of things at 63 Bank Street but never again those perfect, inked Saturday night puzzles.

5 • Mrs. Swanson and the Browders

The vaudeville dancer in apartment 2A swore she'd been a spy for the FBI.

Mr. and Mrs. Swanson had rented 2A since the 1930s as a rest stop between vaudeville circuit tours around the world. "And when we worked the Paramount," a Times Square theater, "it was easy from here," she told us. They'd performed exhibition ballroom dances like the tango.

By the early 1960s, when I was five or six, Mr. Swanson was long gone. Mrs. Swanson was tiny, with rheumy blue eyes, usually wearing a housecoat. Her old dancing feet were splayed and twisted, so she crept around in brocade slippers. She read her *Backstage* and *Time* magazine with a magnifying glass. Her apartment was full of soft silk Oriental rugs and exotic trinkets like porcelain dolls. She gave my mother some exquisite ivory miniatures from 1920s Japan.

A battered touring trunk in the basement had the words "Swanson & Swanson" written in blazing gold loops. It swung open like a walk-in closet, with faded red satin-lined drawers, stuffed with costumes and props. Mrs. Swanson let me play with them on rainy days. She taught me the Charleston. I did sidekicks by the furnace with a rhinestone tiara slipping over my eyes, a doomed flapper on the Titanic, dancing as the waters rose. Mrs. Swanson told me that the musicians kept playing until the end. "Imagine, all those poor people in that freezing water," she said, shaking her head. It seemed very sad and romantic.

"That big American Communist, the top one, lived directly below us, under our feet, in 1A, during the war," Mrs. Swanson insisted to my parents. This was World War II. "I had FBI agents right here in the house listening and watching him and his wife," she continued. "The FBI was in the first floor of 66 Bank too." I was too young to pay attention to the story back then. But I knew that Mrs. Swanson was lucid until her sudden stroke and death in 1967, since I brought groceries in for her several times a week. In my thirties, when I was thinking about the stories of people in 63 Bank Street, I dimly remembered Mrs. Swanson's Communist tales and called my parents. They remembered them well. "Definitely," Dad said. "She told us a number of times that there were high-ranking Communists living downstairs and that the FBI used her place to watch them in the '40s." I caught the scent of a juicy story. But where would I start?

Earl Browder, I learned, poring over archives in the New York Public Library, was the head of the American Communist Party in the 1940s. The most complete source on Browder I found was a book called *Earl Browder: The Failure of American Communism* by Dr. James G. Ryan, a history professor at Texas A&M University in Galveston. He is regarded as one of the nation's leading experts on Browder. But his book did not mention Bank Street.

I decided to email Dr. Ryan describing Mrs. Swanson's claims and asking for suggestions, but I didn't really expect an answer from such an obviously senior authority.

A few days later, the phone rang. It was Dr. Ryan. He sounded young, humorous, and modest about his intimidating knowledge of political history. We chatted for an hour as I frantically scribbled notes. That call was my dream jackpot, proof that Mrs. Swanson knew exactly what was going on with her neighbors, the astounding Browder clan.

Earl Browder himself never lived at 63 Bank Street, Dr. Ryan said. But Earl's brother, William "Big Bill," and his sister-in-law, Rose Browder, did, renting apartment 1A from 1940 through 1944 under false names. Bill headed the New York State chapter of the American Communist Party in the 1940s. Earl's sister, Margaret, was a member too, and so were Earl's lover and assorted other Browder relatives and in-laws.

* * *

Earl's parents were farmers in Kansas when Earl was born in 1891. The farm went broke, and Earl, who had never done anything but work the land, learned the harsh realities of industrial America's brutal but, at that time, completely legal treatment of workers. Miners destroyed their lungs inhaling coal dust for pennies a day. Grumblers and labor organizers, if they survived at all, lost eyes and teeth thanks to beatings by company security goons.

The shock changed Earl's life. He was outraged that America allowed wealthy capitalists to dehumanize its poorer, helpless citizens. He refused to support the US government as a soldier and spent part of World War I in prison as a conscientious objector.

In Earl's eyes, America's government was a failure. He had followed the 1917 Russian Revolution from afar, reading whatever he could about the oppressed peasants and how they rose up against their corrupt tsar. Then Joseph Stalin helped set up and lead a Communist government. Millions of workers, Earl read, had been freed from centuries of social and political slavery.

The indifference of Russia's royals to their starving fellow citizens seemed little different from the situation in 1920s America, where, as Earl saw it, heartless opportunists like the Rockefellers made millions, living like emperors off the labor of poor Americans, many of them uneducated women and children, who had few work choices aside from laboring for starvation wages in dangerous and unhealthy mines and factories. Why couldn't Americans free themselves too? Earl wondered. Communism seemed to him like the morally correct way to fight America's injustices towards the working class.

In 1923, Earl joined the newly formed Communist Party of America, and by 1932, he was their star. He ran for President twice during the 1930s, in the middle of the Great Depression, a time when millions of Americans were out of work. His slogan was "Communism Is Twentieth Century Americanism."

• • •

Back in 1908, a fledgling US government agency had formed that would play a huge part in the lives of Mrs. Swanson and her downstairs neighbors. It was an anti-crime unit that, after several name changes, evolved into the Federal Bureau of Investigation (FBI). When it started, the FBI operated independently, without presidential or senatorial oversight. It set its own rules and ran its own clandestine missions. And that was just fine with the man who headed it from 1924 on, J. Edgar Hoover. The FBI was his personal kingdom and took orders from him alone.

Hoover, a choleric conservative, definitely didn't see communism as America's salvation in the 1930s. On the contrary, he wanted to send that dirty communist Earl Browder *and* the liberal pinko US President Franklin Delano Roosevelt to Siberia, along with all the other lefties. Liberals, as he saw it, were unpatriotic cowards and soft on crime. Hoover was sure that Earl was neither an honest American citizen nor a clean politician. And he was determined to prove it.

Years of FBI surveillance eventually produced enough evidence to allow the government to jail Earl for passport fraud in 1940. Hoover had finally gotten Earl behind bars. But why, I wondered, did Hoover then send agents to Bank Street to spy on Bill and Rose Browder? It didn't make sense.

Then I discovered another plot twist. It turned out that President Roosevelt had his own plans for Earl, plans that had nothing to do with Hoover's delight that Earl was now a convicted felon. Roosevelt had commuted Earl's sentence and set him free in 1942. The action represented another salvo in the continuing power struggle between Roosevelt and Hoover, and as a result more FBI field agents scurried after the Browders.

They began watching in 1940, I discovered, when Bill and Rose moved into 1A, a cramped one-bedroom apartment on the first floor of our building. My grandmother rented 1A in the 1960s when I was a kid, and I lived there for several years after her death, so I knew it well. The front door opens into a tiny galley kitchen. One of the two living room windows has a street view and, on very sunny days, a bit of sunlight comes in. All the other windows face the dark, gloomy courtyard of 65 Bank Street, the tenement next door. And since 1A runs parallel to the first-floor entrance hall, the space is narrow and claustrophobic.

I could imagine Earl thumbing his nose at Hoover as he strolled out of prison. Timing was definitely on Earl's side. He'd bounced from jailbird to World War II White House confidante. Soviet Russia was an American wartime ally against Germany. Roosevelt had released Earl so that he could serve as a private link between the White House and the Soviet leader Joseph Stalin. Browder, Dr. Ryan told me, carried off-the-record communiqués between Roosevelt and Stalin as the two leaders fought Hitler together.

Given these events, Earl and his Communist Party of America seemed at an all-time height of influence and power when his brother Bill was living at 63 Bank Street. The FBI's interest in us was making more sense.

. . .

I was dying to know what the FBI had seen and heard from Mrs. Swanson's Bank Street apartment. Dr. Ryan helped me request the FBI files for William and Rose Browder from 1940 to 1944 under the Freedom of Information Act.

Eight weeks later, the postman rang the bell, complaining about wedging an eight-pound parcel into the mailbox. The files were so juicy that I read for hours, ignoring phone calls and my dog's outraged dinner grunts.

Bill and Rose, I learned, had indeed moved in with fake names, as "Mr. And Mrs. William E. Branch," as Jim Ryan had said. Occasionally, the reports stated, Rose called herself "Olive Branch." They told the building rental agency that they were stationery store clerks.

Hoover's agents recorded every move at 63 Bank Street from 1940 to 1944. The reports described Bill as a thickset, five-foot-nine white man with gray hair and gray eyes, a slight stoop of the left shoulder, and a light complexion. He was also a "heavy cigarette smoker." Born in 1895, he was in his forties. Rose, born in 1897, was five feet ten and a half inches with blue eyes, dyed blonde hair, and a scar on her forehead. She had a high-pitched voice, dressed "plain," and was uncharitably judged "rather heavy."

Earl and Bill had opposite styles. Earl was short and quiet: a fastidious eater who neither smoked nor drank. Bill was a heavy smoker and a hard drinker. An informant characterized Rose and Bill's crowd as "a bathtub gin drinking bunch." The FBI reported that wild parties were routine in 1A.

Connections started to click. Mrs. Swanson, I remembered, had complained bitterly to my parents about the Browders' noise. When I called them, Mom recounted a story I'd never heard. Late one night, Mrs. Swanson, tired of banging on the pipes yet again, threw on her robe, and stomped downstairs. A man leaned against the open apartment door, drink in hand, and whistled. "Hey, guys! They're coming in already undressed!" Mrs. Swanson glared at the crowd. Bill, surrounded by listeners, was telling a joke. He waved his cigar as he delivered the punch line. His friends roared and slapped their thighs as Rose pushed through the living room, smiling.

"Mrs. Swanson! How nice of you to join us! What would you like to drink?"

"Nothing, thank you," Mrs. Swanson said. "What I would like, Mrs. Branch, is what I always want. Some sleep. Can you quiet down, please?"

"Of course," Rose replied soothingly. "I'm so sorry. Are you sure you won't have a nightcap?"

"They always ignored me," Mrs. Swanson huffed to Mom. "They didn't really give a damn about others, those big-talk reformers." Noisy neighbors of any political persuasion can drive you crazy, and she was still mad fifteen years later. Maybe Earl's cozy standing with President Roosevelt made Bill and Rose reckless, not caring if someone called the cops.

· · ·

Another memory surfaced. I'd been fascinated by people's lives and family histories since I was a kid. Besides plying my grandmothers with wine to get 1800s family scandals on tape, I'd shamelessly used my insider status as a 63 Bank Streeter known to everyone since birth to capture neighbors' stories on tape and paper. I dug out my notes on free-spirited Alice Zecher, who had moved into apartment 3C as a young secretary in 1937 and lived here for fifty years. She loved good times, even in her middle and older years, which was when I'd gotten to know her.

Sure enough, according to my notes, she'd gone to "many great parties" in apartment 1A, hosted by what she described as "the fun couple who moved in a couple of years after me." "I don't remember much about them really, like what they did," she added. "I just remember that their bashes had a lot of booze and a lot of interesting men." Wow! I thought. Alice was one of the Browder party dogs! I wondered if she'd ever giggled her way upstairs to her own place with a lucky Communist comrade. Knowing Alice, I wouldn't have been surprised.

While Earl was still in prison, a parole officer wrote to Bill asking for family information. Ever the comedian, Bill gleefully wrote back, describing Earl as a placid accountant who enjoyed playing the flute. The two didn't have much contact, Bill said, adding that he had no idea where their other six siblings were except for a brother who was farming in Missouri.

Hoover's men shrugged. They knew perfectly well that Bill and Rose were running *The Daily Worker*, a Communist newspaper, out of a New York office and had "daily contact" with Earl as well as with many other Browder family members. Names are blacked out in the files, but an FBI "informant" reported frequent daytime visitors to 1A and a deluge of Communist literature in everyone's mailboxes after the "Branches" moved in. Phone records and mail were examined. Vacations were monitored.

Today, Hoover is portrayed as a right-wing extremist, and in many ways I agree with that assessment. But I feel uneasy, decades later, judging either Hoover *or* the Browders. How, I wondered, would I have felt back then, when American workers were so mistreated?

As I pondered this question, Jim Ryan briefed me on yet another bombshell: the Venona Documents. US government interceptions of Soviet secret cables sent from the Soviet embassy to the USSR during World War II had mysteriously appeared after the breakup of the Soviet Union. Around 2000, the US Library of Congress purchased copies of these cables and put them into the public domain.

Now I could fully understand Hoover's obsession with the Browders. It has always been legal for American citizens to affiliate with any political party, but it is quite another matter to work against the US government. The Browders had stepped far and hard over that line. They were, Earl, Bill, Rose, in-laws, lovers, all of them, running an international espionage ring for the Soviet Union.

The more I learned about the Browders' secret life as spies, the more I wanted to learn. What about Earl's lover, Kitty Harris, and the other Browders? What did they do as spies? I read articles and books like *Kitty Harris: The Spy With Seventeen Names*. When Kitty met Earl, she was a teenager, a Russian Jewish factory worker. In 1927 they left the US together on forged passports. For several years they organized Soviet spy cells in Shanghai, the Philippines, China, Jakarta, and Hong Kong, financed by smuggling jewelry and counterfeit currency from Moscow. Their love affair ended in 1929, but the spying continued. Both Kitty and Earl's sister, Margaret Browder, studied advanced espionage at Moscow's Lenin School in the 1930s. Classmates at KGB spy school, I thought. What next?

In the 1930s, Kitty was assigned to London to handle a high-ranking Soviet spy in the English government, a British diplomat named Donald Maclean. Although she was thirteen years his senior, Harris and the gorgeous, aristocratic Maclean fell in love. Looking at photographs of Maclean, I fell in love myself. When the British government reassigned Maclean from London to Paris, he begged the Russian KGB to send Kitty too. They worked together until the 1940 Nazi invasion of France, when Kitty's KGB superiors ordered her back to America to spy on America's secret nuclear bomb project.

Since fake names and passports were part of the game, Hoover's FBI agents had followed Earl throughout his travels, patiently collecting the evidence that led to Earl's conviction for passport fraud in 1940. Passport fraud wasn't what Hoover was after, but it served to get Earl behind bars. Hoover believed that Earl was running a ring of at least forty spies for Soviet Russia worldwide during World War II, both before being jailed and after Roosevelt commuted his sentence. As it turns out, the Venona documents support Hoover.

By the 1940s, Earl was a married father of three. He was careful to keep his family away from politics. According to Jim Ryan, he secluded his Russian wife and their children in Yonkers, a quiet New York City suburb. Given Earl's insistence on domestic privacy, Ryan found it "quite credible" that Earl used the Bank Street apartment of his affable, childless brother Bill as a convenient place to rendezvous with agents. Since Earl was also in and out of Washington and Moscow at the same time, there really must have been a three-ring FBI circus in Mrs. Swanson's living room. No wonder Hoover was in an uproar when Roosevelt gave Earl a get-out-of-jail-free card, I thought. Maybe Hoover had Roosevelt and Browder dartboards side by side in his office.

"What about Earl and Bill's sister, Margaret?" I asked Ryan. Of course he knew her story too. Stocky Miss Browder lacked Kitty's sex appeal, but she was a star spy, too. She left the States in 1931 as "Jean Montgomery" and was a leading Soviet informant in Nazi Germany during the 1930s. She was so valuable that when she became ill,

Moscow refused to release her until Earl intervened. Margaret came home, took a job as a hospital clerk in the Bronx, and died in 1961.

I felt sorry for Kitty Harris. She fled to Russia as World War II was ending. Despite her years of dedicated service, her suddenly indifferent Soviet handlers dumped her into dilapidated public housing and left her to rot. Donald Maclean, her British lover, defected to Russia hours ahead of British agents who were closing in on him. No one even bothered to tell her. Kitty died in Russia in 1966, destitute and alone, still wearing her one treasure, a locket from Maclean.

Earl lost an internal power struggle in the American Communist Party in the late 1940s and was expelled. Bill appealed to Stalin for help. But Earl had served his purpose. Neither the White House nor the Kremlin cared about Earl anymore. After his wife died, he lived with a son in Princeton, New Jersey, writing books and articles, until his death in 1973.

Bill and Rose, expelled from the Party as well, remained in the Village. The FBI continued to interview the Browders in the 1950s, trying to gather evidence of espionage, but could not trip up Earl or Bill, while agents complained that Rose and Margaret were "arrogant, uncooperative, evasive, and abusive." One agent wrote that "should any one of the Browders talk it will undoubtedly deeply involve all of them in Soviet intelligence activities."

The FBI closed a perjury case against Rose in 1961, but her eventual fate is unrecorded. The cigarettes caught up with Bill in 1964 when "William E. Branch" of West Ninth Street died of a heart attack.

When Jim Ryan came through town I invited him over for a firsthand look at the place. Before he arrived, I asked my neighbor Al in 2A if we could search for evidence of the FBI's presence. We rolled back his rug, and right in the middle of the floor, directly above the living room below, the boards had been sawed in a square and neatly replaced. No other apartment in the building had anything like it.

When a Bank Street vaudeville dancer tells you something, you should believe her.

6 • John Lavery

Exit Shakespearean actor Franz Bendtsen from apartment 1A stage right, in 1962. Enter John Lavery. John was in his mid-thirties, tall, slender, and mustached, with reddish hair, sensitive eyes, and a sweet smile. John was an actor and Off-Broadway director at avant-garde theaters like Café La MaMa. The Laverys, Dad surmised from their chats, were an old New England family of artists and academics. John had the easy grace born of breeding and education.

My parents enjoyed his warm good humor and invited him up often for home cooking. We passed the rigatoni, chatting about theater, politics, science, and whatever popped up. When feminine hygiene sprays came out, John, waving his wineglass, declared that a crotch should proudly smell like a crotch. Since he was smiling and nodding at all three of us, I, age six, agreed, as wholehearted as I was clueless. My father coughed and changed the subject.

No romances were mentioned. Once in a while a male friend came upstairs with John. The event was too unimportant for comment. Although I was foggy about what went on in people's private lives, I did know that it was never the measure of their worth in our home.

John's day job was adapting chemistry research for college textbooks. He had, Mom said, a distinguished reputation in this arcane field. He was shifting, he told us, from acting and directing to writing plays and novels. Written, spoken, or performed, he loved words and language. He worshiped James Joyce and once gave Dad a copy of *Ulysses*. "Anyone can 'get' Joyce if they try," he said. "The reader just has to work harder for the payoff."

Since John never spoke down to me or excluded me from his remarks, I wanted to show off my grasp of Joyce to him. After all, I thought, he always complimented my choices in books. When he left, I took *Ulysses* and settled into my room. It was a battle. I slowly reread every sentence, and fought like hell to discern a plot. Unbeknownst to me, I was tackling one of the most demanding books in the English language, and Joyce wrestled me to the floor. For the first time in my life I was forced to give up on a book. I was too embarrassed to tell John.

· · ·

Over time he got more and more involved with textbook editing. Deadlines piled up. Several times he called us in the middle of the night, and Dad rushed him to St. Vincent's Hospital. He became gaunt and his skin yellowed. The AIDS epidemic was decades away, and John's symptoms, in retrospect, were different. He was evasive, though, and we never learned exactly what was going on. My parents encouraged him to accept fewer assignments, go on vacation, and take more time for his own writing. But he stuck grimly to his day job.

He started to turn down our dinner invitations and gradually drifted away. When he announced that he was not going to renew his lease, Mom rented his apartment for her mother. My grandfather had died, and Grandma was alone in Brooklyn. Mom let John stay on as she organized Grandma's move. He was morose and taciturn. The only thing he would tell us was that he had inherited a lighthouse in New England from a relative and was going to live in it and work on his novel. This struck me as a daring and romantic move, the perfect life for John, who came alive in the world of books and theater. After years of enjoying his extraordinary discourse and easy wit, I wanted to be exactly like him. I too wished to be a writer and dwell in a solitary tower by the sea.

We never heard from John again, which made us all sad. We wondered what we could have done to keep his friendship.

7 • Grace Bickers

If Grace Bickers had not lived, Tennessee Williams would have created her.

She was petite, with delicate white skin. Her soft red hair was cut in a pageboy. Her winter coat was a luxurious camel hair in a classic '40s swing style that swirled around her tiny ankles. She always wore stiletto heels, even in the snow.

An almost Japanese sense of privacy kept neighbors apart in our building except by invitation. We had a vague idea that Grace came from Southern money and had been married to a prominent journalist. No one knew if they had divorced or if he had died before she moved into apartment 3A in our building in the early 1950s. She never mentioned family or friends.

But this much we did know. She smiled warmly and loved discussing politics and the arts with neighbors like the writer John Kemmerer or Franz Bendtsen, the actor. She preferred American literature to British, declaring that American writers like Faulkner cut close to the bone with less affectation.

She liked President Kennedy but thought it was more important to continue FDR's social programs than to put a man on the moon. "The Russians are no threat to us," she told Dad in her soft drawl. "Stalin destroyed that country. People are unemployed and starving right here in the States. What about that?" She waved a newspaper at the neighbors, cheering, on the stoop on the day President Johnson signed the Civil Rights Act of 1964. "This'll stir some pots back home in Dixie."

There was no job or mention of a former career. It's hard to say how old she was in the late 1950s when I was about four and became aware of her, but probably in her forties or fifties.

Back then the Village had working factories, docks, and rough, no-nonsense bars. The White Horse Tavern, two blocks away, was celebrated for playing host to the poet Dylan Thomas, but most of the customers were blue-collar locals. One of those bars was around the corner from my building. Once, I glanced inside as I sped by on my bike and saw Grace perched on a stool.

The image had no meaning. I dimly understood that bars were a place to drink liquor, but that wasn't a big deal to me because my Italian-American family served alcohol as a part of meals and socializing, and grandkids got a splash of wine in 7 Up with Sunday dinner. Since I only saw Grace at 63 Bank Street, it was simply unusual to see her in another setting. So I meant nothing when we met and I mentioned it. But Grace was clearly angry. She narrowed her eyes, and said through gritted teeth, "Well, now, why would that be any of your business?"

My face flamed, and I slunk away. At home my mother seemed sympathetic but suggested casually that Grace probably just felt that I was being nosy.

• • •

A few years later, I understood. Grace was cultured and friendly, but her life was savagely bleak. She emerged every late afternoon, sober and impeccably groomed, down to her good kidskin gloves. Then she spent her evenings drinking in local bars.

She generally returned around 8:30 p.m. and always alone. My parents knew she might not make it up the steps so they'd prop open the front door. She'd wobble to a landing and rest. After panting and leaning on the banister for a few minutes, she'd move on. When they heard her apartment door close, they knew she was safe. If she faltered, they'd help her upstairs. Proud and fragile, she always claimed to be tired after a long day. My parents pretended to believe her.

In time I learned to pretend, too. It felt odd the first time I helped her to her apartment, but it wasn't scary. Besides, Grace was still my friend, just weaving and slurring her words. She'd ask how school was and tell me how pretty and smart I was getting to be as I steadied her up the stairs.

Strange, I knew, was not always dangerous. A cross-eyed young man with a vacant look used to sit on his West Fourth Street stoop or in his first-floor window every day as I walked to grade school. He smiled and waved as I passed, and I waved back. We waved for decades until his hair turned gray and his family moved. Glenn, a musician friend, had periodic panic attacks and couldn't be alone in his place on Jones Street. I'd step over him as he slept in the hallway outside my bedroom door, his only choice in our small apartment. Isn't this fun, my parents said. Glenn is sleeping over and he brought onion rolls for breakfast. Sometimes I saw tears on his cheeks, but I wasn't afraid of him, either.

• • •

One day in 1968 police were in the hall of our building when I came home from school. Grace had had a stroke. She had cried for help, and eventually someone heard her. I ran upstairs and wriggled through the officers to get to her apartment.

I stopped short when I got to the door. Her apartment, which I'd never seen, was a labyrinth of garbage. Towering stacks of newspaper edged a tiny pathway through the narrow hallway. The cops could barely wedge the door open enough to talk to her. Even I couldn't squeeze through. She heard me and called my name. "I'm coming, Grace!" I yelled. "Don't worry!"

The cops boosted me on top of the papers, and I crawled down the hallway and into the bedroom like a squirrel in a tree. Another stack of papers covered half of the mattress. She'd left just enough room to sleep. I held on with one hand and reached down with the other, stroking her arm, telling her everything was going to be OK as the cops and Ramiro cleared away enough debris for a rescue.

• • •

Grace was hospitalized for weeks. While she was gone, Ramiro and the neighbors filled bag after bag with rotting newspapers. The stacks wound throughout the entire apartment. There were trails from the hall to the refrigerator, to a teeny Grace-sized place on the sagging couch, to a chair at a table by the window. I gagged as I shoveled black fungus out of the refrigerator. It felt like a crazy dream until the stench kicked me back to earth.

Ramiro set off roach bombs by the case to destroy the Biblical generations that ran everywhere, finally flung from Paradise, ending years of finger pointing as we secretly blamed each other for those disgusting bugs.

Beneath the newspapers, objects appeared. Broken cameras. Window screens. Cracked mirrors. Machine parts. Grace had apparently dragged home anything that took her fancy. The mattress had rotted down to its springs. The newspapers on her bed started at 1968 and descended to 1952. Dad and Ramiro threw it out, and everyone in the building chipped in for a new mattress and box spring. No one wanted to hurt Grace's pride, so we agreed to say that we'd just covered her bed with new sheets.

Even after days of sweat, none of us could believe what we'd seen. The adults talked about the Collyer brothers, who were crushed to death under piles of debris in their 1940s Harlem mansion. Still, who would have imagined a situation like this, even in our admittedly eccentric building? Grace always looked so clean and well groomed.

It may seem strange that we lived so close to her without knowing anything about how she lived. But Grace's home had always been her own world. She had politely refused invitations to drinks or dinner for as many years as she had lived in our building.

We cleaned feverishly, anticipating Grace's pleasure when she returned. Bags of vacuumed dust piled up. Twenty years of window grime was peeled away. She had some good furniture and knickknacks, perhaps relics from her former life, whatever that had been. We kept anything that had any conceivable use or beauty.

The day she came home we tried to pretend that everything was normal. But Grace was furious at us. She didn't like people going through her home. Her important papers were missing. Why were we such nosy parkers?

It was a last show of pride. She was barely able to stand up and needed home aides to prepare meals and help her dress. She couldn't walk well enough to leave the house. Mom, like other neighbors, cooked extra and sent me up with dishes.

During visits she complained about her lost possessions. "I'm sorry," I told her. "We meant well. How are you feeling today? I'm reading *The Grapes of Wrath*. Do you like John Steinbeck?" It was easy to move her onto another topic. There was still a vestige of bright mind left. But she was now an old lady with blue-veined hands, hunched in a sunny spot by the window. If she had friends or relatives, she still never mentioned them. None of us saw any visitors.

Grace died later that year. No one remembers a funeral or a memorial service or even who found her body. Workers were throwing her possessions into garbage bags when I came home from school one day. I salvaged a brass floor lamp and a silver vanity set with her initials on it. Years later I had a tailor copy her swirling camel hair coat. I still think of her and her lonesome, fierce pride with love even though none of us ever really knew who she was.

8 • Lena

Back in 1822, West Fourth Street, which crosses Bank, was called Asylum Street. It still deserved the name in the early 1960s as I walked to first grade. New York had begun to close halfway houses that provided beds and social support for mentally fragile individuals and to release tractable patients from psychiatric institutions under a policy known as deinstitutionalization. This policy was later seen as a disastrous mistake. But during my childhood, people who couldn't care for themselves filled Village stoops and parks.

That was nothing new. By 1675, with only five thousand settlers elbowing each other in the tiny colony below Wall Street, the colonists had already built an insane asylum. Queen Anne, their English queen, sent a potential inmate, by Colonial standards, when she sent her nephew, Lord Cornbury, to be the governor. He swept in to his first meeting wearing a hoop skirt, declaring that he represented Her Majesty, and should, in all respects, portray her faithfully. He also hid behind trees in his frocks, leaping out to startle passersby.

Colonists might have tolerated a cross-dressing prankster but certainly not a thief. Astonishment turned to outrage as Cornbury embezzled funds and cheerfully took bribes. By 1707 he landed in debtors' prison with the approval of his mortified aunt. When Cornbury's father died, he paid off his debts and fled to England.

Thomas Paine, the lauded incendiary writer whose words helped fuel the American Revolution, also later descended into mental illness. Sailors and whores watched, laughing, as Paine was kicked from Village dives. Shortly after that, the former Bellevue Farm, hidden in the woods up the East River, became the site of New York's first psychiatric hospital.

My matter-of-fact parents trained me to cross the street to avoid odd behaviors and to run away or into a store for help if anything happened. But giving strange a wide berth was very different when it lived upstairs. Lena moved into apartment 4C of our building in the early 1960s. Soon afterwards she accused all of us—especially Irene and her parents, who lived down the hall from her in 4B—of Satanism. Irene was seven and I was five.

Lena was a heavy, middle-aged woman, about five-foot-four, with coarse black hair tied in a bun. Her olive complexion was sallow, her teeth yellowed. Moles and brown spots dotted her face. She had a fat white cat, which I glimpsed as the movers carried her furniture in, before she hurried to close the door.

· · ·

Her extended family knew our landlady, as did we. The landlady, a former singer, chatted with us when she came around. She told us that Lena and her sister were orphans from Sicily who had immigrated to the States as teenagers and worked their way through high school and college.

For the first few weeks after Lena arrived, I smiled and said hello when we passed. Back then, everyone in the building greeted one another. She returned my greetings a few times. Then one day she scowled and turned her head away as I opened my mouth. "It's this kid again, bothering me," she informed the wall. I froze. Other tenants got the same treatment.

After that, Lena usually muttered to herself as she walked by, too. If we passed her on the stoop, she'd skulk to the sidewalk, picking up bits of litter and mumbling about folks getting in her way. Irene and I sometimes saw her put her own garbage into other buildings' cans along the street piece by piece.

Over the next few months, she became unkempt. Her hair stuck out as if she'd jabbed her hair pins in at random. Her clothes became wrinkled and dirty. She often smelled bad. Her antipathy to the neighbors was obvious. If she was in the downstairs hall and couldn't get to the stairs without passing us, she'd run to the unlocked door to the basement in the back of the hall, lunge into the stairwell, slam the door, and yell, "Children of Satan! Devils! Evil! Save me, Jesus! Shut up and go away! You're all going to hell!" Irene and I stopped playing in the hallway on rainy days. She'd open her door and scream, "Shut up, you goddamned noisy kids!" so we didn't feel safe there anymore.

Lena sometimes gave us the same treatment when she was inside her apartment. It could go on for hours. When she was really on the boil, she'd open her door and slam it shut over and over. Plaster cracked and floor tiles came loose. Sometimes she sang. A mangled *Ave Maria* came through the backyard and into my bedroom where I did my homework. It sounded as if the Virgin Mother were being dragged through the streets by her hair.

• • •

Our parents had given Irene and me orders to leave Lena alone after the aggravated landlady called Lena's sister, asking her to come and help. Mom and Irene's mother, Annie, heard the sister banging on Lena's door and came out to the fourth-floor hall. The sisters were yelling at each other in Italian. Lena refused to open her door.

The sister wore an elegant white suit and heavy gold jewelry. She was sobbing as she pounded on Lena's door. Black lines of mascara dripped down her jacket as the Annies led her downstairs to our living room. Mom made espresso and sent Irene and me to play in my room while the women talked. We could hear them, of course. There were few secrets in this building, with its small rooms and echoes.

"I don't know what to do," Lena's sister sobbed. "She started acting this way in her late twenties. Before that she was fine. She had a good job. She had friends. The doctor says she'd be all right if she'd take her pills. But when she feels better, she thinks she doesn't need them anymore. I beg her, Lena, please, you know what happens when you stop. But she doesn't listen."

"Believe me, this is not really my sister," she continued tearfully "She is so smart and educated. She loves me and my family. She had a good life before all this. It breaks my heart, but I can't keep her with me on Long Island. My husband fights with her and she scares my kids." When we tiptoed in to get sesame cookies, the ladies, to our annoyance, switched to Italian.

Lena's sister finally left with hugs and thanks. We listened as she went upstairs and tried again. This time Lena opened the door.

Our mothers herded us into the living room, the table still set with espresso cups, now edged with red lipstick.

"Sit down, girls," my mother said. "We need to talk to you. Lena needs privacy. It's better if you don't say hello or talk to her."

We'd never been told to do this before. Proper manners to adults were an iron house rule for both of us.

"What if she yells at us?" Irene demanded.

"Just walk away," my mother said.

Irene and I filed back to my room, shocked into silence. We avoided muttering strangers on the street, of course, but the adults didn't seem to understand how terrifying it was to have a neighbor act in this bizarre way. "I'll pull her hair and bite her if she tries to hurt you," Irene whispered as a tear rolled down my cheek. Irene was tough. She was the only kid who fought Rudy, the strongest kid on our block.

Terrified, I decided to flatten myself against a wall and sidle off if Lena came in sight, and for years that's exactly what I did. I never volunteered another word or looked her in the eye.

· · ·

Bank Street and New York in general offered kids daily lessons in survival, with a wide assortment of perverts and criminals. A man lurked in a doorway during my walk to first grade, snapping his fingers to catch my eye and wagging what I thought was a raw fish in his pants. A teenager grabbed my allowance dollar and ran off as I was handing it to the Good Humor man. The fuming vendor gave me a Creamsicle for free. A group of girls surrounded me on a subway platform, shoving me from one to the other like a beach ball. When I darted for the next train, they finally let me go, laughing and sneering. A friend and I watched from her stoop as her brother and his friends punched a man who'd licked his lips and rubbed his groin at us.

· · ·

I saw Lena's sister on and off for the next twenty years. We could hear the shouts as the two of them argued. Lena usually combed her hair and stopped muttering for a while afterwards. Sometimes the sister brought attendants who pulled Lena downstairs as she screamed about devils and took her away for a few weeks. She was better when she came home from that, too. Once in a great while she'd even smile and ask me how school was going. I'd mumble something and skulk off fast, sure that the wrong response would make her howl and yank my hair.

"I'm stuck," the landlady told us. "She pays the rent and hasn't actually hurt anyone, so the courts won't do anything. Believe me, I've tried." It was true. New York City had strong laws protecting tenants. It would take years to evict her, if it could even be done. Acting crazy was not cause for eviction, especially in the Village.

Lena reserved her greatest enmity for the Frydels in 4B. They were leading our Satan cult, she screamed from behind her front door, and Mimi, their poodle, was a demon dog. Fat old Mimi worshiped anyone, saint or devil, with food. If our door was open, she knocked us over barreling to our dog's dish. If you lacked culinary potential, Mimi ignored you and waddled away. But whenever Frydels appeared, Lena crossed herself and shook her fist in their faces, yelling, "Satan, be gone!" There was a decided shortage of loving thy neighbor on the fourth floor.

Every few weeks, thick chalked crosses showed up on our apartment doors, leaving a powdery morning mess. Lena was a champion at sneaking around the building at night. No one ever caught her, not even the early-rising white-collar workers or the performers who came home after shows. At moody age twelve, I slammed back into the house one morning, snapping at my parents as I furiously brushed my new Afghani suede coat, all the rage in 1968, with a washcloth. I'd forgotten to check for a cross before rushing out.

"Why don't they evict Lena?" I demanded. "My coat is dirty, and I'm going to be late for school. You make me live in this stupid building with crazy people! What if my friends see her?"

My mother blotted the suede with a towel and told me it would dry quickly. "It's just chalk," my father said calmly over his *Times*. "It's harmless."

Lena also accused the Frydels of spying on her from the peephole in their apartment door. They'd wake up smelling paint and find their peephole cover painted black again. Since the covers were little metal disks that swung open, it was merely a statement. Lena's own peephole was barricaded with wood.

Lena lived below Sabine, the artist, in 5C. Sabine had her own mental problems, and the two women often screamed at each other as we covered our ears. One day Irene and I ran out to a police commotion in the halls. Sabine had turned on her water full blast, plugged the drains, and hidden in her closet with no clothes on. She had broken down this way at least three times by now. It was always easier on us when Sabine called the White House and threatened the President, as she had several times. No one had ruined paintings or soggy carpets, and Ramiro's basement didn't flood when the muscular Secret Servicemen in their cool sunglasses pulled up and ran around the building. But now I could hear Ramiro banging pipes, yelling and cursing, and hoped he wouldn't run upstairs with his leaded baseball bat while the cops were here.

The young policemen in the fourth-floor hallway asked our advice. What about 4C? Would that tenant let them climb up to Sabine on the back fire escape?

Irene and I looked at each other and grinned. "Lena is probably home," Irene said sweetly. "But if you think the lady in 5C is nuts, wait until you meet *this* one. She'll call you devils and come at you with a knife." Inspired, Irene yammered on as I nodded sadly, trying to add an air of sympathetic gravitas and veracity.

The cops squared their shoulders and knocked.

"Yes?" came a musical trill. "Who is it, please?"

They explained their mission through the door and it swung open.

There was Lena, neatly attired, hair combed, and smiling broadly. "Hello, officers. Of course you may come in, of course. Anything to help."

Years later, I asked a psychiatrist about Lena's astounding act. He said that many mental patients who had been involuntarily committed learned to fake normalcy to get themselves sprung, especially those who, like Lena, had been hospitalized repeatedly.

The cops thanked her and went in, throwing disgusted looks back at us as they went.

After graciously ushering them by, Lena glanced over her shoulder to make sure that they were out of earshot, then glared at Irene and me. Thrusting her face forward until she was nose to nose with us, she bared her teeth and hissed, "Satan's children! Die and burn in hell!" Then she calmly shut the door.

• • •

Several years passed. I left for Boston University and, two restless years later, moved to Italy, where I studied for two years and finally learned to speak Italian. Then I flew home and married my high-school sweetheart. My parents were moving to the suburbs, and I traded my lease on my late grandmother's apartment, 1A, for larger and sunnier 2B.

When Lena saw me, she sighed and muttered, "Oh, great. Look who's here again." I respected her space, stepping back into 2B and closing the door as she passed, but she didn't terrify me anymore. In fact, I was startled to discover that I felt sorry for her. I had tried to backpack solo through Sicily and found it, in the 1970s, to be a darkly unwelcoming place. I could not imagine a mentally ill woman who cursed her neighbors surviving there.

I divorced and got a master's degree in special education but moved from teaching to Wall Street to TV production and back, unable to settle down. My twenties became my thirties. Still a travel addict, I spent long stretches of time in other countries. There were new jobs and new relationships, but I kept apartment 2B and practiced my Italian whenever I could. By the mid-1980s, when I came back for another stretch in New York, Lena was gray-haired and stout. Now she pulled herself up the steps one at a time, grunting and stopping for breath.

Like a veteran dance couple, we continued to perform our hallway pas de deux. She seemed to understand that I wouldn't intrude on her space. She fought with some of the young new tenants, but I'd explain her story. Most left her alone after that.

One day, I came home worn out and cranky. I saw Lena ahead of me on the second-floor landing, but I was too tired to wait. Screw it, I thought. I walked up to the second floor, a flagrant violation of our rules because Lena was less than halfway to the third floor. She turned her head and gave the wall behind me a nasty look.

"Oh, God!" she snapped. "What a fucking nerve this one has!"

"Lena!" I said before I knew that words were coming out of my mouth. "Stop! You know who I am, and you know I'm not going to bother you. I'm tired and I want to go home, just like you."

Her head jerked up, and she shifted her gaze so that we were eye to eye for the first time since my childhood. Only then did I realize that I'd spoken in Italian.

"Oh, OK," she answered in English. Sighing, she grasped the banister and pulled herself upstairs without another word.

"I don't care if you spoke ancient Greek," Irene, who now lived in Vermont, barked when I called and told her about the encounter. "She's nuts, and if she ever touches my parents I'll come back and put a stake through her heart."

• • •

After decades of fear and hostility, Lena and I were now having a guarded relationship of sorts. I still gave her space and privacy. But where as a child I'd seen a monster, I now saw what my parents had seen, a scared, fragile person who was desperately lonesome. She seemed to welcome an innocuous exchange about the weather, but she flinched and hurried away if other neighbors came by. She sometimes checked in, making a comment about some imagined issue or another, watching my reaction, waiting to see if I was experiencing it too. She understands that her perceptions are wrong, I realized, but she doesn't know what to do. If I answered with soft, gentle words—and only in Italian—I could get through to her and calm her down. Now I saw that she was pitifully confused by her hallucinations, which were so very real to her.

"Lei non possa sentire l'odore della cucina di Anna Frydel, Signora Lena" ("You are not smelling Annie Frydel's cooking, Lena"), I said one day in 1997, after she complained that her house smelled nasty because Annie had burned her tomato sauce. "They moved out. Annie passed away and John lives in Vermont with Irene. It's OK, Lena. They're gone."

Lena stared at me with dull uncertainty. "But I smell her tomato sauce," she insisted. "I know it's hers."

You poor thing, I thought. Old, tired, alone, afraid. Her sister had given up on her or maybe died, and as far as I knew there was no one else to help her. The landlady had handed the building's affairs to a management company. What a bleak and savage life this schizophrenia has given her, I thought. In prison forever for a crime she didn't commit. Imagining evil in this crazy city, where real troubles lurk in every corner.

One friend said it best: "We weren't brought up in the Village. We were yanked up." It's true. Someone asked how many times I'd been bothered before I turned twenty-one. I tried to come up with a number, but it was hard to calculate because there are so many categories. Besides muggings (at least ten), and burglaries (three), should I include people spitting or hissing as I walked by? Masturbators? Flashers? Stalkers? Gang threats or violence? Angry drunks? Addicts shooting drugs in our hall? Trash-talking street prostitutes by the river? And how about men in cars yelling, "Oh, baby, I wanna f*** you so bad!"

It was scarcely the most genteel childhood, but those hard-won street smarts have saved my hide, like when I was hiking on a deserted Indonesian beach and a man glided out of the woods, blocking my path. When absolutely cornered, with no avoidance options, go nuts! I dropped to the sand, bouncing and gibbering like an ape while he stared, eyes wide. When I started flinging sand at him, snapping my teeth, he turned and ran.

Thank God for Greenwich Village, I thought to myself.

· · ·

One evening in the late 1990s Rose in 2C told me that an ambulance had again come for Lena. This time, she didn't come back.

It was one of the rare mercies of Lena's life that she was not on the streets on 9/11. Her demons screamed through the blackened air as I watched people burn alive and jump to their deaths from the towers. I locked myself away in my apartment, as Lena had, while Bank Streeters, with quiet sympathy, brought food and took me to doctors. It was a long struggle, but in the end, with a newfound respect for Lena and her years of daily courage, I came out and faced the world.

9 • Sabine

I stared at the young woman in the hall. "Do you know Sabine, my grandmother?" she said. She had the tawny eyes, high cheekbones, and golden brown hair of her mother and grandfather. As she peered at the mailboxes, I had asked if she needed help. It was 2009, and she clearly didn't know that Sabine, a resident of 63 Bank Street since 1949, had died several years earlier.

I was a few years younger than Sabine's two daughters, Ava and Chloe—too young to understand what the screams from apartment 5C were doing to them in the 1950s and 1960s. Decades later, the daughters by then long gone, Sabine was indigent and bedridden in her apartment with only a city health aide to help her. I visited, bringing food, and listened to her story.

• • •

Sabine was born, she told me, in 1921 in upstate New York. Her father died, and her mother moved to the city and took a factory job.

Sabine came of age in the Village of the 1930s and '40s. She watched artists at work in Washington Square Park and wandered through local galleries, determined to celebrate beauty and live the artist's life.

Bohemia and working-class Greenwich Village glared at one another a lot in those days. Sabine's mother frowned at artists as she trudged home. Scruffy good-for-nothings, all of them. What would they live on when they got old? She fought to instill sensible values into her daughter, but it was a losing battle. By her late teens, Sabine was a vivacious beauty with creamy skin and thick black hair. She had a lithe figure and loved to design dramatic clothes. She wanted to dress like her idols Frida Kahlo and Georgia O'Keeffe.

Sabine's art school friends rang the doorbell at all hours. Sabine's mother grumbled. "Life is serious, Sabine. Art doesn't pay the rent. That nice young butcher likes you. A woman needs a steady man, not one of those artsy bums." Sabine laughed and kissed her mother as she draped a shawl around her shoulders and twirled in the mirror. She'd made the shawl from a thrift-shop skirt. "We'll be fine, Mom. Everything will be great."

. . .

Sabine kept taking art classes during World War II. A rangy young man named Levi with gold-brown hair and tawny eyes watched from his canvas as she swept into the studio. Levi, a war veteran who had grown up on a farm in Washington State, was studying art too.

Sabine lost her job as a waitress and left art school. Levi, who had been working up the nerve to speak to her, searched through coffeehouses and galleries all over the Village. Finally he sidled into the art school's office, twisting his hat with long, bony fingers as he mumbled a request to the manager for the address and phone number of "that girl, Sabine."

The manager, a tough woman from the neighborhood, frowned and said that she wasn't allowed to give out such information. Then she hesitated. "I saw the scars on his face and hands," she told Sabine later. "He fought for us, and now he wants to meet a girl. What the hell." She glanced around and scribbled on a pad. "Here," she said. "But don't say where you got it."

Because Sabine had no phone, Levi walked to her Perry Street apartment the next morning. It was a Saturday. Her friends had thrown her a birthday party on Friday night, and the place was still draped with streamers. Levi rang the bell and stammered an invitation for a date. Sabine wasn't dressed yet, but she put on a housecoat and invited him in for leftover cake. Her mother, scandalized, kept a beady eye on them from the kitchen.

They went to Gertrude Vanderbilt Whitney's museum of American art on West Eighth Street. The Whitney, which is now downtown near the Hudson River, was cutting-edge, packed with artists and collectors on the lookout for new trends. Levi was so nervous that he left his new hat behind. Sabine was amused and intrigued. She decided to give him a chance.

Sabine's mother worried. "He has no job," she pointed out. "How can you live on art?" But she had to admit that Levi was a steady fellow with old-fashioned ways. When he asked for her permission to court Sabine, the mother reluctantly said yes but only if he earned enough to support her. He got a job with the post office.

Sabine was torn. She liked extroverted young men. Levi was mature and quiet, not the life of any party. But he was kind and gentle, and most of all he was determined to live the same unfettered artistic life she wanted. She began to fall in love.

• • •

In 1946 the couple married in St. Veronica's Roman Catholic Church on Christopher Street. His parents sent a little gift money in a letter, apologizing that they couldn't afford the trip from Washington State. Their friends threw flower petals as the wedding party paraded to a reception at the Stonewall Inn, which several decades later would become an icon of gay life in the Village.

That summer the couple borrowed a friend's place in Cape Cod for a week. A photographer walking through the dunes saw them painting side by side. His photos were published under the title "Up and Coming New Artists at Work in Provincetown." Sabine was designing clothing too, and the Schiaparelli couture house was interested in her work. Schiaparelli bought some sketches and asked for more. Both Sabine and Levi exhibited their paintings in galleries and attracted buyers. Sabine's dreams, she told me, had come true. She had it all: love, friends, and a career that was taking off.

The couple lived in a cramped studio until 1949, when baby Chloe was due. Their eyes lit up when a realtor brought them to apartment 5C. The place was perfect; quiet, cheap, and sunny. A second daughter, Ava, arrived in 1951. Sabine was delighted, she told me, that Ava had Levi's lanky frame and coloring since Chloe looked so much like her. They painted while the girls slept.

• • •

When my parents moved to 63 Bank Street in August of 1955, Sabine saw my pregnant mother struggling to carry boxes up the steps and helped her as they chatted. She painted a mural in Annie Frydel's kitchen. "Sabine was a sweetheart back then," the Annies agreed. "A beauty with an open heart."

At the time we still had Mr. Simmons, the wiry old super who lived in the basement apartment. In 1957 he retired and prepared to go back home. Part of his preparation was making sure that his job went to his 18-year-old nephew, Jimmy, who was coming up from their small town in rural Mississippi. The uncle wanted Jimmy to live in New York and get the opportunities he'd never have as an African American man down South. "Crackers keep their boots on a man's neck," he told Larry over goodbye drinks. "A man has nowhere to go and all his life to get there."

Because the job paid little, Sabine knocked on everyone's doors, asking them to chip in for Jimmy's furniture and food. She also worried about the temptations of the city, since he was only a kid. His uncle was concerned too, writing to Sabine that he'd told the family to find a proper Mississippi wife.

Everyone blinked when the bride arrived. Doris was a doe-eyed beauty, but she was only fourteen. Ann tried to make conversation while Doris stared silently at the ground. "The poor child was scared to death," Sabine told me.

Sabine took Doris sightseeing and taught her to haggle with pushcart vendors. Two babies arrived in quick succession. Doris was barely sixteen when her second child was born, but she smiled and talked with us now. Sabine decorated bureau drawers as bassinets. The Annies cooked soups and strained baby food. Sabine and Doris herded the number 63 kids—her girls, Irene, and me—down to the Hudson River for picnics. Doris walked behind, making sure we crossed the street safely, pushing her baby carriage. One night an arsonist set fire to several doors in the Village where black families lived, including the one to our basement. Sabine, crying and furious, brought Doris and the babies upstairs that night and kept them until Jimmy fixed the door and repainted.

I painted with Ava and Chloe while Sabine coached us. "Look at the sheen on the apple, girls," she'd say. "Draw that light." Both of her daughters had real talent. My work was awful, but Sabine inevitably found something nice to say.

· · ·

I sometimes saw Levi struggling up the stairs as he came home from work, gasping and stopping every few steps. He was hospitalized for a year and finally died around 1963. He'd never really recovered from his combat wounds, when shrapnel tore into his face, throat, and lungs, Sabine told me.

Maybe Sabine could have coped if poverty, Levi's constant illness, and motherhood hadn't pushed her over an edge. We first heard her screaming at the girls when Levi was in the hospital. After he died, her outbursts became a daily affair. The girls stopped smiling and playing with me or the other kids on our block.

Chloe was fragile and shy. She had buck teeth and could be made to cry and run back upstairs with one taunt. The Bank Street kids, shamefully including me, who played tag and jump rope together, smelled a wounded animal and were unmercifully cruel. Years later, Chloe told me that she'd sit on the wooden steps above the fifth-floor landing that led to the roof and read, hiding from everyone. I felt horrible. We'd been mean for no reason at all.

Tough, wiry Ava was a different story. We heard her yell back at Sabine, bang down the stairs, and run out to the street. She smoked cigarettes on Bleecker Street with the bad boys, the ones who cursed and joked about tits and pussies.

One day Ava came down Bank Street as I was jumping rope with my friends. My jaw dropped. She wore a strange, embarrassed half smile. And her belly was huge.

At eight I was clueless as to how this had happened, but I knew that it was not good. The baby's father was a lifeguard at the nearby public pool, where we all swam. Ava was barely thirteen. The lifeguard was almost thirty. My grandmother poked her lower lip out, but Ann sighed and shook her head. "It isn't that simple, Mom. Not with that family."

. . .

By now Sabine was completely unable to function. Doris and Annie Frydel coaxed her to a clinic for some pills. A social worker got her a job at the Greenwich Cinema around the corner. The pills shut her up, but they made her a zombie. She pushed our tickets through the window of her booth without a flicker of recognition. If I said hello in the hallway, she blinked at me without saying a word. If she stopped taking the meds, she'd telephone the neighbors in the middle of the night, screaming. She'd keep calling until we took our phones off the hook or until the police got Dr. K., the psychiatrist in 4A, out of bed to talk her down.

I was still in high school in 1971 when the photographer Diane Arbus slashed her wrists in her apartment down the street. I had seen her at one of her exhibits, a slight woman with big expressive eyes. Her work stunned me, although I was too shy to walk over and tell her so. But her bleak photographs lacked hope. When I heard that she had committed suicide, I could understand why someone who saw the world as she did wanted to leave it. Sabine's paintings expressed joy, but she was unable to live that way.

Ava lived nearby with the lifeguard and their baby, Elaine. We hardly ever saw her. She and Sabine fought no matter how medicated Sabine was. I met Ava on the steps of our building after a visit in the early 1970s. She was shaking with rage and swore that she would never again make her child endure a visit to hellish 5C. Little Elaine watched me fearfully, clutching her mother's leg.

A few years later, Chloe told me that Ava had run off with another man, leaving Elaine with the lifeguard.

I saw Ava on the front steps again around 1985. She lived in the Virgin Islands, she reported proudly, and had two more children. She was making money in construction. But this had been another bad visit. She spat out that she still hated her mother.

"When will my sister escape?" she demanded. "She's a slave to that lunatic. Why does she stay?"

I never had any answers.

When I asked Ava how Elaine felt about having been left behind, Ava snapped that she was a great mother to Elaine no matter where she lived.

"That bastard hit me," Ava continued. "Did you know that? He was an animal to me. He loves Elaine and would never hurt her. But I was another story. And I was a kid, for God's sake. He raped me. They can both rot, him and my bitch mother."

She looked wounded and defiant, and I kept my mouth shut. Who the hell was I to judge? I had heard about the beatings from another pool lifeguard. It was so lovely and fun, I thought to myself, back when Sabine cooked and laughed and taught us to draw. But Ava had lost her father, endured a screaming, psychotic mother, and had a child at 13 with a man who beat and raped her.

Ava disappeared again.

. . .

Chloe, now a textile designer, got pregnant by a casual acquaintance who, she said, wanted nothing to do with her or the baby. She moved to Queens with her infant son. "I miss my mother," she told me. "But the apartment is too small for all of us. Mom needs quiet." And you need a life of your own, Chloe, I thought. I'd seen many single mothers fail, their kids running wild, and it was impossible to imagine timid Chloe disciplining a child. But it was wonderful to see her with her baby, smiling and happy for the first time since we were kids. Sabine was over the moon in love with her beautiful grandson. As usual, I kept my reservations to myself.

. . .

Since Sabine couldn't function on her own, Chloe hired a companion to come in for a few hours a day, an elderly Village actress with elaborate crocheted hats, who struggled up the stairs with groceries several times a week. She was tiny and looked worn out herself. But they seemed to do OK.

I moved abroad again for several years. By the time I returned to Bank Street in the late 1990s, Sabine had a home health aide from a city agency, a pleasant West Indian woman. "Please come up and visit," the woman urged when we introduced ourselves in the hall. "I am here five days a week. Please, come up." It took a few weeks, but I finally walked upstairs and stopped at the door, too shocked to move.

The actress was there, wandering around in filthy underwear. She'd had her own mental breakdown and had moved in, uninvited and unwanted. She'd made a urine-soaked nest of pillows and blankets on the couch. The kitchen table where we kids used to draw now lurched on three legs, propped up by a radiator. Sabine lay in her bed covered with a ripped sheet. She was so medicated and obese that she couldn't even get up. The West Indian woman was doing her best, she said, but her bosses told her to mind her own business and she was powerless.

I called Chloe. "You just have to get this woman out of here," I said. "I'll help you."

It took a lot of red tape, but the actress was moved to a nursing home. The apartment was still reeking and squalid, but Chloe and the home helper tidied as best they could. I visited Sabine, and we chatted about the good old days. "I've had a fascinating life," she said. "So rich, so full." She gave me a self-published book of her poems. She talked about her daughters and four grandchildren: how smart and good-looking they all were and how lovely it was that they were all living with her in 5C together as a happy family. How she told them every day over dinner how much she loved them. I was glad that her delusions were happy ones. When she became tired, she'd tell me that Blue Boy, the figure in a framed painting by her bed, was floating overhead, waving at us. It was my cue to leave.

• • •

One morning in 2003 I heard the aide crying in the hall. Sabine had died in the night. She'd called Chloe at work and told her to come but hadn't told her why, so we waited for her together in apartment 5C.

Chloe was so distraught that I finally led her down to my apartment. We got plastered on Scotch while we waited for the coroner and tried to figure out what came next. Neither of us had ever handled a death before.

Chloe slumped on the couch. "I don't have any money to bury her," she moaned. "My son is out of control. He curses me. I can't make him go to school. I'm supposed to go to court about him tomorrow. What am I going to do?" she implored. "I can't just dump my mother in a hole."

I thought of Sabine helping Doris and Jimmy and my pregnant mother. Laughing and painting Annie's mural. Our kiddie art classes. My shame-faced memories of cruelty to Chloe as a child. And I thought about growing up in 2B with unstable, angry parents, like her. But I had had help. There, but for the grace of Bank Street saviors like Annie Frydel and others, went I.

"Don't worry about the money," I told Chloe. "Your mother will have a proper funeral."

The service at nearby St. Joseph's Church on Sixth Avenue, where Chloe and I had been baptized, was small but dignified, attended by the few Village friends who were left. Jimmy had quit the job at number 63 for a bigger Village building decades before, but Doris remained friends with Sabine, as sad about her mental illness as the rest of us. After Jimmy died of a heart attack in his forties, Doris had moved back to Mississippi, but she called and sent flowers. "My father was buried in a special cemetery because he was a war hero," Chloe told us proudly. "I can reunite them now." She insisted on taking us out to lunch afterwards in a café around the corner from the Stonewall Inn, where Levi and Sabine had celebrated their wedding fifty-seven years earlier. How sad but lucky, I thought, that they hadn't known that day what the years would bring.

Chloe invited me to choose one of Sabine's paintings as a memento, and I took one of Ava as a pensive child. Months later I called Chloe, but her line was disconnected and she'd left her job. I never heard from her again.

· · ·

All this was whirling in my head as I stared at Sabine's granddaughter in the hall. "Ava lives in Florida now," Elaine said. "We haven't gotten along so good for most of my life, but we're trying. She hates my grandmother and tells my brothers and me that Sabine was a crazy bitch who ruined her life. I can't find Aunt Chloe. I remember my grandmother as a screaming old lady who scared me. I was afraid to visit her after my mother left, and anyway my dad didn't let me. He died a few years ago."

"Your mother is telling you the truth." I said, searching for words. "Sabine was horrible to her. Her childhood was hell. I have to say that. It's all true. But that's not the whole story. Your grandmother was also a nice person who did good things for people. She was kind. Not to your mother, that's true, but to many others. Your grandfather was a tall, rangy man, sort of like Gary Cooper. You look like him, do you know that? He grew up on a farm in Washington. Your great-grandmother lived around the corner on Perry Street. She was petite, like a little doll. She made apple cake."

Elaine was expressionless. "I never heard any of this," she said.

I kept babbling. "I have Sabine's painting of your mother. And a book of her poetry with a wonderful photo of her on the back. I have your grandmother telling stories on tape. I'll give it all to you. Your mother is right, but it's not the whole story."

Elaine scribbled my phone and email on a slip of paper and promised to come back. I never heard from her, but Ava called a few times. At first, she thanked me for validating her. "My children thought that I was crazy, that I made it up," she said. "Elaine told me how sorry she is about that, now that she's heard it from you."

We reminisced. Ava was talkative and animated. "I'm proud of my life," she said. "It was a struggle, but I've made it. I help kids who were abused. Elaine and I weren't close for a long time, but we're getting there now. And as for my mother, she could do it all, painting, clothing, even interior design. She was amazing. If she hadn't gone crazy, she would have been famous."

It was wonderful to hear her sound happy, but like everything with that luckless family, it didn't last. Late one night Ava called again, a completely different person. "How dare you offer my child that filth from my mother!" she screamed. "My mother was the devil. You're sending the devil to my daughter's house. You and your fancy words, you patronizing bitch. Who do you think you are?"

It was an assault, just like Sabine's shrieking night calls. I leaned against the wall, trying to breathe and stay calm, but she kept going and I finally broke.

"Everyone in this building had to put up with your family's insanity!" I yelled. While you're feeling sorry for yourself, imagine how it was for us! We didn't sign up for screaming calls at 4 a.m.! For floods and cops dragging your mother downstairs again and again! And you know what, Ava? You may hate your mother, but you sound exactly like her! Don't you dare call again!" I slammed down the receiver. I will regret that cheap outburst for the rest of my life.

Some real healing, I thought sadly, had to come to this family sooner or later. Sabine sought beauty and joy, for others as much as herself, I wanted to tell them. She was kind. She loved you. It was never enough, but it was all she had. Ann was right. It isn't simple.

10 • Sid Vicious

Some neighbors are better on your T-shirt. Sid Vicious, for one. We got our own Sex Pistol, the former lead singer for the punk band, at 63 Bank Street after the group broke up, sometime in late 1978 or early 1979.

After the Sex Pistols parted ways, Sid's girlfriend, Nancy, was stabbed to death in their room at the Chelsea Hotel on West Twenty-Third Street in October of 1978. The police found Sid wandering aimlessly around the hotel, too high and dazed to make sense.

Sid and Nancy were heroin addicts by then. The other Sex Pistols and many of Sid's friends hated Nancy. They called her a sick, obnoxious bitch, and blamed her for getting Sid hooked on heroin and breaking up the band. Sid, they told reporters, ignored everyone's entreaties to dump Nancy. It looked, friends said later, as if they had each other by the heart and throat. No one could break her hold on him no matter how hard they tried. Nancy attempted to manage Sid's post-Pistols solo career, but between her acidic personality and Sid not showing up for the few gigs she landed, money was draining away by the time she died.

Sid was arrested and forced to kick heroin cold turkey in jail. A cop friend whispered that Sid tried to kill himself in lockup every chance he got. The police didn't want an embarrassing high-profile suicide on their hands. They made it easy for him to make bail, and Sid left jail, clean and newly single, pending trial.

• • •

My parents were still in living in apartment 2B at 63 Bank Street, but by 1978, since I'd inherited apartment 1A from my late grandmother, I was living down there, sharing the apartment with Andrea, a childhood friend from the Village. It was the glittering disco era. Andrea, who designed trendy clubs and restaurants, had connections that whisked us past the bouncers at Studio 54 and every other hot spot in town. When we got tired of dancing, we'd invite people home to party. Everyone was happy to jump into a cab and come to Bank Street, and we shamelessly bribed Ramiro in the basement apartment below us to ignore the noise.

Andrea knew how to dress. She took nerdy me shopping for sexy, glamorous outfits I would never have had the nerve to buy on my own. I loved the heady rush of power as we glided into clubs and men fought to buy us drinks. Discos like Hurrah's and Paradise Garage were full of movie stars, models, Andy Warhol divas, poseurs, socialites, and folks like me, a nobody with well-connected friends. I wore a black lace bustier with long black Audrey Hepburn gloves and danced next to stars like Margaux Hemingway, Bianca Jagger, and David Bowie.

One of Andrea's friends was head chef at the new Odeon restaurant, *the* destination in the late 1970s for socialites and celebrities slumming over nouvelle French cuisine in then-seedy Tribeca. We sipped wine at the bar and watched while Liza Minnelli, Grace Jones, and Jackie Onassis laughed and waved to their friends at other tables. One night I opened the door of the ladies' room as a blonde Vogue cover girl in a sequined dress threw up and slid down the wall, platform shoes twisting her long legs into a convoluted yogi pose. Cocaine and a silver mirror fell to the floor, along with a tiny beaded purse. A rolled-up snorter, probably a $100 bill, was dripping in her nose. I felt terrible for the staff that had to clean up her mess and hoped that her date, Mikhail Baryshnikov, a Bolshoi Ballet star who had defected from Russia, was a generous tipper.

The gritty clubs where punk rock bands like Sid's Sex Pistols played were another story. At CBGB a plastered girl with a nasal bridge-and-tunnel accent dumped beer on Andrea's head. At the Mudd Club, a biker wannabe shoved me to the floor. He was aiming at the guy next to me but was too stoned to reach him. Random violence and snarling attitude was de rigueur for everyone, including the performers. Andrea and I always ended up dashing out and hailing a taxi. Discos and entertainers like Bette Midler, a young nightclub singer our gay friends had introduced us to, were more our style.

· · ·

Sid's post-prison lady friend, Michele, had inherited apartment 1B across the hall from mine after her own grandmother's death. She had curly dark hair, brown eyes, and dramatic, full-lipped features. Michele was our age, and we once went clubbing together. She told us that she wanted to be an actress or a rock singer.

She beamed as she introduced me to Sid. I was underwhelmed. He was stork tall and emaciated, with pasty white skin and wearing studded pants and a ripped T-shirt. He mumbled greetings, then stared absently into space, blinking. Civil enough, I thought, but definitely not on the planet. I wondered where they'd met, but didn't bother to ask. New York native girls like us whirled through the night, through secret parties in lofts and deserted buildings, and underground gambling casinos. We met people everywhere.

One night, shortly after that, Sid followed Dad up the stoop and into the front hall. This was pre-Giuliani New York. Anyone who lived here then knows how dangerous the city had become. We peered under the stoop at the dark basement steps before going inside at night. I'd been mugged several times that year. Andrea had had a gun to her head. Our 1A apartment had been ransacked. They'd pried the window burglar bars apart.

Dad whirled to face Sid, squaring for a confrontation with a drug-addict mugger. "Excuse me, sir," Sid murmured to Dad's amazement. "I'm staying here. Sorry if I startled you." They shook hands and introduced themselves.

Dad was impressed by Sid's manners. "He's a decent guy, even if he looks like a clown," he said to Mom. Maybe it was good breeding. Sid's father was a guard at Buckingham Palace.

Andrea and I saw Sid in passing. Michele asked us never to lend him any money. "He's clean," she explained. "I don't want him to get back on heroin." We promised, but he never asked for anything. If we happened to meet, he'd say something politely unintelligible in his soft British garble, look over my head at the sky, and wander off, lost in his own world. Nothing at all like his rough onstage persona. Andrea and I did wonder, though, about the murder and his temper. At some point he cracked a beer bottle on the brother of the rocker Patti Smith in a club fight and did another stretch in jail. We hoped that Michele was safe.

. . .

We stopped wondering in February of 1979. Andrea had been ill all night with a bad flu and woke me up to go to the drugstore and get medicine. I woke up fogged and grumpy as usual. She shook me, then backed away, knowing my invariable morning mood. I was furious until I realized that she was sick. More asleep than awake, I pulled on boots and an ancient ski hat, threw a coat over my pajamas, and stumbled through the hallway onto the stoop, eyes closed behind my thick glasses.

They popped open when flashbulbs exploded in my face. Reporters surged forward, microphones pushing towards me, as I blinked, trying to make sense of what I was seeing. News trucks and police cars jammed the street in front of the building.

"What's your name?" the reporters demanded. "What do you know about Sid Vicious's death? Is it true that he overdosed here last night? Was there a party here last night? Do you know Sid?"

I was on the news all day, dirty old ski hat and all.

"Oh my Gawd . . . oh my Gawd . . . Ug, aah . . . my name is Donna Florio . . . dead? Well . . . I know he is . . . was . . . ummm . . ."

The reporters had truly sandbagged me into being a stuttering idiot, complete with my horrible Noo Yawk accent. They surged closer as I stood rooted, mouth open.

In the 1970s, Villagers my age danced along razor edges. Everyone took chances. But I was still young enough to believe that we were immortal. No one I knew, even as casually as I knew Sid, had died in our dance before.

The reporters kept hammering.

"Were you at the party?"

"He's really dead? Ohhhh . . . What? Oh my Gawd!"

"Miss Florio, did you know about the drugs here?"

"Oooooohhhhhh . . . dead . . . my Gawd!"

"Were you in the room when Sid Vicious took drugs?"

Drugs. Parties. Next door. Oh my Gawd, indeed. I didn't hang out with Sid and Michele and had no idea what they did or where they did it, but I was having plenty of my own dubious fun right across the hall. It wasn't hard to get crazy at that age in this neighborhood.

As I blinked stupidly at hands with microphones pushing one another out of the way, neurons finally fired, and my street reflexes kicked in. The last thing I wanted was cops or the press in my apartment. These reporters didn't know or care how peripheral I was to Sid's story. They just wanted raw meat. They'd happily twist me into the punk drug queen next door to sex up their coverage into a lead. Besides, I was still in my snarling morning wake-up mood. There weren't enough reporters on Bank Street or the entire city to make me care about dead Sid Vicious or kidnapped Patty Hearst or anyone else just then.

I shoved down the steps, pushing microphones out of my face. "No more questions!"

The reporters put that on air all day as "Miss Florio refused to deny being at the party where Sid took his fatal dose."

Neither Andrea nor I wanted to face that crowd, but she needed to see her doctor and there is no back door out of 63. We draped ourselves in scarves and sunglasses. Although we'd heard cops going in and out of apartment 1B all morning, they—thankfully—hadn't bothered with us.

The reporters went wild as we came out. Andrea, beautiful and tiny and now pallid and stumbling, could have easily been a wrecked rock starlet. Given her Jackie O camouflage and buckling legs, the mob was sure they'd scored one of Sid's friends or maybe even Michele herself.

A young reporter with orangey pancake makeup and a cheesy turquoise suit grinned avidly and blocked us, holding her microphone to Andrea's mouth.

"Miss, I'd just like to ask you a few questions about your friend Sid Vicious," she said brightly. We knew that if we cursed or made a scene it would only make her news bite a hit, so we kept our mouths shut and tried to head away. But she had us trapped.

"Just a few questions, Miss. Were you a *very* close friend? How are you feeling now?"

I believe that there is a punk rock god up there somewhere because he came to our rescue as only a punk god would. The tea and toast I'd mistakenly coaxed into Andrea before we left had made her queasy. Now she wasn't getting enough air. She gagged and suddenly vomited over the reporter and her microphone. We laughed about Orangina, cursing and wiping herself, for weeks.

We returned before Michele emerged to face the crowd. Before she left she appeared at her apartment door in full rock makeup and a tight striped shirt. I watched from across the hallway as a female retinue, including Sid's mother, surrounded her, patting her arms and urging her to be strong. The women were carrying on as if Michele was a suttee widow in India, set to be roasted on Sid's funeral pyre. She lifted her chin, squared her shoulders, and walked slowly down the hall towards the building's front door.

I was still punchy and in need of sleep. Now Michele's theatrical looks and demeanor made her look like Gloria Swanson as the demented 1920s actress Norma Desmond, rolling her eyes towards the cameras and what she thought were hordes of adoring fans in the final scene of the movie *Sunset Boulevard*. There was even a dead lover, although poor Sid was hardly heart-throb William Holden, Norma's murdered boy toy. I watched Michele sweep down the steps, tossing her hair as she was surrounded by shouting reporters.

Reporters rang our doorbell until we disconnected it. They called until we unplugged the phone. A camera poked through the blinds of our front window. We locked the window and draped the blinds with sheets. Just in case.

Andrea felt a little better and I took a nap. After some sleep, I woke up feeling human. I sipped coffee, watching the TV coverage and thinking about how sad and lost Sid had seemed whenever we passed him. I started to feel sorry for him.

• • •

Over the next few days, the coroner told reporters that Sid had shot up without being used to it anymore. Happens a lot after heroin addicts detox, he said. Michele's friends came and went, some tossing gossip our way like bits of gold. One whispered that Sid's mother had given him money for drugs. Or maybe he'd stolen it from her, I thought. Mommy Vicious, who'd been hanging around number 63 a lot, looked like a withered groupie from some backwater 1960s group: half-bagged and easy to fool. A cop told me that Michele had fallen asleep in the crook of Sid's arm and awoke in the same position to find him dead. Perhaps. We never asked, Michele never said, and to her credit she never sold her story.

Michele's grandmother, someone I'd known for years, had died in that same tiny bedroom. I'd heard the police and gone in. Her mouth was hanging open, which bothered me. I asked them if I could fix it before rigor mortis set in. Mrs. N. met her maker with my purple spangled scarf wrapped around her jaw but her mouth decently closed. I wondered if these two wildly different ghosts were circling each other in the air. If Tuffy, Mrs. N.'s slobbering, nasty Boston Terrier that bit everyone, is there too, I thought, Sid doesn't stand a chance.

Like Andrea and me, the other tenants hadn't cared about Sid's presence one way or another. But the B-line tenants sighed with relief. Sleep at last! Whether it was Sid's stalwart British manhood, great drugs, or an act, howls of joy from 1B had blasted up the walls for hours every night. Walter, the artist in 3B, stuck his head out the window, yelling, "Shut the fuck up already!" Irene rolled her pillow around her head. My parents in 2B laughed about it. "Again? That skinny wreck?" They'd go sleep in the living room.

For months Sid's mourners blocked our way up the stoop and littered the building, leaving flowers, beer, letters, and candles, and writing messages to him on the walls. I ran to stop Ramiro from beating two cowering leather-clad boys with his leaded baseball bat. They'd spray-painted the hall that he'd repainted twice since Sid's death. Ramiro was truly dangerous when he was that riled, and he'd be the one who'd get in trouble for hurting what were likely suburban kids from New Jersey. I grabbed the bat, yelling at them to run.

· · ·

The mystery of Nancy's murder will probably never be solved. Sid may well have been innocent. He never stood trial and there were other plausible suspects. But it astounds me that people still dress up and pose for pictures on our steps. Gray-haired tourists play Sid's cover of "God Save the Queen" as they take selfies. Our mailman delivers letters to "Occupant" in apartment 1B from all over the world, saying that the writer will be visiting New York and could they please see the apartment. The young men who now live in 1B found me on YouTube, forever bleating, "Oh, my Gawd!"

to a gaggle of reporters with microphones. It had never occurred to me to look.

Theories about Sid, and Nancy, and his final night here at 63 Bank Street, I discovered, still fill the internet. The most opinionated theorists sound like people who weren't even alive then. If they were, they sure don't know about young 1970s Manhattan life, let alone the size or acoustics of 63 Bank Street. Besides, it was almost fifty years ago.

But they have a right to their opinions and so do I. The ending of the 1986 movie *Sid and Nancy*, when his spirit simply rises to join hers, is the truth to me. He tried to kill himself in jail long and hard enough to alarm New York cops, not the easiest thing to do. When I close my eyes and see the vague, skinny boy who mumbled proper greetings while his eyes wandered the sky, it makes me think that Sid had already let go of his life by then. Maybe it happened when Nancy died. Maybe before.

In any case, I hope that he wafted to the hereafter and that they've both come to peace, whatever happened that night at the Chelsea Hotel. No Michele. No reporters. No Bank Street. I don't believe that Sid was ever really here.

Artistic Bank Street

11 • John, Yoko, Rex, and Many More

Long before Sid Vicious died, the fickle nature of the Muses was nothing new. Edgar Allan Poe wrote his 1845 poem *The Raven* while he was a Villager. It brought fame but not fortune. He lamented that writing kept him as poor as he ever was, "except in hope, which is by no means bankable." Even so, Poe at least had that advantage over an unpublished young 1920s poet from 60 Bank Street I read about in the *New York Times* archives who drowned himself in the Central Park reservoir.

Harlem Renaissance poet and African American social activist Langston Hughes fared better. In the 1920s, he co-founded the Golden Stair Press with the printer and illustrator Prentiss Taylor. Taylor, working out of his 23 Bank Street apartment/art studio, handset and illustrated Hughes's works, including the poem *Scottsboro Limited*, based on the true story of the Scottsboro Boys (nine young African American men convicted of rape on sham evidence by an all-white Alabama jury). Taylor remained on Bank Street while Hughes toured, giving readings and selling their collaborations.

• • •

Over the decades Bank Street has made remarkable contributions to either American culture or its downfall, depending on one's view. The Western Electric Company built a cavernous research building (later named Bell Telephone Laboratories) at Bank Street by the Hudson River in the 1890s. Their first focus was a telephone. The inventor Alexander Graham Bell called San Francisco from his lab there in 1915, his invention an instant success. A 1920 Christmas phone call from distant family to a young girl at 65 Bank Street on the new Bell system was truly a gift. Her neighbor, who had the phone, smelled gas as she knocked on the girl's door. Firemen rescued her, unconscious but alive.

The year 1921 brought another new creation from the Western Electric building, the public address system, which blasted President Harding's inaugural speech to his astounded audience in Washington, DC. Broadcasts from Bank Street on Western Electric's new radio system started in 1920, playing music and inviting listeners to send comments. The costs of replying to the resulting flood of letters pushed the company to invent commercials. The first one trumpeted the merits of a realtor in Queens.

During the 1920s Bank Street radio broadcasters sent football games, classical music, and Broadway tunes to a delighted public, who kept demanding more. As broadcast connections were set up with stations in other cities, Bank Street technicians sketched them on a map. One connection chain was red and another was blue. By the 1950s the colorful chains became NBC, ABC, and CBS.

Still inventing, Western Electric showed new talking movie technology to a Hollywood producer in 1925. He hustled the equipment to California while technicians set up a studio, tinkering to further improve audio quality. Their sound stage still exists today as the Bank Street Theater. For good measure, they invented coaxial cable and stereo recording before the 1929 stock market crash that precipitated the Depression.

A teenaged Lauren Bacall, crowned Miss Greenwich Village, lived at 75 Bank Street in the 1940s before she became a Hollywood star. In the 1950s and early '60s I played jump rope as streams of Western Electric (now Bell Lab) employees walked by on their way home after work. The place closed in 1966, but in 1970 the old research complex was turned into an artists' residence called Westbeth, attracting the dancer Merce Cunningham, the photographer Diane Arbus, and the poet Muriel Rukeyser, among many others. Action film star Vin Diesel is the Bank Street child of Westbeth artists too.

I watched movies like *The Parent Trap* and *Bye Bye Birdie* in the 1921 Loew's movie theater across from Bank Street on Greenwich Avenue (demolished in 1969). The plush seats and carved, gilded woods of grand movie palaces like Loew's inspired Village resident Edward Hopper to produce works such as his 1939 painting *New York Movie*. But his slender young usherette, dreamily alone in her thoughts as the audience watches a show, had nothing to do with the roped-off Loew's kiddie section of twenty-five years later. Parents dumped kids at weekend matinees and fled for a few hours of peace. A matron in orthopedic shoes, lower lip poked out, patrolled the aisles, scolding and shaking her finger as we bounced in our seats, pelting each other with spitballs and popcorn. No Hopperesque reflections in *our* crowd.

• • •

Bank Street's resident celebrities, who mainly lived in brownstones on our fancy first block by Greenwich Avenue, were low key at home. Charles Kuralt, host of the CBS television show *On the Road*, who owned 34 Bank Street, came to our rescue when Mom's spike heels sank into melting street tar on Greenwich Avenue and Bank Street one hot day in the 1950s. She leaped out of them as Charles grabbed her with one hand and me with the other, the three of us dodging traffic to the sidewalk. We watched, in stitches, as passing cars flattened her pumps to pulp. The actor Theodore Bikel, who lived at 25 Bank and was the perennial star of the hit Broadway musical *Fiddler on the Roof*, was just another pleasant neighbor.

Actor Alan Arkin was an exception to the friendly Bank Streeter rule, silently glowering at me across the wooden bins of Feldman's old five-and-dime one Saturday morning when I was twelve. I was floored. It was 1967, and he'd just bought 30 Bank Street. His son Adam and I had exchanged casual hellos, but that was it. To make matters worse, I'd just seen the scary movie *Wait Until Dark*, with Audrey Hepburn as a blind Villager and Arkin as a sadistic creep who terrorized her.

My friend Jack at 15 Bank Street later told me that the actor Anthony Perkins lived here for a while. Anthony Perkins? Forget Alan Arkin. I would have fled screaming if I'd seen Perkins, the crazed motel shower stabber in Alfred Hitchcock's 1960 movie, *Psycho*, giving me the stink eye.

Young actors have paced and muttered lines outside of the HB (Herbert Berghof) Studio at 120 Bank Street for decades. Berghof fled Nazi Germany in 1938, and in return his school has given Americans excellent, affordable acting lessons on Bank Street since 1945.

HB Studio trained Joe Pesci, Robert De Niro, Al Pacino, Anne Bancroft, and Jeff Bridges, among many others, and is doubtless preparing future stars who are pacing the street as I write.

Neighbors John Lennon and Yoko Ono took me by surprise, and vice versa. Someone mentioned that they'd moved to 105 Bank Street, across from HB Studio. It was 1971, and I was occupied with high school and my own life. Nor did I know or care that John, an outspoken peace activist, was fighting the US government's efforts to deport him and that the avant-garde composer John Cage, who also lived at number 105, let them use his phone to avoid possible FBI wiretaps.

I forgot about Lennon until a warm Sunday morning as I watered flower boxes on our fire escape. Two unmistakable, hairy people were wandering down the street beneath me, holding hands. Dumbfounded, I leaned out to keep watching, my watering can forgotten. A shower of water hit them, and they looked up.

"Oh! Ohhh! I'm so sorry!" I stammered, my mind blank. Was there even a category for stupid enough to pour petunia water on a Beatle?

Yoko scowled and stalked on silently, but John smiled up at me. A Beatle looking right at me! My knees buckled.

"No worries," he said in a soft voice. "It's OK." He shook his long, bushy wet hair, still smiling, as I stared in frozen shock. I watched him catch up with Yoko, so mortified that I never told a soul about the episode until my twenties. At least, I consoled myself, I hadn't upended the can onto George Harrison. John was all right, but George was my Beatle true love.

Years later, I met a TV producer who had briefly worked for them when they lived on Bank Street. "Yoko didn't like men, or maybe me," he said. She'd fire him every few weeks and he'd trudge home. A call invariably came from John, who had sneaked out to a pay phone.

"We haven't seen you. Where've you been?"

"Yoko fired me."

"Oh, Mother has her moods. Come back. What were we paying you? Add $100 a week to it."

He claimed that his salary, during that eight-month gig, went up 500 percent.

· · ·

Jack Heineman, at 15 Bank Street, was a friend of the actors Christopher Plummer and Tammy Grimes when they rented 24 Bank, across the street, in the 1960s. After the Plummers divorced, Tammy and their daughter, Amanda, stayed. Early one morning Jack paused in his doorway on his way to work, watching as the actor Rex Harrison closed Tammy's door and tiptoed down the stoop, still in top hat and evening cape. Perhaps Rex hoped to discreetly avoid Theodore Bikel, a co-star of his film *My Fair Lady*, who might emerge from his 25 Bank Street home a few doors away to run an errand.

I sat behind Harrison in the audience of a performance in 1973. I was eighteen and he was sixty-five. I'd seen dozens of actors on Bank Street and never felt a flick of interest. At that age, any man over twenty was a toothless wreck to me. Rex was a different matter. Movies, I realized as I gazed at him, didn't even begin to convey his magnetism and sex appeal. I imagined caressing his elegant, broad shoulders and wanted to heave his infuriatingly sleek young companion into the orchestra pit.

Bank Street was deserted that morning as Rex tiptoed from number 24, Jack said, except for our 78 Bank Street neighbor, Mrs. Ryan, the house cleaner, trudging towards Tammy's place, pulling out the keys. No one remembers Mr. Ryan, who may well have fled to save himself a lifetime of marital misery. Mrs. Ryan polished silver and scrubbed windows like a grim Olympic athlete, but everyone on Bank Street, even customers like Jack, gave her a wide berth. She haggled over prices with fellow Irishman Pat Mulligan in Shanvilla, his Bank Street grocery store, insulting his tomatoes and celery as he turned red with fury.

Mrs. Ryan blinked at Rex. She was as unpolished as cockney Eliza Doolittle, but she clearly wasn't expecting to meet Professor Henry Higgins, tails and all. Rex tipped his top hat as he opened the gate, then bowed and said, "Good day, Madame. Please, allow me." Jack swore that an actual smile cracked Mrs. Ryan's face. She paraded through Tammy's gate and up the steps like the queen of New York.

• • •

Addie, an heiress who moved to number 27 with her companion, Ruth, in the 1940s and has outlived her for decades, made a friend from around the corner in their geriatric exercise class in her nineties.

As we played Scrabble, she mentioned that this new acquaintance was coming for tea. "Ollie is quite cultivated," she said brightly. "*Most* interesting." After their tea, she showed me two books that he had presented to her. "He wrote these, but I really feel that I should pay him for them. Authors don't make much money."

I looked at the books. "Addie, he wanted to make a gift to you. Let him. Oliver Sacks can afford it."

• • •

Bob Dylan sang in Washington Square Park in the early 1960s as my friends and I played tag. Aspiring artists like Joni Mitchell and Billy Crystal played local clubs. Waiting girls squealed as rock stars like Jimi Hendrix and Mick Jagger left the Electric Lady recording studio and beckoned one of them, the night's lucky pick, into a limousine. As far as I was concerned they were, artists, groupies, and all, just irritating tourists getting in the way.

That changed in 1968, when I was twelve and a new kid came into sixth grade. David's dad worked at the Fillmore East, a rock music theater. Groups like the Doors, the Grateful Dead, and Eric Clapton played there. Sometimes David and I watched rehearsals. One day he introduced me to Grace Slick, lead singer for Jefferson Airplane, and mentioned that I sang opera at the Met. "Hey, that's amazing," she said, smiling. Her earthy cool was enchanting, but as I watched her, in lacy skirt and Frye boots, belting "White Rabbit" I saw amazing, and it sure wasn't dull, opera-singing me.

I liked waitressing in local cafes for fast cash, and one night three New York University students on LSD babbled about a disturbing film, set in a mental hospital and called *One Flew Over the Cuckoo's Nest*, that they had just seen. One of them glanced at my other table and spit out his espresso. "It's the inmates! Oh, my God, they're fucking here!" Villager Danny DeVito and his fellow *Cuckoo's Nest* actor friends smiled and nodded to us as the students stared, petrified. The comedian John Belushi lived nearby too. He and his castmates outdid their own *Animal House* movie in 1978 when they took over the Village Gate, site of another of my waitressing gigs, for their opening night party. Balancing armloads of dinners through table dancers, coke sniffers, and tangled couples left me staggering home at 5 a.m., clutching a $700 tip.

During the 1970s I was a spirited young native with her own Village place, and I worked the power it gave me. While that magic lasted I danced and partied with celebrities, all of us dressed up and shining. Artists, whether it was Luciano Pavarotti at the Met, Christopher Plummer in *The Sound of Music*, Alan Arkin in *Wait Until Dark*, Charles Kuralt hosting *On the Road*, or John Lennon with guitar in hand, radiate a frisson when they're on. They emanate an energy that gives them a glow.

But on Bank Street they walked their dogs, bought groceries, and went out with friends. They wore comfortable shoes. They rescued neighbors from traffic. They read the *Times*. They played clarinets off key. Idiot neighbors dumped water on them. Without applause, makeup, reviews, or magazine profiles, they rejoined everyday humanity. Everyone, perhaps, except Rex Harrison.

12 · Al

One day in 1970, when I came home from high school with a friend, beautiful pieces of furniture were lying on the stoop.

I was a well-trained bohemian kid and knew the drill. Nobody in our circle bought furniture. We found stuff, dragged it home, and figured out where it belonged afterward. If we didn't want a particular item, someone else invariably did. We had marvelous antique mirrors, brass lamps, and solid oak tables, all from the street. If we put something out ourselves, it was gone in an hour.

We hustled bamboo side tables and framed art up to apartment 2B, sweating and gloating.

After the third or fourth trip, an attractive couple came out of 2A, and smiled at us. "Vhat luffly helpful neighbors ve havff, Al," the woman said. They were hauling that furniture upstairs too. Except, of course, they were moving in and it was their stuff.

Mortified, I grabbed a bottle of wine and made a big show of pouring welcome drinks in our living room, while my friend sidled into 2A with our loot. Neither of the new neighbors, Al Calvi and Crystal Pelikan, blinked as a fifteen-year-old knocked back Chianti with them at four in the afternoon.

Al was definitely both Italian American and local, I thought. He had that *I smile but I don't take crap* air that comes from running New York streets as a kid, plus the looks and casually warm affect of southern Italy. Sure enough, he had been born and raised in nearby Little Italy. He was, he said, a freelance commercial artist and also a staff photographer for *Time* magazine. He wasn't quite as tall as Crystal, maybe five-foot-nine, with a slim build. He had lightly toned olive skin, brown eyes, and thick brown hair, cut just long enough to be fashionably artistic but short enough for corporate jobs like his gig at *Time*. He was wearing pressed slacks, a turtleneck, and well-polished loafers. As he talked, easy, chuckling laughs animated his face.

Crystal was Austrian. At first she said she was an office worker, but her persona radiated theater. When I said that she had a strong actress vibe, she said, yes, she'd trained as an actress and had had a few roles, both here and in Austria. "It doesn't pay ze rent, though," she said. "So I verk in ze office jobs now."

What a knockout, I thought, a tall, showgirl blonde with a well-filled blouse and long legs encased in black pants. Like Al, she had a warm smile and a throaty smoker's laugh. This is some pair, I thought.

My parents were equally enchanted with the new neighbors. They were our favorite type—extroverted and theatrical. Playwrights, artists, and Broadway directors arrived for parties every week. Sometimes we were invited. Al, a marvelous cook, banged around in the tiny kitchen, emerging with yet another scrumptious dish, smiling and bowing as we applauded. Lively arguments about art, music, and politics, along with jokes and one-liners, bounced off the walls. Laughter rang into the night, booming and tinkling through cigarette smoke.

Either Al or Crystal mislaid their keys at least once a week and knocked, apologizing, to climb onto our shared fire escape, coaxing their splintered old window up enough to wriggle through. After months of acrobatics, my parents suggested a key exchange. The arrangement lasted for forty years.

. . .

Al and Crystal lived together in 2A for ten festive years. Then one day in 1980, Irene saw Crystal leave the building with another man and innocently mentioned it to Al when he came home a few minutes later. She knocked on our door, close to tears, and told me what had just happened. "Al blew up. He demanded to know what the guy looked like and which way they'd gone. Then he ran after them, swearing like a sailor."

Shouts rang through the walls, and I wondered what would happen. But both Al and Crystal were good friends of the landlady, and all of a sudden Crystal was, literally, living over Al's head. She had rented apartment 3A. The two were still lovers and entertained together a lot, but they now had separate lives and parties too. It was all very complicated to me, now in my early twenties, but I adored them both and was glad they'd stayed together in this sophisticated Jean-Paul Sartre and Simone de Beauvoir–like arrangement. Such Continental style, I thought.

. . .

Crystal retired from her office job in the mid-1980s and moved back to Austria. But Crystal and Al were far from finished as a couple. She came back for decidedly conjugal visits. I heard them laughing in Al's shower as I unlocked my door. "Pass the soap, darlink, I need more. No, not zere, Al, you bad boy!" When I came over for drinks, they grinned and brushed hands over the coffee table. When they were alone in the kitchen, I heard little slaps. "Al, ve have company! Vait until later!"

Al flew to Austria every December for years, spending the holidays with Crystal and her family. That was fine with me, now in my thirties. Every New Year's Eve, in his absence, my friends and I piled my furniture into Al's apartment and rocked out with an all-night, wall-to-wall party in mine. Al thought it was a huge laugh.

In a misguided fit of domesticity I decided to emulate Al's dinner parties and another 2A–2B neighbor tradition was born. With pans of raw chicken and three hours to go, I realized belatedly that my never-used oven was broken and probably had been for years.

I pounded on Al's door in a panic. "Darling, don't worry about it," he said with a laugh. He took the chicken to his kitchen, cooked it, and whipped up a few side dishes. He even provided candles. "Dinner parties are always more festive by candlelight," he explained. "Ladies love the way it makes them look."

The party was a great success. The next day I gratefully knocked on Al's door with a bottle of wine. "The cooking is nothing," he said. "Invite amusing people, smile, and keep the drinks going. Buy more candles. Everyone loves to have fun."

As my thirties became my forties, our relationship reverted more and more to our roots. Al became increasingly like an uncle who lived next door, as relatives do in our Italian American culture. We knocked on each other's doors to borrow brandy, negotiate vacation mail pick-ups, or figure out a new gadget together.

. . .

Years later, around 1990, I interviewed Al for my book. We relaxed over drinks and he told his story.

I was born on Mulberry Street. There were ten of us. My mother came from Sicily in 1901. After six or seven years my mother still couldn't conceive. So they adopted a little Irish boy from the local nursing home. After that she had nine children.

Of course the adopted child was her first love. Grew up to be a handsome guy. He married a beautiful Italian girl from Brooklyn. She was a little toughie, a spirited one. She was the kind of girl . . . once she went to the movies and saw Jean Harlow. She came home the next day with platinum blonde hair. He gave her a whack, and it went back to black the next day.

He had a problem with drinking. During the Depression, you went out to the bar to boost your spirits. He came home one winter night in 1936, and she wouldn't let him in. He died of pneumonia, right outside the door.

I guess I was the only artistic one in the family, although my father used to draw boats. He was a seaman in the Italian navy. He came from a fishing village in southwest Sicily. He was orphaned, or what, it's hard to tell; they always kept a closed mouth. There was a rumor that my father was the love child of an aristocrat, the Marchese of Savoia. Likely or unlikely, who knows, but it's a romantic story.

During World War II I went into the army. After that, in 1950, I went to Cooper Union [a public art and engineering school] in the evenings. I studied painting. Everyone told me I should be a painter. I really didn't know what to do. I came from a working-class family. The whole idea was, get yourself a civil servant job.

I was drawing for muscleman magazines. As soon as they got through with the issue, they fired you. Then they hired you again when there was something else going on. I made up a small portfolio of sportsmen. A man I talked to worked for a Joe Bonomo. He had a project going, a muscle-building exercise chart. It was the famous Joe Bonomo, you know, the old Hercules of the screen? He ran a publishing house. Bonomo is an Italian name, but everyone said he was Turkish. Bonomo Turkish Taffy, that's the guy. The bastard paid about $24 a week. I finally asked for a raise. He said, "Oh, I thought you were training." He was a cheap bastard.

Al and his Cooper Union friends hung out with other artists at the fabled Cedar Tavern and Village coffee houses. He had to work to pay his tuition, while rich students traveled. Al finally said screw it and ran off to Europe with a friend named Bill.

We took a small two-class ship. There were a lot of older people, the ones who traveled in the winter because of the prices. They sent a scout out to look for the young men to fill the first-class tables because there were not too many people in first class.

That's how I met Lena Horne. She was doing her debut at the Savoy and so she was rehearsing and performing on the ship prior to getting into London. Not only was she stunning, but she was a very, very knowledgeable woman.

We stayed four and a half months all over Europe. Can you believe I used only $900?

I wound up renting a room in a bordello in Bologna once, where some toothless wonder came into my room asking me for cigarettes. And was there anything else I needed? Since that didn't work, she says, "Well, maybe you'd like my friend." And I looked at her and said, "Darling, I just arrived. Give me a chance."

I got another job in publishing when I got back. That's when I met Crystal. She wasn't anything like what we had in New York. When we got together, she was living in a six-story walkup. We had an editor friend, the music editor of the Herald Tribune. We used to go to all the openings on Broadway. He always had extra tickets. He died of a heart attack at the Times Square subway station after a night at the theater. We came down here after that.

• • •

Al rarely mentioned his family, but he kept a silver-framed photo of his father, lean and good-looking like Al, in the living room. That and one of his mother were the only family pictures he displayed. He was still sad, he told me, that his mother had been too worn out to be affectionate by the time her last children, Al and his fraternal twin brother, arrived. "If I tried to climb on her lap, she pushed me away," he said. She'd died when he was eight, and he was, he said, raised by his older siblings.

His non-relationship with his family was the one emotional pain I ever heard him express. If he had other regrets, he kept them to himself. He had close friends who invited him to weekends and holidays. He was never alone except by choice.

By the late 1980s and '90s Al, retired by then, along with Rose Moradei, the elegant widow in 2C, and I were 63 Bank Street's second-floor Italian village. Al hated to cook for just himself so he fed Rose and me several times a week. We kicked in for groceries and wine and I knocked on his door for requests before I went to the A&P.

Al gave me advice about hair and clothing but only if I asked. He and Rose paid the same careful attention to grooming and fashion as my parents, aunts, and uncles. Unlike many of the Villagers around us, they left the house with well-styled hair and a neat outfit, even if they were just going to the bank. Their first generation had had far more to prove to America than mine did.

I loved having Italian elders and enjoying our ethnic warmth and casual togetherness without the chop-busting that came along with my real blood kin. I would never hear the end of it if I'd ever dared walk into a relative's Sunday dinner in jeans and sandals. Al squinted as I hemmed pants with masking tape and wore ripped T-shirts, but unlike my actual family he didn't scold. And when I was decked out, he'd praise me to the skies.

· · ·

We knocked on each other's doors for anything from salt to card partners. We'd stand in our doorways and chat, and if we wanted to keep our conversations private from passing neighbors, we switched to Italian. We had movie nights at my place. I supplied the wine and Al brought snacks and the special pillow for Rose's back. Old Italian comedies like *Divorce Italian Style* and *Seduced and Abandoned* were our favorites.

Low-key Al, who—unlike so many Italian men—didn't flirt shamelessly, was nevertheless irresistible to women. From the day he walked into 63 Bank Street in 1970 until his death in 2012, I watched him enchant the ladies. It was easy to see why they adored him. He had saturnine good looks that improved as he aged. He was a sophisticated, witty dinner companion. He read *The New York Times* and *The New Yorker* and stayed up to date. If a theater production didn't meet his standards, he could tick off the problems on his fingers. He frequented museums and galleries. He was also a great listener, that rare treasure who enjoys other people's stories without trying to top them.

His ex-girlfriends married and had families but stayed in his life as friends. They ranged from Village writers to Brazilian opera singers to wealthy matrons with beach houses in Montauk. He left for weekends toting bags of groceries and shooed hostesses out of their own kitchens.

The attractive widow who owned 64 Bank Street, across the street, had eyes for him. We'd have coffee in her big sunny kitchen and chat.

"Why don't you bring that nice man next door—Al, is it?—over too?" she asked several times, smoothing her hair.

Al responded with his dismissive hand wave.

"She's a *commare*" (a housewife type), he said, "Not interested."

"Al, that's not true! You've never even talked to her! She's smart and funny. And she's right here. Quite convenient. You two could do a lot of, ahem, *cooking* in that big kitchen of hers."

He waved his hand again, refusing to rise to the bait.

Al didn't need money. What he had, no one could buy. His hearty laugh made guests feel witty and special. His dinners were delicious, stylish, and fun even though he'd gotten the foods on the cheap. He could walk into a thrift store, pick out a perfect designer jacket, drape his cashmere scarf around his neck, and look like his fabled grandfather, the Marchese of Savoy.

When Rose died, the second-floor family became just Al and me.

• • •

Corky, the bowlegged old shelter dog I brought home one night, became Al's buddy once he realized that dog walkers meet women. Al would cook supper for the lady du jour and invite Corky too. Sometime after midnight, when I was already asleep, Al opened my door so Corky could pad in and climb into his bed. When Al started dating Betsy Palmer, a glamorous 1950s star, Al and Corky took the subway to her Central Park West triplex for candlelit dinners *à trois*. When local boutiques brought in sexy models as Christmas elves and Easter bunnies for customer photos, he used Corky to enchant the models and get shots that he framed and displayed in his living room. No movie-star dinners or glam photos for me, however. I was never invited.

By around 2005, the visits between our apartments were constant and family-like. I knew it would drive me crazy, and probably him too, if anyone else knocked four or five times a day, but we had evolved our own, very loose boundaries.

"Al, wait! I'm on the toilet!" I yelled as the door lock clicked.

"But I left a lasagna in your freezer. I need for tonight."

"OK, but you have to give me a minute."

One morning before work Al knocked, his lower lip trembling. "My twin brother just died, down in Florida," he said sadly. "We were the last ones. We never saw eye to eye, hadn't seen each other in years, but it's just me now. Feels strange. There were ten of us, for God's sake. I've never been alone like this in my life." I left Corky on his couch and brought our favorite Chinese takeout when I came home that night.

. . .

By 2010 Al was in his eighties, and he seemed to be aging more quickly. One day I ran to fetch his keys as gas fumes blew out from under his door. Sauce dripped down the stove, the flame out, as Al slept on the couch. "God Almighty, what a thing to do!" he said, his face red, after I woke him up. "I guess I owe you."

"Forget it, Al," I replied. "You'd have done exactly the same for me."

Although he still put on a great show at his dinner parties and on the phone, I knew that he was increasingly confused and helpless. His knocks on the door for help were almost hourly. Given his life of glamorous independence, he privately admitted that his new limits were driving him crazy.

"He's probably developing dementia and perhaps geriatric depression too," said my husband. It sounded right, but what could I do? I worried, finally calling Crystal in Austria, hoping she'd invite him for a stay. They hadn't seen each other in a long time, although they still spoke. "Vell, darlink, call Bittsy Palmer," Crystal sniffed. "Bittsy is his girlfriend now." Crystal is pissed about the sexy blonde competition, I laughed to myself. She's the one who left. Serves her right.

My father had lectured Al about working off the books too much as a freelance artist and he was right. He got next to nothing from Social Security and had no savings. I made excuses to give him the aperitifs, virgin olive oil, and taralle (biscuits) that he loved. When his worn-out sandals hurt his feet, I bought four different pairs until he liked one. His hearing was now awful, but he refused to wear the hearing aid his doctor gave him. I found a headset amplifier that he liked for watching TV. In return he picked up clothes for me on his thrift store prowls. I bought the groceries, but he did all the cooking.

His circle made his birthday a celebration every December. One friend took him to her family for Christmases and Easters. Others took him to shows. He appreciated us, but he no longer held back his feelings about his family. "I have thirty-four nieces and nephews, and not one of them calls, invites me over, or sends a goddamned birthday card," he told us. "If it weren't for you guys, I'd be all alone."

We had an amazing run from 1970, Al and me. But by early 2012, when Al was 84, the end of our partnership was near. I had come home from a trip and didn't hear his usual puttering sounds. I unlocked his door, steeling myself, but the place was empty. I called around but no one knew where he was. Really worried now, I called the Veterans' Hospital, his medical facility. Al was in the intensive care unit. I dropped the phone and ran.

Apparently he had fallen several weeks before and hit his head, coming home with a lump and some cuts. Unbeknownst to anyone, the fall had triggered a bleed in his brain. Tough old Al trudged around town with a constant headache but finally got weak and dizzy. True to form, he had walked from Bank Street to the VA hospital on East Twenty-Third Street.

When I got there, he was confused and angry. They'd asked him about next of kin, the nurse said, and he'd told them that he had no friends or relatives. And he was refusing to let the doctors drain blood to relieve the pressure on his brain. I watched a bedside conference, realizing that clever Al, minus the hearing aid, of course, was fooling them. He was making such a great show of nodding as they spoke that none of them realized that he couldn't hear a damned word they said.

"You're free to refuse the surgery," the neurologist was saying. "But without it you're walking around with a death sentence. You live alone, in a walk-up. Another head bump, even on a doorway, might trigger a bleed that could leave you dying on the floor with no one to help." She was sorry, she said, but without surgery she was sending him to a public nursing home in Queens.

My beloved Al in a nursing home? Not if I had to do the surgery myself. I alerted his circle, and we spent the next seven weeks trying to talk him into treatment. Between the brain injury and being confined to a hospital bed, he was ornery and stubborn. "What about Betsy?" I pleaded. "Don't you want to get out of here and see her again?" She was at her daughter's place in Connecticut, and he couldn't make long-distance calls on the hospital phone. I dialed her number on my cell phone and handed it to him as I stepped out of the room. "Hiya, baby," I heard. "No, I haven't forgotten about you. Not at all. I just had a little accident."

Even after he agreed to the procedure, there was another hurdle. "If his apartment has trip hazards," the doctor told me, "the Visiting Nurse Service will revoke home stay and he'll still have to go to a nursing home. I see that he has great friends, but I'm sorry. I have to protect him." She gently explained that the treatment delay had injured his brain, and that Al going home would be dicey in many ways. I was too stubborn, and too hopeful, to listen.

. . .

Al's apartment, crammed with his photographs and paintings, plus exotic street finds like an Arabian camel saddle, was nothing *but* trip hazards. We took up rugs and threw out bags of magazines, worn clothes, and spoiled foods, working for hours at a stretch. It was a mission of love.

Al finally came home, slowly hobbling up the stairs. Unfortunately, as the neurologist had tried to warn me, he remained angry and un-reasonable, accusing me of throwing out valuables. "Well, you knew I was sick," he growled when I reminded him of why I'd done it and the endless phone calls I'd made, asking him to decide on item after item.

His other friends didn't get thanked as they deserved, but they didn't get kicked in the heart the way I did. They weren't in the same category. Our singular relationship made me the closest thing to a daughter that Al had, and Italians, I well knew, took their rage out on their kids, logic be damned. Even knowing that it was our very inti-macy that now made me a target, I was crushed.

I finally accepted the fact that Al's behavior was the result of the brain damage his doctor had warned me about. It was, I realized, time to let go and leave him to the care of home health aides and his other loyal friends. However he was behaving, I vowed not to let it cloud my memories of the most extraordinary relationship with a neighbor I've ever had.

Anyway, I had been given a priceless reward, one I'll always trea-sure. After forty amazing years of movies and martinis and frantic chicken bakes and daily laughs, I'd gotten to honor Team 2A/B as it deserved, when it mattered the most. My Al, artist, consummate host, lover of glamorous women, and great friend, spent the last six weeks of his life as a free man, still walking to Little Italy and still at 63 Bank Street.

13 • John Kemmerer

I was petrified of the serial killers in 5B.

By day John and Ruth Kemmerer seemed innocuous. He was tall and gaunt with thin white hair, usually wearing a wrinkled trench coat. She had long gray hair coiled in a bun. Her clothes were artistic, made with fabrics from Africa and Bali. He tipped his hat to my mother when he passed her in the street.

In 1962, when Irene was eight and I was six, we stared at photos of dead girls in her father's *Daily News* as the Boston Strangler struck over and over. Rose, in 2C, woke up one night as a burglar ransacked her place. There are bad people in the world, our parents said. Never speak to strangers. Night after night, Irene, whose bedroom was right below John and Ruth's, in 4B, cowered under the covers, listening to the dragging sounds coming from upstairs. It could only be John and Ruth pulling murder victims across the floor, she decided. The squeaks and slams that came after the dragging must be the bodies being shoved into trunks.

Irene looked away from John and Ruth in the hall, trying to be nonchalant. If she told her parents, she thought, the Kemmerers might kill them, too.

She shared her awful discovery with me as we hid in the wings at the opera, waiting for our cue during *Hansel and Gretel*, and I went stiff with fright. After the show we lined up in the lobby, as usual, to greet members of the audience. Irene nodded somberly at me as kids shook our hands and touched our costumes. I checked that our door was locked that night, guiltily glad that we lived down on the second floor. Maybe I was safe.

• • •

None of the neighbors were killed, and Irene learned to ignore the noise. One morning in 1968, when I was twelve, my parents and I heard cries in the hall. John was sitting on the stairs, sobbing. Ruth had died in her sleep. My parents poured him a brandy although it was 8 a.m. Dad patted his back as he sobbed on our couch. The two had met in 1920, in college. She was his whole life. They'd wanted children, but none came. How was he going to live without her? They listened and refilled his glass.

My parents invited him in often after that. He had old-school manners and waited to be asked twice. "I don't want to intrude," he'd murmur. But he always accepted. He was starved for company, they said later.

I was a bookish child who came alive as I read and wrote poetry and stories, and I never stayed in the living room when John and my parents had cocktails. Years later I asked them about him. He'd retired as a structural engineer just before Ruth died, they told me. After her death, he wandered the city alone all day, going to lectures and movies. He read Socrates and Plato in the Metropolitan Museum's Greek sculpture galleries. He sipped whiskey in the lobby of the Algonquin Hotel and imagined the writers of the celebrated Round Table trading witticisms and vitriol. He gazed at the East River and sniffed the air as the Fulton Fish Market vendors shouldered by with crates of iced fish.

He never ate a single meal at home after Ruth died. He dined out three times a day and never repeated a dinner restaurant. The only exception was the Waverly Inn down the block, then a shabby local hangout with rickety chairs and fireplaces. John liked their Southern fried chicken.

The scraping sounds had ended after Ruth died. When Irene and her mother paid a condolence call, they saw an enormous loom in the bedroom and piles of raw wool on the floor. Spectacular hangings covered the walls, next to African masks and hand puppets from Indonesia. Ruth had been a weaver. She worked at night when she was not too tired from her office job. It never occurred to them that the loom, something they had saved carefully to buy, could be heard outside the apartment. John apologized when Irene told him about the noise, and they laughed about the murders. He gave Irene a leather-bound book of poetry with hand-painted illustrations that had belonged to Ruth as a memento.

It was another bad day when John dismantled Ruth's loom. He cried in the hall again and my parents poured more drinks. Taking her loom apart felt like burying her bones with his bare hands, he told them.

• • •

As a moody pre-adolescent, I'd stomp off to the library, making selections after close, narrow-eyed inspection, like Grandma when she picked her vegetables from sidewalk vendors. My parents' fights often boiled onto me. As the smallest, least powerful contender I buried myself in books and writing. When they yelled at one another, I opened a book or journal and fled to my imagination, hiding in plain sight.

In 1969, at the age of thirteen, I had been among the first girls admitted to formerly all-male Stuyvesant High School. My young English teacher, Frank McCourt, famous a couple of decades later for his memoir *Angela's Ashes*, encouraged us to find our inner voices, although if he'd had a few at lunch he could be moody and mean. "Just read the feckin' Norton Anthology and be quiet!" got tossed our way now and again. Like some of the other girls, I occasionally amused myself by flirting with him. He was still young enough to think that we would find him, a geezer in his thirties, attractive. We laughed about it in our one bathroom, a boys' room with the urinals boarded up. But McCourt, a tough judge, always knew when I'd hit it in my writing. One word of his praise made me glow.

I loved to travel and fussed for hours over letters home, working to shape the characters and descriptions. Your writing is wonderful, friends and family said. They'd save the letters from Paris or Tokyo and return them to me. I'd reread them endlessly. But I never considered writing as a career. I lacked the self-confidence to even try.

• • •

John and I continued to nod in passing. One day in 1977 we passed on the stoop. He stared at my armful of library books, and then looked at me as if he'd never seen me before: "What did you think of Carson McCullers, Donna? *The Heart Is a Lonely Hunter* shook the literary world in the forties. Did you like it? Do you like social realism?"

I was twenty-one. John was seventy-six. Although we'd lived in the same apartment building three floors apart for my entire life, this was our first real conversation. Being onstage as a kid had made me an extrovert on the outside, a good cloaking device for an insecure girl who held most people at arm's length. Anything I felt deeply went onto pages that I shared with no one. And all of a sudden, my elderly gray neighbor, a stranger, really, stood at the door to my secret world. I was floored.

We spoke awkwardly at first. Durrell's *Alexandria Quartet*? I liked the plot of *Justine* best. He preferred the character development in *Balthazar*. Doris Lessing? He hadn't read her *Golden Notebook*, but since I liked it he would seek it out. Mark Twain was one of the greatest American writers, we agreed. Neither of us liked Hemingway. He was too determinedly artless, and his one-dimensional women were parodies.

We sat on the stoop as the super swept the sidewalk and neighbors passed. By then we were beaming. Finally, John admitted that he was a writer and had published a book called *Along the Raccoon River*, along with some collections of poems. As my eyes widened, he hastily explained that they'd been self-printed, by a vanity press. *Raccoon River* was autobiographical, he said, inspired by his journals of the 1920s to the 1940s. Would I care to have a copy of *Raccoon River* and a book of his poetry? I'd never been given books by an author and uncertainly offered to pay. He smiled and said no, he wished to give me a gift.

· · ·

Like any Villager I passed celebrities every day. I checked them out, of course, but that was all. Actress Marlo Thomas had perfect skin and a warm smile. Rock singer Roger Daltrey was unexpectedly short. Lucille Ball really had a raucous parrot laugh. I'd keep walking.

Good writers were different. They'd give me a world. We ran off together for hours: special, magical friends. And if one was unlucky enough to actually cross my path in person, they faced a maudlin, babbling idiot. As a teenaged cashier, I burst into tears when James Baldwin came in for cigarettes. "Oh, sir, the hours we've spent together! The places we've been!" Baldwin smiled with his moist basset-hound eyes as I tenderly pressed Pall Malls into his hands. Years later I blubbered my gratitude to a stiffly proper Oliver Sacks at a reading as he hastily autographed my copy of his book.

I had the same awed reaction to John's book. I was enchanted as I wandered through his world. *Raccoon River* mixed John's musings on nature and history with character sketches. He had a dry wit and a steady, crystalline writing style. Erudite, observant, and a bit sly, he produced simple, evocative phrases and exquisite portraits. His writing had the elegant simplicity of Annie Dillard or E. B. White's *This Is New York.*

I told him so the next time we met. "You knocked me out," I said. "Your writing is pure and clear. You give characters in brushstrokes, like a haiku poem." His face lit up.

"I just read good authors and try to copy them," he said modestly but still beaming. "I've been at this for a while."

I'd never seen him so happy before, not even after Dad poured second tumblers of Scotch. John was shy and guarded too, I realized. He took a chance sharing his work with me. It didn't occur to me until it was much too late that he would have been a wonderful first person, other than teachers or professors, to ever allow to read my deep writing, where I hid my feelings.

. . .

Raccoon River starts in the 1920s when John, born in 1901 on a farm in Panora, Iowa, has finished college at Grinnell and graduate school at Harvard and returned home to write.

Under the winter sky, between snowbound bluffs, the river lies like a glacier in a gorge. The ice is gray, cracked, and frozen shut again; the here and there on the surface the snow, lifted by the wind, whirls into little drifts. On the bands the cottonwoods and willows stand bare and stiff. On either side the white bluffs loom through scattered oaks. The wind blows steadily from the northwest, swinging down from the Dakotas and Canada, coming straight down the valley.

In the latter part of August, when our own wild plums are ripening, the farm slows down. The hay has been made; the oats have been threshed. After the rain the cornfields go on maturing, but farmers worry about an early frost. . . . How does my father feel when he walks past his fields and pulls a weed that nobody else would notice? Probably the way I feel when I go through a manuscript and pull out a wrong word. Tomorrow more weeds will appear; wrong words too.

As I read, I envied John his graceful writing. He'd learned a lot more from Mark Twain, I thought, than I ever had.

When Mr. Smith talks, he likes to tell of his travels, for he has been West several times, to see how they live out there. He likes to state his opinions as to what is right; he would be satisfied, he says, if people only used a little horse sense now and then. . . . He himself would be glad to be young again and start all over. He would be a farmer again. He reckons that then he would pitch in and show the present generation a few things. Probably he would, too.

• • •

In the years that followed, between work, graduate school, and travel, John and I didn't have much more contact. I sometimes thought of inviting him in to chat, as my parents had, but full of my own young life, I never followed through. I wrapped up his books and put them away. There were jobs, romances, and adventures. I still fussed over my letters from abroad. I thought of writing letters to John, but felt shy. He's an accomplished author, I thought. My words can't measure up.

Six years passed. In 1982, when I was in Rome, Irene wrote and told me that John had died. I sat in a café, thinking about him. The times we'd discussed books were the only times I could remember seeing him smile. Did he have a proper funeral? Had anyone read his works over the coffin? I was angry at my own stupid shyness. We should have become friends, and now it was too late. I'd really wanted to understand his dedication to life as a writer on Bank Street, and I'd waited too long. I wished John's spirit a safe journey as I got up to join my date, waving from his Vespa.

Years passed. Still restless, I moved to Asia. I remarried, redivorced, taught, wrote TV scripts, and kept traveling. I kept writing my own stories. I wrote more letters to friends. I wrote travel pieces for magazines. Back home, I used my leverage as a native of Bank Street to coax stories from my neighbors; whom they'd loved, where they worked, whether they'd fulfilled their dreams.

This building of mine, I came to realize, this 63 Bank Street, holds the stories of America. We are linked across the decades, and far more than we know. What, I wondered, have I learned about life from those who came here before me? As I tried to translate the lives of my neighbors into stories, I thought again and again of John, the master of clear, shining prose. I reread *Raccoon River*, running my fingers along the thick textured paper and admiring the crisp, spare layout. Who was John really? How did he live and write?

I pestered my parents, Irene, and every neighbor who'd known him. They couldn't tell me much. You remember how he kept to himself, they said. I called Kemmerers in the Panora phone book, searching for his family, without success. I spent hours in the rare-books room at the New York Public Library, poring over all of his self-published books, which he had donated to them. Why did we have to be born a half century apart, John? I fumed. You walked past a silly kid for too much of our time together. I need to connect to you, John. I have to know how you lived your writing life so deeply and for so long.

• • •

By the late 1990s I was an administrator in the New York City public school system. I stood facing the fourth-story window of a Lower Manhattan school on 9/11, holding a girl as her mother, a security guard in Tower 2, died in front of us. The schools were on emergency lockdown and I'd had no place to hide. None of us did. White ash, all that remained of people I may have passed on the street that day or gone to school with, drifted into our eyes.

I had worked in foreign slums and refugee camps but I was a free person with an American passport, a first-world do-gooder, able to leave chaos behind with the swipe of a credit card. Suddenly, unimaginably, I was in a dark parallel reality of my privileged life, where no one knew if further attacks—maybe bombs, or poison gas—waited for us if we tried to flee in subways or across bridges. There was no credit-card escape that day. We, the staff and students, stayed on lockdown in our building, high in the air, with unbearably clear views of the towers. Sirens ripped my ears for hours as police and firemen drove past, many to their own deaths. I watched nearly three thousand people die as the towers collapsed. Mumbled words, maybe prayers, fell from my lips, but I don't know what I said.

The principal prepared to bunk us there that night, but as evening approached we watched the news, got through to parents, got the kids home safely, and numbly parted ways. As I walked home, I passed people coated in white ash, staring ahead and shuffling slowly, their faces blank. I went to friends, none of us wanting to be alone. Finally, home alone in my apartment by 2 a.m., I wrote an account of what I'd seen, wincing and crying as I wrote, and sent it to everyone I knew. It is the only thing I've written that I've never reread.

The breakdowns that followed made the next years a collage of doctors and recurring nightmares of people burning alive at my windows as I tried to break the glass and save them. I wanted to flee but could not leave 63 Bank. I was imprisoned in my own skin.

I did the only thing I could. I wrote. Words spun into a thread, gradually pulling me out of my nightmare. My shadow self, the writer, stepped through the blackened landscape, unafraid. Our fingers touched on opposite sides of the page.

John had cried and written alone at 63 Bank Street, and so did I. Slowly, it worked. A sympathetic librarian at Grinnell College, John's alma mater, mailed excerpts from the personal journals he had bequeathed to them. The material threw flickers of light on him, as if I was watching him pass by on a night train. I reread John's book, this time seeking a path back to life.

Electricity had arrived in Panora, Iowa, in 1925. The town, one thousand strong, was "honest but not nearly as honest as it used to be." It had a grist mill, four churches, carpenters, mechanics, one blacksmith, and three sellers of gasoline.

His grandfather Kemmerer gave him an 1868 arithmetic primer with tiny pictures for adding two acorns plus one acorn. His mother taught him the alphabet and the Lutheran catechism. "She liked almost any book, including her Webster's Dictionary. My father, in his younger days, gave her Browning's Poems." Other relatives contributed *Robinson Crusoe, David Copperfield,* and *Tom Sawyer.* I'd read them too, curled up backstage.

In high school, John translated Caesar's *Gallic Wars* and read Shakespeare. He "spent many hours alone. For a boy the landscape was vast. My parents were busy, and other people lived at a distance. This was one reason why I read books."

He left for nearby Grinnell College in 1919. "At this time I was six feet tall, tanned like any farmer, and full of confidence. I weighed around one hundred and sixty pounds. My hair was brown and parted on the left side. My eyes were blue. My dark necktie, silk shirt, brown serge suit, and black oxfords were such as a small country town provided. When someone said that I was bright eyed and bushy tailed, I was surprised. I did not dash around like a squirrel in the timber. I myself supposed that I was sensible and laconic, slow, but not very slow. Being already a reader of etymologies, I knew that 'laconic' came from Sparta."

At Grinnell he studied engineering and typography and wrote poetry. He noticed as a Miss Ruth Chamberlain walked by. "The exploration of English and French literature interested me the most. . . . We studied Maupassant, Chekhov, Hardy, and Conrad too; and the Americans Poe, Hawthorne, Henry James, Stephen Crane, Ring Lardner, and others. To me their sad lives seemed incidental." The tragedies of life are unimportant compared to writing, John? I thought. Maybe I'm starting to find you.

• • •

After Grinnell he "had a grand year" at Harvard studying Latin and Chaucer. He watched John Barrymore play Hamlet and spent evenings with pipe-smoking friends discussing literature. They sought the purity and bohemian romance of the writing life. The "vast panoramic masterpieces" of the nineteenth century had passed away. Here now were *Ulysses* and *Nostromo*. John respected Joyce and Conrad but did not care to emulate them, he wrote. He wished to evoke a clear scene with a few perfect words. In 1924 he bought Twain's new two-volume autobiography. He'd read other Twain works at home in Panora, left by a horse-and-buggy bookseller as payment for his dinner.

> The young man at his writing perhaps learns to write. Quite a lot may be learned. But what can he say? In time, if he is lucky, he discovers what depth writing must have. He senses this without much logic, the way he selects one word out of many, the way an experienced farmer

looks at his fields and knows what to do. If the writer is still lucky, he does not then proceed to devise a set of rules. He even abandons his notebook. He writes and he revises.

He wandered the countryside, taking long walks along frozen rivers and through thick oak stands. He talked to a very old man who thought it was good to be young in a new country.

There were many solitary evenings on the farm with his books. John's college friends had encouraged one another to move to New York and live the writing life. You knew that a farm life in Panora was impossible for you, I thought as I read. It was just a matter of time. Right now, John, I thought, I wish I were walking through those thick oak stands in the Iowa that you left behind, safe from terrorist attacks.

• • •

Columbia University offered him some sort of a scholarship in 1924, although he did not specify. "By chance I had come to New York along with a wave of new Middle Western literature. In the 1920s many of its authors were being published here . . . Edgar Lee Masters, Theodore Dreiser, Willa Cather, Carl Van Doren, Sinclair Lewis. . . . Most of them came from the country or some small town. Just to know that they were active made the city more exciting and more like the America that I knew." He commuted to Columbia from Brooklyn Heights, reading Walt Whitman and soaking up New York.

John may have been an Iowa farm boy, but he was not always dazzled by the city.

Meanwhile the New York wits were sharpening our language and criticism. Day and night, especially night, new jests would be circulating in conversation, newspaper columns, and magazines. Since 1920 the speakeasies had solved the Prohibition problem, and brightened their bars with women. Not much attention was given to other national problems. Usually a wit would attack personal faults and difficulties, his own or those of this drinking companions. . . . Besides he was clever at tricks with matches and cards, at impersonations or solo dance, at puns, bawdy limericks, Broadway gossip, Wall Street tips. In this acrid atmosphere I myself could detect the flaws in my novel 'About Sundown'. Several editors and I agreed that it should not be published.

In 1928 he moved to the Village, to 3 Weehawken Street, "by the Christopher Street ferry." His writing shifted from fiction to narratives about people, places, and events. He published in small local journals and presses. I'm so envious, John, I mourned. You were here when this *was* the Village.

Not long afterward, the shy young man found love with the girl from Grinnell. "In NY in November [1929] I married Ruth Chamberlain, the New England girl, the daughter of the late anthropologist Alexander F. Chamberlain. She was a few months younger than I. . . . she liked dancing, Vermont hills, Christmas trees, little tiger cats, comedies, books, pictures, indeed all the arts. Now as I put one year after another I see again how good her company was."

John joined a Midtown engineering firm. Although he worked there for thirty-six years, he had the Village habit of ignoring the day job after 5 p.m. He'd rarely mentioned it, my parents recalled, and ignored it in his journals too. The Great Depression wiped out the small journals and publishers and propelled him back towards the typography he had studied at Grinnell. He loved fonts and the feel of fine thick paper. No wonder *Raccoon River* is such an elegant book, I thought.

Throughout the 1930's I continued writing my kind of prose in which, as times passes, men and the landscape too are passing. Mainly I proceeded with Along the Raccoon River. . . . In the spring of 1937 we moved from 3 Weehawken Street to 63 Bank Street. We came to a better part of Greenwich Village and a newly remodeled building. Ruth had found this place. Our apartment was on the top floor, up four long flights of stairs, which we were glad to climb. The living room windows looked south across the roofs to trees, including an old pear tree, and to the distant towers downtown. In the sky we saw the great clouds above New York harbor.

I envied the Kemmerers because their fifth-floor B-line apartment is the only one that rises above the dark narrow alley we share with the house next door. What did it feel like, I wondered, to write in sunlit Bank Street rooms and to feel breezes drifting through your kitchen window?

. . .

And what did Bank Street look like in 1937? Did the pear tree bear fruit? Did John see many more of the street peddlers I loved, like the rag man with the wooden wheelbarrow who still came around in the 1950s? The rag man would ring a little cowbell, and Mom would wave to him and give me her cache of used clothes to bring downstairs. He'd smile and tip his cap. Was Jimmy's uncle Mr. Simmons, the smiling 63 Bank Street super I vaguely remembered from my baby days, just as nice as a younger man? I knew that our 1889 building had indeed been remodeled in the 1930s. I had copies of the permit and the plans, according to which gas ovens and radiators replaced coal stoves and braziers (small cast-iron coal heaters that fitted into shallow wall alcoves). John and Ruth were among the first to enjoy their own private bathroom, with a "flushometer" too. No more communal privies off the kitchen.

> During the late 1930's I was still given to digressions that an efficient man would have avoided . . . in the summer Ruth and I raced model sloops. Hours of thought went into their sails and the weighting of their keels. At Bank Street we played tabletop battles with toy soldiers and artillery which shot pellets. . . . But as the real [World War II] war arrived, our games seemed heartless, and we stopped. We never resumed them.

John appeared closed and laconic to others, wrapped in his words. "Some evenings they [writing and printing] kept me in another world. . . . Once a smart young guest told Ruth that she was charming, but as for me, he'd be damned if he would bother with anyone so unresponsive. I had neglected to inquire about his paintings. She hardly mentioned this matter to me. By chance in 1973 I saw an indignant note on that guest among her papers."

. . .

He loved to climb the creaky wooden steps to the roof and watch the sky, he wrote, as I did later on. In 1950 he and Ruth bought an old farm, a weekend place, in Litchfield, Connecticut, where he set up a printing press. My 1955 arrival went unremarked in his journals, although perhaps he "discovered recordings of Germaine Montero singing Spanish songs" that year to drown out my newborn wails.

. . .

Unbeknownst to my parents or the other neighbors, John's writing was being recognized just as I entered high school in 1970. The accolades were modest, but in his journals he savored what he described as "several hundred friendly responses: from veteran critics of the Twenties; from generations in their prime; from pretty girls and young men with beards. Thus in a Dark Age the poems, author and printers had lively company. And the books were in great libraries in New York, Iowa, Massachusetts, Rhode Island, and Connecticut; and in the homes of collectors whose books may go anywhere." Good for you, John, I thought as I read. Your writing certainly deserved it.

By 1972, Ruth had been gone for four years. I was in high school. John sold the farm and "simplified the Bank Street apartment." That was when he dismantled Ruth's loom and cried in the hall again. He focused on his poetry. During the decades when I studied, traveled, threw parties, and fell in and out of love downstairs, John was alone up in 5B, hard at work.

His rent was probably not even $100 a month. He had friends. Genteel, erudite Village ladies would have welcomed the companionship of a tall, well-educated widower. John, in his retirement, was free to travel to the Greece and Rome of his beloved classics or down Twain's Mississippi. Why did he stay here, all alone? Why did he go on writing doggedly for years without any real rewards while far less talented writers were applauded? I read and reread his works, groping through time towards my quiet neighbor.

A reader asked me how I came to write poetry, and how I then survived in New York and Connecticut. The question set me to thinking. In November I began to retrace my long expedition into the world of letters. During the winter in New York City I wrote an answer, a draft of this narrative. I am living alone in my Bank Street apartment. From the south windows I see low roofs and bare trees, on which a few brown leaves dangle. It is November again; November 21,

1973. The towers downtown are gray, and the sky is full of gray clouds. Why should I still be elaborating my narrative? Some old scholar has remarked that few poems are made better by biographies of their authors. But there he exaggerates a little, I think. The inquiring reader could be right. . . . But all the time, in fact I have been remembering and describing what I have learned earlier in the day, last week, and years ago.

New York City. . . . Strange people crowd the sidewalks and bright restaurants. . . . This New York is closer to London, Paris, Rome, and Moscow than to the Mississippi Valley. Still, the City is not entirely alien. Many Middle Western writers and scholars work here; Leonard Gross, Carl Van Doren, Hamlin Garland, Ring Lardner. . . . Here littera scripta manet. [The written word remains.] What is so good about these bookmen? They understand that words may throw a long and sharper light across our landscape, on fortune and misfortune, on dark wilderness campaigns, and even on the fairest weather, which in a day will vanish.

A wise person once said to be a poet at twenty is to be twenty, but to be a poet at forty is to be a poet. John's words and why they mattered to him above all else throws that long and sharper light on my elusive neighbor, the gray-haired loner in the hall.

14 • George and Gloria

George and Gloria rented the carriage house behind the brownstone next door when I was six or seven. My bedroom window faced their front door. Gloria was tall, with a dancer's lithe figure and thick black hair cascading down her back. She wore long scarves and swirling capes. George had the almost ridiculous good looks of a blond George Hamilton, right down to his gleaming smile, and the casual insouciance of a leading man in old black-and-white movies like *The Thin Man*.

George had appeared on Broadway in the musicals *1776* and *Funny Girl*, he told my parents. He didn't seem anxious about getting roles, unlike every other actor we knew. And the only other actors I knew about on Bank Street who rented entire houses were stars, like Christopher Plummer.

My parents assumed that he came from money. "Look at their clothes," Mom said. "And that carriage house, even as a rental, isn't cheap." Gloria had danced on Broadway and was now working on a nightclub act as a belly dancer. I watched her twirl in the yard, clinking her finger cymbals. When I applauded, she bowed and we laughed. George assembled a harpsichord from a kit in the living room. Bach and Mozart tinkled through the summer air.

Over the years, Gloria and I chatted as I hung out of my bedroom window. She listened to my social quandaries like an older sister. She praised my voice and cheered when I passed auditions.

The year I turned 11, Gloria got a show tour and was gone for months. I missed our chats. George must be lonesome, I thought, since he brought in a man to live with him.

The breakup, like everything else they did, was civilized. Gloria waved goodbye as I hung out the window and she promised we'd stay friends. She visited George sometimes. It wasn't the same without my sympathetic big sister, but George kept me up to date on her career and sent news back and forth.

His taste in men was awful, though. Between the Village and the opera, I knew plenty of classy gay men. Gay people from all walks of life congregated in Village bars and clubs: one of the largest, most diverse scenes in the country in the 1960s and '70s. Places like One If By Land had piano bars and elegant fireplace nooks where everyone, gay and straight, was well dressed and behaved with decorum, even if they were at the bar picking someone up for the night. My friend Mila, whose father was gay and wealthy, treated us to festive dinners there with his lover on her birthday.

The closer you got to the Village docks, the more you found rougher bars and S&M leather clubs. George, who draped cashmere sweaters over his shoulders and summered in Bar Harbor, had a penchant for the tricks, the low-class hustlers who hung out on lower Christopher Street or on the docks. I couldn't get over it, given his immaculate taste and manners. As a one-night stand, perhaps, but letting them move in for months at a time?

Cheap hustlers were at the bottom of the gay Village hierarchy, and I was not shy about my disdain, letting their efforts to join my conversations with George fall away, pointedly keeping my attention on George. Insulted, they threw attitude, rolling their eyes, crossing their arms, and sucking their teeth. That was as far as they dared go in front of their meal ticket. George serenely pretended not to notice. I decided that George's smooth, upper-class approach was even more bitchy fun and emulated him, the two of us chatting while they seethed.

When I was in high school, George got an offer in Hollywood and moved away. I've searched for both of them but never knew their stage names, so they're gone. Even so, I never forgot George or Gloria, or their lessons on class.

The Amato Opera, 159 Bleecker Street, 1950s. Author's private collection.

The author and Ann in the Amato Opera orchestra pit. Author's private collection.

Backstage at the Amato Opera, 1950s. Courtesy of Irene Frydel.

Larry directing at the Amato Opera. Author's private collection.

Irene (*far left*) and the author (*second from left*) in their snazzy parochial school uniforms rehearsing Hansel and Gretel at the Amato Opera. Author's private collection.

Larry running lights at the Amato Opera, 1953. Author's private collection.

Ann Florio backstage at the
Metropolitan Opera House.
Author's private collection.

Annie Frydel onstage during an Amato Opera production of *The Marriage of Figaro*, 1950s (*center, facing audience, and inset*). The author's father is in the upper far right, wearing a bolero jacket. Author's private collection.

Irene and the author on Bank Street. Author's private collection.

Ann Florio and John Frydel backstage at the Metropolitan Opera. Author's private collection.

Irene, John, and Annie Frydel, 63 Bank Street, apartment 4B. Author's private collection.

Franz Bendtsen, 63 Bank Street, apartment 1A. Author's private collection.

Earl Browder, circa 1939. Courtesy of Universal Images Group/Getty Images.

Sid Vicious, 63 Bank Street, apartment 1B. Courtesy of Mirror Pix/Getty Images.

Al Calvi,
63 Bank Street,
apartment 2A.
Author's private
collection.

John Kemmerer
of 63 Bank Street,
apartment 5B, at
Grinnell College,
1923. Courtesy of
Grinnell College
Libraries Special
Collections and
Archives.

Jack and Madeline Gilford. Courtesy of the Jack Gilford Estate.

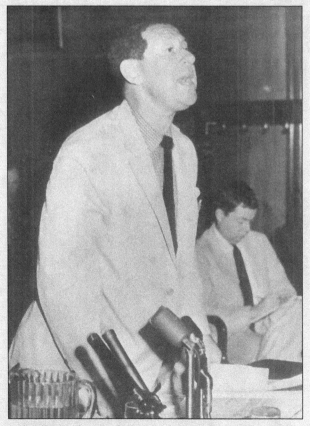

Jack Gilford addressing the House Un-American Activities
Committee, 1953. Courtesy of the Jack Gilford Estate.

Marion "Auntie Mame" Tanner, 72 Bank Street, on her attic floor with her sleeping bag. Courtesy of Jack Manning/*The New York Times*/Redux.

Marion smiling with Roz Russell photo on wall. Courtesy of Bettman/Getty Images.

The author before Larry and Bella threw her graduation into a riot, 1969. Author's private collection.

Bella Abzug, 37 Bank Street. Courtesy of Leonard McCombe/Life Premium Collection/Getty Images.

Debating the Issues of '72

LIFE

McGOVERN vs. KLEINDIENST ON CRIME

WOMEN IN POLITICS

How are they doing?
Where are they going?

Bella Abzug fights
to stay in Congress

JUNE 9 · 1972 · 50¢

Tish Touchette, 51 Bank Street, in his nightclub act. Courtesy of Tish Touchette.

Stella Crater, One Bank Street, with her attorney, Emil Ellis. Courtesy of *New York Daily News* Archives/Getty Images.

Yeffe Kimball,
11 Bank Street.
Courtesy of
the estate of
Dr. Harvey L.
Slatin.

Before there
was AIDS: The
author and one
of her beloved,
now deceased
Village friends
on Halloween.
Author's private
collection.

Marty Braverman, 75 Bank Street. Author's private collection.

Roz Braverman, 75 Bank Street. Author's private collection.

Marty's Harem: (*left to right*) Madeline, the author, Becky, Amanda, Chloe.
Author's private collection.

Commare Peschiola in
her 409 Bleecker Street
fish store. Courtesy of
Anita Isola.

Stylish and Splendid Bank Street

15 • Jack Heineman Jr.

Bernard ("Jack") Heineman Jr. turned my stereotypes about wealthy Bank Street upside down. When a friend mentioned him in 2003, I put a letter under his 15 Bank Street door, explaining my Bank Street stories project and requesting an interview. He called with an invitation to afternoon tea. The door opened to a trim, cordial man in his late seventies, wearing casual WASP chinos and loafers, as if ready for a dock party on Martha's Vineyard. Interesting, well-framed paintings lined the walls. We settled into a parlor full of comfortably worn oak and marble furniture.

Although I hadn't known his children, his son sent a message through our mutual friend, warning me to brace for temperament. Jack was indeed a curmudgeon at times, huffing when I misspelled prominent names from our taped interviews or when the quality of my transcripts did not please. Perfect accuracy and grammar, I learned fast, were important. But he was also charming, razor sharp, and hysterically witty. My Bank Street stories idea intrigued him. We took to each other during that first meeting and ended up having many more. His wife, Ruth, had died before we met. They had bought 15 Bank Street in the 1950s as their babies arrived.

To my astonishment, Jack loved the art of the raconteur, keeping me in stitches or on the edge of my seat. Since storytelling was my territory, too, it became a friendly contest. Wine glass or teacup in hand, we'd sit in his living room entertaining each other as hours passed.

Since Jack had developed an eye for then-obscure Ashcan School artists such as John Sloan and Edward Hopper in the 1940s, while he was in college and had the means with which to buy their works, his pleasantly old-fashioned brownstone was filled with extraordinary art. He had collected widely and well. In the early 1960s, a Bank Street neighbor inherited a Sloan watercolor of her father on a Manhattan balcony and asked Jack to appraise it. She had hoped that the picture would be worth at least $2,500. Jack arranged its sale for $80,000.

Jack wasn't my first socialite. As theatricals, my parents and I were invited to soirees at Back Bay townhouses, Atlanta mansions, Dallas ranches, and Detroit auto magnate castles when we visited my mother on the Met's annual six-week tour. We were the entertainment, dishing backstage dirt and insider stories over dinner. I learned young to arrive with anecdotes and jokes at the ready.

Nonetheless, Jack was a revelation. He had lineage, money, *and* razor wit. We traded backstage gossip, solo travel stories, and obscure tidbits of Bank Street history for hours at a time. When I read his 2006 obituaries (he died at eighty-two) I realized that for all of our fun, he had modestly withheld large portions of his life. He had been a decorated World War II hero, for example, but had never mentioned a word of it. He was a true gentleman, letting me show off when he could have steamrolled my paltry adventures. Instead, he'd listened gleefully, laughing and asking questions.

. . .

Jack was born in 1924 New York to Central Park West elegance. The Heinemans had arrived in New York in the 1600s, among the country's first Jewish settlers. He was a Morgenthau on his mother's side. One cousin was Henry Morgenthau Jr., FDR's secretary of the treasury. Another was Robert Morgenthau, Manhattan's longtime district attorney. Jack never mentioned what his father, Bernard Sr., did for a living, but it was obvious that the Heinemans had multigenerational wealth too.

Although my unusual opera life amused him, he was formidable competition even there. Eleven-year-old Jack played bridge in the 1930s with Metropolitan Opera star May Irwin. The opera singer Geraldine Farrar was a frequent family guest. His childhood nurse was accosted by Enrico Caruso as she wheeled baby Jack through Central Park. Her boyfriend, an Irish cop, arrested Caruso and threw him in jail.

William Danforth, another famous singer of that era, was a neighbor at the family's Thousand Islands summer home, he said (neglecting to mention that his family owned the largest island in the chain).

Later on, Jack met young soprano Beverly Sills when she was a dental hygienist working her way through Juilliard. She confided that her real name was Belle Silverman but asked Jack not to mention that to her anti-Semitic boss.

During a college vacation in the early 1940s, Jack and some friends drove through California. Their car broke down in front of the Hearst Castle in San Simeon, built by the newspaper magnate William Randolph Hearst. A limousine pulled up. "Gorgeous legs uncurled from the car," Jack recalled. They belonged to the actress Marion Davies, Hearst's adored mistress. She invited them to spend the weekend—no hardship since the castle, now a major tourist attraction, had more than fifty bedrooms. The young men dined with Gary Cooper, Tyrone Power, Claudette Colbert, and Norma Shearer. Jack and Davies corresponded for years.

Other friends were composer Richard Rodgers and his brother, Morty. Poor Morty, Jack snickered, had unfortunate taste in extramarital flings. He'd had an affair with the film star Mary Astor, which forced him to appear at her lurid 1936 divorce trial. Astor's diary, key evidence, was purportedly so full of the names of prominent lovers, with explicit reviews of their sexual prowess, that it was sealed by the judge and later burned by court order.

• • •

In the 1930s, before World War II, Jack's father received a letter from a man named Benno, who was Jewish and who lived in Germany. Although Benno's wife was a Heineman, the two Heinemans were not related. Benno, who had gotten the name from a Manhattan phone book, pleaded for help, fearing that the growing Nazi persecution would destroy his family.

Bernard Sr. called a family meeting and candidly told everyone that sponsoring Benno and his family's migration to America would cost more than $50,000 (nearly $900,000 today). If Benno was a con artist, they could lose it all. Benno and his family would be not helped, he said, unless every member of the Heineman family, including the children, agreed to take the risk.

Everyone voted to help. Bernard booked passage, signed affidavits that they were related, and posted bonds to ensure that the refugees would not become public charges in the United States. Bernard's only stipulation was that they live someplace other than New York City. He felt that there were already too many Jews in the city and that they would have a better life elsewhere. Benno settled in the Midwest, worked three jobs, and repaid every dime. At Jack's memorial, Benno's son declared that were it not for the Heinemans he would not be alive.

• • •

Jack's passions were travel, the arts—and butterflies. Bernard Senior wrote a book titled *Jamaica and Its Butterflies* that is still in print. Jack had siblings, but it didn't seem that anyone else had caught the bug from their father. He and his parents went on collecting expeditions several times a year after World War II when Jack was in his twenties. During one trip they socialized with Noel Coward at his villa on Jamaica, where young Jack turned down the elderly composer's advances. "It's entirely your loss, dear boy," Coward huffed.

After taking their leave of the spurned Mr. Coward, they drove to the exclusive Shaw Park Hotel in two open Packards. One was driven by their chauffeur from New York. The other carried gear, luggage, and their maid. Jack's mother had brought a trunk of evening gowns. The Heineman men had tuxedos and tails. It was, Jack said matter-of-factly, "how things were done."

They had been asked to check in before the cocktail hour but arrived late. The terrace glittered with guests in formal evening wear. Jack and Bernard strode through the crowd in expedition gear: pith helmets, nets, killing jars, and all. The terrace had neon lights, a rarity then, which were swarming with moths. Bernard spotted a prime *Erebus odora* butterfly hovering over the bar. Only one obstacle, an elegant woman draped with emeralds and diamonds, stood between him and his prize.

"Madam, would you kindly remove yourself?" he demanded. "I need your chair." When the lady obliged, Bernard leaped onto the bar, deftly netting his prey as the bartender ducked. Cocktail chatter ceased as he jumped down, bowed to the lady, and exhibited his treasure to general applause and laughter.

The obliging lady was Millicent Rogers, a Standard Oil heiress and one of the world's richest women (Jack, a delicious gossip, added that

Millicent's lovers included the Prince of Wales and Clark Gable). She thought that the butterfly hunt was all very exciting and bought the Heineman men, still in muddy jungle gear, a drink. Jack's mother looked at her unruly two and "promptly fled the entire scene."

On another outing, the Heinemans docked in Cuba as a young Spanish woman in black mourning clothes walked by. A prime katydid was hanging onto her swaying buttocks. Bernard crept up and grabbed for it. She leaped and screamed as he held it to her face, saying "cricket, cricket" by way of explanation. Jack understood, he laughed, why his beleaguered mother frequently assured onlookers that she had never met either Bernard or Jack and had no idea who they were.

• • •

Jack went butterfly hunting on his own in 1952. Since he was representing the American Museum of Natural History, he had letters of introduction from board members for his journey. His ultimate destination was Ceylon (now Sri Lanka), but along the way one letter yielded an invitation to meet the King and Queen of Thailand. He spent a frantic day running through Bangkok looking for a white suit. When he reached India, another letter led to dinner with Prime Minister Jawaharlal Nehru. Far more important, India was where he met Ruth, the daughter of missionaries.

At the time Ruth had two Indian beaux. One, an Ivy League graduate, later headed the Indian navy and murdered his wife's lover in their bathroom. The other became Prime Minister Nehru's private secretary, solicited money for dead people through a nonexistent charity, and landed in jail.

Once he and Ruth were married, Jack dutifully settled into a day job, as a founding partner in a fabric house. Business was, he said, strictly for the money. His love remained the arts and butterflies. He lunched at the Algonquin and nodded to Dorothy Parker and Robert Benchley. He met his father for drinks at the elegant Lambs Club. Even with a happy family life and many activities, the day job, lucrative as it was, bored him to tears and he eventually quit in order to devote himself to his passions. Another example from Jack, I mused. Follow your heart. Of course, he could afford to.

Jack settled my childhood fears that Tom Iacovone, the elderly Italian iceman who lived at 51 Bank Street, was poor and alone. I'd always worried about Tom. Who would care for him, I'd worried at the age of eight, when he couldn't deliver ice anymore? And since refrigerators were fast replacing iceboxes, what if Tom became indigent?

"Tom was a friend of mine," Jack told me. "He had two daughters. They were far older than you and you wouldn't have known them. He had a happy home life."

Jack was right, I discovered. To my surprise, Tish, the female impersonator who lived at 51 Bank Street, told me that one of Tom's daughters, Rose, was still around. Right upstairs, he said. One day I knocked on Rose's door and introduced myself. As it turned out, she had been born at 51 Bank Street ninety years earlier and still lived in *her* family's apartment too. Given our thirty-three-year age difference, I must have taken her for just another tenant as we passed. Neither of us recalled the other, but it didn't matter. We understood each other. She has her father's eyes too, I thought.

I was thrilled to be thoroughly bested in the "oldest Bank Streeter in her original dwelling" category. Rose was still sharp. She remembered Jack, a staunch Reform Democrat, working the voting polls with her. "He was at 15, that's where he lived," she said. "He was a lovely man. He entertained us all with hilarious jokes and stories."

Jack was also a friend of another Italian iceman, who lived near Bank and Waverly. That iceman, who could neither read nor write, worked "like a dog," Jack said, to give his children excellent educations, and his son, Wally, became a lawyer.

Jack was asked to be a trustee of St. Vincent's Hospital, a block from home. He served for twelve years, the token non-Catholic on the board of this very conservative Catholic hospital. When a new member was needed, Jack raised his hand.

The chief trustee hesitated before recognizing him. Jack's liberalism had quickly become an embarrassment to this conservative group. They were doubtless sorry, he said, that they'd brought him in. "My impression is that New York has Catholics from Puerto Rico, Spain, and Italy," Jack said. "I look around the room, and you are all English, Irish, and German. Correct me if I'm wrong. Since the Village neighborhood we serve has a great many Italian residents, I think it would be an appropriate gesture of respect to bring an Italian Catholic onto the board." Monsignor Clancy and the others were stiff. But, Jack exulted, he had them cornered. And so Wally, the illiterate iceman's lawyer son, joined the board.

After Jack died, I watched, furious, as St. Vincent's, a beloved Village institution since 1849, was ground up into yet more Village luxury housing under what many hospital employees insisted were shady, controversial circumstances. Some Bank Streeters had worked there for their entire careers and their parents before them. Jack would have dug deep and, if he'd found wrongdoing, used his power to fight like a tiger. That's what privileges were for, in his eyes. I can imagine his acid comments about the later next-door resident of 13 Bank, movie mogul Harvey Weinstein, and his abuse of power, too.

Jack changed my attitude towards the rich. Money and social connections are great, I thought, looking around his lovely home. They buy brownstones and art and butterfly expeditions. And used properly, they also rescue refugees and help the children of illiterate immigrants move up the ladder. Being rich *and* living by deep humanist principles, with laughter, style, and panache. *That's* a life.

16 • Jack and Madeline Gilford

A reading of Madeline Gilford's 1953 testimony to the House Un-American Activities Committee at her funeral in 2008 made us laugh until we cried all over again. Two talents, a rubber face, and raw New York moxie had catapulted one neighborhood couple to fame and history.

The actors Jack and Madeline Gilford lived at 75 Bank Street from the 1950s until the 1990s. Jack had a comic acting role in one Metropolitan Opera production. "All he has to do is crook his eyebrow and the audience is in stitches," Mom said. "He's amazing."

Jack being at the Met was no big deal to me. Like the rest of our little Bank Street gang, I was excited because Jack was the star of TV commercials for Cracker Jack candy. Kids yelled, "Hey, it's Cracker Jack Man!" on the street as Jack waved to them. He was a Real Star in our book. When I was seven, I tapped his elbow one day as we stood on line at Shanvilla Grocer. "Mr. Gilford, you don't know me, but I'm Sam's friend, Donna, from 63 Bank," I said shyly. A smile lit his face. "How sweet and grown-up of you to introduce yourself," he said. "It's a pleasure to meet you, Donna."

Jack's warmth made me float on air as we shook hands. His son, Sam, in my block's play group, was exactly my age. I neglected to mention that Sam and I, red-faced and avoiding each other's eyes, had kissed, on a dare on Bank Street, egged on by cheering kids. Jack's other son, Joe, was a few years older than me, so we just passed each other with a nod. His daughter, Lisa, a teenager, was already out and about. I didn't even know that she existed until years later.

The Gilford kids went to nearby private schools—Little Red School House and its upper school, Elisabeth Irwin High School, both notable as among the city's most progressive institutions. We shared Bank Street and show-biz parents, but our school cultures were worlds apart. My Catholic parochial school, St. Joseph's School,

JACK AND MADELINE GILFORD · 135

on Christopher Street, had local blue-collar and working-class kids, and my family's theatrical ways definitely didn't suit the dismally misnamed Sisters of Charity teachers.

"Mommy, what's a slut?" I asked after school in third grade, on the verge of tears. I'd come offstage late the night before, too sleepy to wash before bed. In my next-morning rush, I'd forgotten about the Max Factor pancake makeup on my face and throat.

Ann stopped breading her chicken cutlets and stared at me. "Why are you asking me that?"

I pointed to the makeup. "Sister Richard says only sluts wear this. She made me say three Hail Marys before I could eat my lunch. She says I should be ashamed of myself. Am I a bad girl?"

Ann mashed breadcrumbs into a cutlet, her mouth tight. "No, you aren't. You didn't do anything wrong. It's a misunderstanding. Sister Richard didn't know that you had a show last night. I'll talk to her."

I survived one more year as a trollop until my parents put me out of my misery and sent me to public school.

• • •

Little Red, on Bleecker Street, was only blocks from my nasty nuns, but in reality it was in another universe. Little Red and Elisabeth Irwin were known as schools for the children of left-wing parents, a.k.a. "red diaper babies." In the early 1950s, before Sam and I were born, Jack and Madeline became acquainted with the tactics of Senator Joe McCarthy and his House Un-American Activities Committee (HUAC) anti-Communist witch hunters up close and in bleakly personal fashion. HUAC went after American citizens with Communist Party affiliations (a perfectly legal tie but one that many considered un-American) in all walks of life during America's Cold War with the Soviet Union in the 1950s. HUAC summoned Jack and Madeline, who, like many others, had been named as possible Communist Party members by the choreographer Jerome Robbins, to come to Washington to testify.

Jack stormed at his interrogators and invoked the Fifth Amendment, refusing to answer the committee's infamous question, "Are you now or have you ever been a Communist?"—or any other question, for that matter. His stance took enormous guts. People who refused to cave in and cooperate, as Robbins had, risked being found in contempt of Congress, blacklisted from employment, and often sent to jail.

Jack was the committee's easy Gilford. When committee members interviewed Madeline, a petite blonde beauty, she demurely misheard and stonewalled every question during that unforgettable exchange we heard at her funeral. She offered respectful but utterly oblique answers to members of the increasingly baffled committee members, staying sweetly but firmly in ditzy, wide-eyed character until her interrogators threw up their hands in despair.

Unlike Robbins and others, like the director Elia Kazan, future President Ronald Reagan, and the author Ayn Rand, the Gilfords refused to be bulldozed or cowed into pointing fingers at others to save their own careers. Their principled defiance landed them both on a nationwide employment blacklist, HUAC's lethal punishment for the uncooperative. Hiring a person in any profession whose name was on that list brought serious political pressure on employers, and few were brave enough to even attempt such a thing. Actors changed professions. Authors wrote scripts under assumed names. Others fled the country. More than a few committed suicide.

• • •

The Gilfords, made of sterner stuff, struggled through the blacklist at 75 Bank, never altering their politics or their professions even as jobs and friendships died away. In 1952 Jack rushed to a resort in the Catskill Mountains, one of the few places that would still employ him, to do his stand-up comedy act. Unless the Gilfords paid their bill, the hospital wouldn't release their newborn son, Joe, lying in his maternity ward bassinet like a hocked watch. The couple raised their kids and worked wherever they could until Senator McCarthy and his committee toppled from power in 1954 (to the credit of the Metropolitan Opera, the company defied the blacklist so Jack had never lost that job).

Jack made a fabulous comeback from the blacklist, starring in films and shows like *A Funny Thing Happened on the Way to the Forum*, *Catch-22*, and *Cocoon*. Madeline wrote a show-biz memoir with her good friend Kate Mostel, Zero Mostel's wife, and continued her social activism. She was on the platform during Dr. Martin Luther King's "I Have a Dream" speech. When she found herself at a party with Jerome Robbins, she made a loud public toast that concluded, "kiss my ass."

"Lucky Sam," Madeline said with a smile as I told her about our childhood kiss. In the 1990s, after Jack died, Madeline had become not just the Gilford kids' mother but my friend. We were both members of a tight Bank Street group who saw a lot of one another. We had dinner parties at one another's homes. Went to the theater together. Spent weekends at Madeline's country house.

Madeline was a Bronx-born force of nature who juggled numerous lives at once, onstage or onscreen from her 1930s show-business childhood until her death in 2008. She was a shrewd financial manager, a talent agent, a Broadway producer, and a hard-working actress as well as a good Jewish mother who nagged her kids to eat more fruit. She bristled if the subject of the blacklist came up, but her life went on as it always had, full throttle. When I interviewed her about the couple's life in the Village, all I had to do was hit the "record" button.

Jack fell in love with the Village before we met. In 1938, Barney Josephson opened New York's first interracial nightclub here, Café Society. It was on Sheridan Square. Kids, mostly Irish kids, would be throwing eggs, even late at night, when the musicians went home. Jack was the emcee, the only white person on the bill. He was funny and he drew a crowd. Billie Holliday did her first downtown engagement at the Café. Lena Horne debuted there. Jack sort of discovered her because he was doing some benefits in Harlem. Lena was a chorus girl at the Cotton Club. She was very beautiful and she could sing. She and Jack lived near each other in Brooklyn. He used to walk her home and they dated for a while.

The local tradespeople were wonderful . . . there were peddlers in the street, scissor sharpeners, knife sharpeners. Around the corner was this Italian fish lady with gray hair in a bun and a plain black dress. My kids ate clams with lemon from the fish store for breakfast. I got the most wonderful fresh vegetables from the pushcarts. They ate all kinds of things, healthy things. The kids sometimes had trouble with the kids from Pompeii [Our Lady of Pompeii, a parochial school on Bleecker Street]. There was maybe some anti-Semitism, anti-Communism, maybe anti–Little Red.

We went to Washington Square Park after the kids got out of school. I did business on the pay phone. The Fifth Avenue bus used to streak through the park. It went through the arch and around the fountain, going downtown. Kids got hit. We conducted demonstrations, petitions, everything. Eventually we mothers, including Jane Jacobs, staged a lay-down protest—I think it was 1958. It worked. They moved the bus route.

Theodore Bikel was one of the best Bank Street citizens, but he was always on the road with *Fiddler*. We were closer to Alan Arkin. Jack did *Catch-22* with him. When Bella Abzug lived on the street, her husband Martin and Jack would meet in Shanvilla and complain about their absentee wives. Actually, Martin was completely supportive of Bella and just a terrific guy.

Madeline was fiercely loyal and supportive. "This is Donna. She sang at the Metropolitan Opera and she's writing a book. Gorgeous and talented like her parents. Donna, this is Elise. Elise was a fabulous Broadway actress and then she started her own school. Today it's one of the best in the city." That was a typical Madeline party introduction. Her get-togethers were extravaganzas of laughing people and heaps of food. She got us all talking as she circulated, working the room.

Dropping by for coffee was like visiting a boutique where the owner locks the door until you buy. Madeline had not been petite for some years by the 1990s, but she never got rid of anything. Her closets were stuffed with amazing clothes from the Broadway and Hollywood years. "I have a perfect dress for you!" she'd say, pushing sequined gowns aside. "I wore it on auditions, and it worked every time. With a scarf, maybe a hat, it will look great! And take this purse. I haven't used it in years. Italian leather!" I never left empty-handed.

Warmth. Grit. Talent. Courage under pressure. Generosity. Compassion. Outsized, extravagant personalities that fought injustice and adversity with style, wit, and moxie. I'll forget a lot of people before I ever forget the Gilfords.

17 • Auntie Mame: Marion Tanner

The woman at 72 Bank Street smiled and opened her arms as I tod-dled over, already excited. I knew what was coming. She'd toss me in the air and whirl me around. Then we'd rub noses and giggle. She was maybe five feet tall, lean and wiry, with dancing, merry eyes. A few of her teeth were missing, and the rest were crooked and yellowed. Her thin gray hair was twisted into an untidy nest of a bun. But even with wrinkles and ropy, blue-veined hands, she looked like a pixie or a kindly fairy queen. "Let her stay here while you go shopping," she'd say to Mom. "She'll learn that headstand this week, you'll see."

Marion Tanner's four-story brownstone was a crumbling eyesore by the time I was born in 1955, but to me it looked like one of the enchanted kingdoms in my Little Golden Books. Mom brought me over for short visits at first or left me there briefly as she ran errands. But by age six I just ran up the steps by myself and opened the door, which was never locked, whenever I wanted to visit. The entrance hall had a grand curving stairway and huge, gold-framed mirrors. Broken velvet couches flanked a marble fireplace. A crystal chande-lier swayed overhead, too coated with spider webs and black filth to throw light. Roaches scurried up the walls.

Despite appearances, Ann felt that I was safe with Marion, and she was right. My parents had moved to the Village to live the artist life. Their friends were every color, gender, and religion. They ac-cepted people on their own terms. It wasn't surprising that they con-sidered the highly eccentric Marion a perfectly reasonable babysitter.

From the time I can remember, Marion always had a teeming houseful of "guests" wandering in and out at all hours. Beds were full; visitors lived in corners, under rigged tents. The basement was packed like a subway train with snoring, horizontal commut-ers. Most were either weaving aimlessly or asleep wherever they'd dropped.

"Did you bring my clothes?" a young man asked one day. He had arrived recently and asked everyone this question when they came in the door. His army jacket was tattered, and I tried not to cringe as I smelled his foul breath. "I'll bring them next time, Mr. Harris," I said. Marion had coached me to say exactly that, and to smile at him, too. "He's a little confused right now," she said, "but he'll be all right."

Marion didn't wrinkle her nose if someone smelled bad or swayed as they spoke, and therefore neither did I. If they were in her house, I figured, they were probably safe to talk to. If I sensed interest, I'd hold out a book, my usual calling card, and ask them to read or tell me a story. Sometimes they seemed sadly surprised that I wasn't afraid of them. But if someone didn't want to play or was mumbling to himself, I left them alone.

As attentive as Marion was to other people's problems, she completely ignored the problems of her own home. Cracked windows rattled in rotted frames. I held my nose near the stinky toilets. Pigeons flapped through jagged holes in the roof through which rain and snow dripped to the top story, where Marion slept on the floor in a black sleeping bag. Water trickled down the walls to the basement, rotting the plaster walls.

"Oh, this place is a mess!" she would say as she tugged my foot from a hole in the floor or when a mouse raced across the table as we played Chinese Checkers. "I have to do something." But she never did.

Mom and others sometimes called her Auntie Mame. I thought it was a nickname. As it turned out, it was anything but. She *was* Mame, the real-life aunt of the author Patrick Dennis, who wrote the best-selling novel *Auntie Mame*, which would spawn a Broadway play, a Hollywood movie, and a Broadway musical.

But Marion was so much more than the heroine of a campy novel. She was a blueblood, a bohemian, a scholar, and, I believe, a real-life Buddhist avatar. She was a dancing life spirit. Although many, including her nephew, considered her demented, within her unswerving principles, Marion was no more mad than Mother Teresa. She too evolved a social mission to help the down-and-out that was perfectly rational on its own terms, and she lived her life accordingly.

• • •

Baby Marion swept into staid Buffalo, New York, in 1891. The wealthy Tanners had some wild genes in the pool. Marion's respectable brother, Edward Everett Tanner II, endured his sister with gritted teeth and rejoiced when she departed for Smith College in Massachusetts, never to return. His happiness lasted until he himself sired Edward E. Tanner III, later known as Patrick Dennis, the flamboyant bisexual theater personality whose runaway hit novel, *Auntie Mame*, threw the Tanners into the international spotlight.

After college Marion made a beeline for New York City. It was around 1910, and Freud's revolutionary ideas were beginning to cross the Atlantic. Marion was fascinated. She studied his theories, got herself a shrink, and considered becoming an analyst herself. Her patrician lineage, athleticism, and Smith College degree opened doors to jobs like coaching a Park Avenue girls' ice hockey team and giving horseback riding lessons. During the 1920s and '30s she acted on Broadway, sold lingerie at Macy's, and worked as a mediator for the National Labor Relations Board. She married and divorced a writer and then a British engineer. "Don't wonder about anything in life from the outside, Donna," she always said. "Jump in!"

In the 1920s, Marion also studied Buddhism, and it transformed her life. Love in all of its expressions, she decided, was the supreme goal of existence. Everyone carries the divine flame of life. Embracing a high path, she learned, didn't require renouncing the world. The true Buddhist shared his path with as many other souls as possible. Elevating one helped elevate all.

In 1927 she bought 72 Bank Street, an elegant 1890s brownstone, and threw the doors open for book readings, dance performances, concerts, and cocktail parties. A speakeasy that supplied her party gin was conveniently down the street on Bank and Waverly Place. The slinky clothes of the '20s were perfect for her sleek, lithe figure. A portrait over the chipped marble fireplace in the parlor showed Marion, light brown hair bobbed to her chin, draped over a chair, legs crossed, in a shimmering blue frock, a shoe dangling from one slim ankle. Her expressive eyes were set in a small oval face that reminded me of Tinker Bell in my Peter Pan book.

When Marion moved into 72 Bank Street in the 1920s, she may have passed Edith Kitching, neighbor and kindred evolved spirit. In 1916, when Edith made headlines by inheriting a fortune, her home

was a room in a boarding house at 24 Bank Street. Edith, a philosophy teacher, ate one meal of vegetables a day and slept on a wooden
board because it was "sleeping on Mother Earth." Her income was
$300 a year. When an uncle in Brooklyn died and left her $195,000,
she took the executor of his estate to court for trying to force the
money on her. Her uncle, she told reporters, had grown rich in real
estate by evicting penniless mortgagees. That tainted inheritance,
she fumed, could only bring her spiritual problems and woe. "There
are only three things in the universe that have any value and those
are intelligence, love, and will," she told the *Times*. "To acquire these
things I have all the money I need."

. . .

Decades later, when I was in my twenties, Marion was in her nineties,
and as I'd push her wheelchair to Abingdon Square Park she told me
wild stories about her life. As a 1920s flapper, she smoked Gitanes, a
chic French cigarette, in a carved ivory holder. Eugene O'Neill and
D. H. Lawrence read their works at her literary salons. George Gershwin played her piano while movie siren Pola Negri paused just
long enough to grab a drink before slithering upstairs with her date,
a self-proclaimed Expressionist painter. At one soiree, Ethel Barrymore, the doyenne of the Barrymore acting clan, pursed her lips,
snatched her brother John's flask of gin, and dropped it down her
bosom. "He's already acting a drunken fool," she sniffed, "He'll have
to act a Greek tragedy to retrieve it."

The more Marion studied Buddhism, and meditated, she told me
when she was in her nineties, the further she felt herself slipping
from what her gurus called "the chains of existence." She started
to focus on helping humanity achieve enlightenment, one soul at a
time, right here on Bank Street.

"You are a divine flame, a gift from the universe," she told me as
she combed my hair. "You must discover why you came to earth and
fulfill your journey." She was always telling me that, although I never
understood what she meant.

Struggling artists and others began to stay over in the 1930s as
the Depression took away jobs. Marion had a bed and meals for anyone, including the blues singer and heroin addict Billie Holiday. "It
elevates the soul to help others, Donna," Marion told me decades

later. "I was the lucky one." Some gathered themselves together and moved on, thanking her. Others took advantage of her kindness for years. Marion had jobs, Tanner money, and generous ex-husbands, but her helping mission became difficult as the Depression wore on. Marion didn't worry. She always believed, she told me, that the universe would provide for her good intentions.

Her guests were scarcely great neighbors. We had metal garbage cans in the 1950s. Inebriated boarders sometimes capped a night on the town with al fresco bowling, rolling the cans down Bank Street and cackling and slapping their thighs when the cans crashed into cars. Neighbors yelled, but my parents, who came home late from their shows anyway, just wrapped pillows around their ears.

Tiny, ragged Marion passed serenely through it all, reading Kant or the Upanishads. Her nephew, Patrick Dennis, visited often. He was elfin like her; they had a strong family resemblance. During one visit, I sat on her lap at the kitchen table shelling peas while Dennis paced in front of us wearing a starched white shirt, gold cufflinks, and a neat little derby. Dad had just taken me to see *The Pirates of Penzance*, and Dennis, in his prim outfit, reminded me of a character out of Gilbert and Sullivan. Glaring at the grimy walls and broken furniture, he flicked dust off his sleeve as he lectured his aunt.

"Look at this place, Marion. Your friends will burn it down if the roof doesn't collapse first. Have you paid those taxes? I can only do so much." Marion just nodded peacefully, until he snatched up his walking stick and stormed out, leaving a wad of cash on the table. "He has a good heart," she said with a smile as she pocketed the money. His warnings didn't seem to bother her. Nothing did, as far as I could tell.

• • •

One long-term guest was a French artist with a daughter my age named Gabrielle and Gabrielle's little sister, Fanny. I called the artist Maman, as they did.

The three of them shared a bedroom with a disheveled woman who woke up only long enough to curse in French, Russian, or slurred English before she took a swallow from the bottle of vodka under her bed and passed out again. Gabrielle and I mimicked her, drinking and falling down, until Marion intervened. "She is a princess, but she lost her palace during the Russian Revolution, and she is still sad about it," Marion said. We stared at her blankly. "Just be nice to her, please, girls," Marion said with a sigh. When Maman and the princess quarreled, Marion hurried upstairs to mediate in French. "She ees une saint and une geeniuus, zat Madame Marion," Maman always said.

One rainy day when Gabrielle, Fanny, and I complained that we were bored, Marion tugged a moldy trunk from a corner of the basement. Beads and feathers flew about as she dug through it, holding up pieces of clothing and laughing.

"Lord, look at this old stuff!" she exclaimed. A sharp flowery scent filled the air as she swathed us in silk and satin dresses. "That's Shalimar perfume, girls. It was my favorite scent. I even poured it into my bathwater. Can you image anything so silly? Here, put on a tiara. And wave this feather fan. You peek over it and wink at boys, like this."

Marion and Maman laughed as we twirled and showed off. "Darlings, you look très, très chic," Marion said. We paraded noisily through the dilapidated rooms in our ancient finery, eliciting curses and threats from the sleeping derelicts.

Marion practiced yoga in the kitchen for hours, oblivious to everything, as soups bubbled on the wobbly gas stove, random new ingredients tossed in as she brought them home. Even in her weathered fifties, she could drop into a full-leg split and do headstands. The kitchen had a wood-burning fireplace and an enormous hanging cast-iron pot. Gabrielle and I once hid Fanny in the pot, giggling as Maman searched for her.

• • •

Other Bank Street kids made fun of Marion, and teased me for visiting her. "Eww, don't touch Donna!" a tough older girl yelled one day as she snapped her gum. "She got cooties in the crazy house!" The Bank Street kids made fun of Gabrielle and Fanny, so Maman took her girls elsewhere to play outside.

In an effort to fit in, I chalked the words "72 Bum Street" on Marion's sidewalk. Maman saw me from the window and gently asked if I thought that was a nice thing to do. The realization that I was being mean to my friends shamed me. I rubbed it out and slunk away.

Marion charmed wilted vegetables and dented cans out of tight-fisted Pat at Shanvilla Market and day-old bread from the French bakery next to Pat. I sometimes helped Marion carry groceries and talked about operas. I acted out the children's choruses I was doing in her living room, leaping around while she smiled and clapped. One of her guests had been a violinist before the drink took over. He tapped the beat from his spot on the floor when he was in the mood.

By 1963, when I was eight, I vaguely understood that my friend was famous, although it meant nothing to me. I had no idea that Patrick's best-selling novel spawned a hit Broadway play that ran from 1956 to 1958, as well as a Hollywood movie, both starring Rosalind Russell. Dennis's popular sequel, *Around the World With Auntie Mame*, was published in 1958, and the smash Broadway musical, *Mame*, starring Angela Lansbury, opened in 1966.

"How dare he make all that money off her and leave her rotting like this?" my mother raged. Nor was she alone. Marion's neighbors fumed to one another about heartless Patrick Dennis living in luxury from his aunt's story while letting her live like a bum. His name was mud on our block.

The truth is, Patrick Dennis didn't deserve their disapproval. He was supporting his aunt substantially, even though he swore heatedly that his books were creative fiction and not the story of his aunt's life at all. Truth or, as Dennis insisted, fancy, as the *Mame* novels, play, and movie became hits, Dennis paid off her debts and gave her a generous stipend. But whatever his style and proclivities, he was a fiscally conservative New England Tanner, his father's son in that respect, and he tried to set firm conditions. Marion was to either sell 72 Bank Street and move, alone, to a sensible home in good condition, he said, or make her rowdy boarders leave.

Marion was extraordinarily intelligent. But she was also as stubborn and willful as any Yankee mule. She'd make vague promises to him, or, as when Dennis lectured her in front of me, she smiled, nodded, and ignored every word. Even I realized that Dennis was talking to himself.

In case her irresponsibility, as he saw it, didn't rile him enough, Marion the extroverted show-off basked in the limelight of "their" success. She talked to journalists and paraded onto TV talk shows as the "real Mame," cheerfully dismissing the Broadway show, the movie, and Rosalind Russell with a wave of her hand. "They wouldn't have *dared* film some of my real life, darling!" she bragged to me decades later, still full of herself. The stories were legendary, like guests opening a bathroom door to find the flapper movie star Louise Brooks perched on the sink having sex in her fur coat. Dennis had fits about that too, but Marion kept welcoming interviewers as if she were the Queen of Sheba. Even a selfless Buddhist, I realized, can be a diva.

• • •

Along with her remarkable assortment of housemates, Marion had exotic treasures from all over the world. Sometimes guests stole her silverware or her Lalique crystal. I'd see someone weaving down the street trying to sell a familiar tray or figurine. Marion knew, but she didn't care. When I snatched a candlestick from a sleeping drunk on the steps and brought it back inside, I expected righteous indignation.

"It's OK," she said to my astonishment. "He's broke."

I was in Catholic elementary school then and although the adultery and neighbor-coveting businesses were still head scratchers, I understood that commandment.

"He's stealing! It's a sin!"

Marion smiled and waved her hand in the air. I knew that wave: it meant that she was no longer paying attention. "You're right. It is. Thank you, Donna." She put the candlestick back on the mantle and walked away. Later in life, I understood. She had let go of her attachment to worldly goods.

They were not all thieves, not at all. Some, like Maman, tried hard to help Marion run the place. One night Maman rang our bell, holding out a stunning topaz brooch. She was close to tears, and Mom shooed me into my room. But I could hear Maman, who refused to come in, stiffly asking Mom to buy it. "Marion sent me. Everyone in the house is hungry." Maman refused to accept money without leaving the pin, but Mom sent it back with me the next day, although to no avail. "Tell your mother to please enjoy it," Marion said quietly, folding the brooch back into my hand. "We needed food."

Another guest tried to set up a fair living arrangement. His friends were willing to buy the house, renovate it at their own expense, and let Marion stay on in half the space. Marion airily rejected the idea, just as she rejected her nephew's boring insistence on paying bills.

Her refusal to regulate her situation, coupled with problems in Patrick Dennis's own life, finally made it impossible for him to continue his support. The two eventually had a huge fight and never spoke again.

Even the brightest eyes can't charm the Internal Revenue Service. In 1964, after a legal battle, Marion's house was seized for nonpayment of taxes, and city marshals came to evict her. Camera crews filled the sidewalk. Some Bank Streeters rubbed their hands together, anticipating sleep at last. Others shook their heads. I was nine, and my friend was leaving, along with Maman and the girls. I crouched on her steps, crying. Suddenly Marion was sitting there too, with her arms around me. She hugged me and told me that she was just going to take a little vacation from her messy place. "Don't you think it needs cleaning, Donna?" I shook my head and clung to her waist as she stroked my hair.

Former residents, some of whom had been part of a campaign to save the house, showed up to support her. They swore to reporters that she had given them dignity and comfort when no one else would. Even the city sheriff who reluctantly locked her out told *The New York Times*, "She's an amazing woman. There's no place left in society for a person like her." And he added, "In an earlier time, she might have been a saint."

•   •   •

A friend had arranged a room and counseling job for Marion at a women's shelter in nearby Chelsea. I disappeared into adolescence and lost touch with her. But Marion returned in 1977, as a resident in the Village Nursing Home on Abingdon Square Park, just around the corner from her old place. I saw a short article about it in *The Villager*, our local newspaper, and ran over. I was twenty-one and hadn't seen her since I was nine. She was in her nineties and bedbound. But it only took her two minutes to remember me. "It's darling Donna, the little opera singer," she told a smiling aide. I'd seen enough grins as I asked directions to her room to know that she had wrapped the staff around her little finger. I hugged her carefully. She'd become as frail and tiny as a newborn bird.

I laughed and straightened Marion's wrap as she held court at Abingdon Square Park in her wheelchair, waving her arms and gabbling about her famous friends to the elderly clique that gathered on the benches every day to take the sun. The Village cognoscenti, retired professors and the like, smiled and nodded as she talked. But the fiercely clannish blue-collar locals sniffed and pointedly ignored her.

I had grown up with many of their grandkids so I was all right, and they enjoyed bragging about their families or complaining about their aches and pains to me. But Marion, who for all of her saintliness had the tact of a rock, would cheerfully interrupt their stories to laugh about how grumpy her dear friend, the world-famous dancer Martha Graham, was about *her* aching feet, as I tried to steer the conversation back to good, affordable shoes for bunions.

They didn't appreciate her grandiose ways, but who could blame her? She was the star of novels, plays, and musicals, played by stars like Rosalind Russell, Angela Lansbury, Ann Miller, Ginger Rogers, and Lucille Ball. She had been a beloved friend to all, from Nobel laureates to nameless broken souls. She was still news; publicity about her presence in the nursing home headlined two fund drives that saved it from closing. Even First Lady Rosalynn Carter came to call.

Marion Tanner blew kisses and danced away in 1985 at the age of ninety-four. My darling Auntie Mame looked fragile, but she was pure fire and steel. When I wear her exotic topaz-and-silver brooch I do feel très, très chic and free-spirited. And she will always be the luminous sprite who wrapped me in satin and taught me that I am a divine flame from God.

18 • Bella Abzug

Cowboy star Gary Cooper faced off to a death duel in the movie *High Noon*. Dad gunned up in 1960 when the political activist Bella Abzug stomped onto Bank Street, renting a garden apartment in 37 Bank, a beautiful 1800s brownstone.

Politics aside, Bella grabbed your attention. She was a fierce, scary neighbor, sort of a two-legged nuclear plant, radiating power. She was strong-featured and heavyset and looked as if she'd won some street fights in her day and was ready for more. She didn't walk like other people. She stomped to her waiting car, glaring around the street like a homicide detective about to grill a quivering perp.

For all this, she wore impeccably tailored suits and stylish, improbably feminine broad-brimmed hats that became her signature. At five, I'd never seen a woman even remotely like her and was unnerved. But when I worked up the courage to smile, she'd smile back and we'd wriggle fingers at each other. It felt like waving to a tigress. Even when I saw her standing on her stoop in a housecoat, her dark, curly hair wrapped in a turban as she chatted with a passerby, her eyes darted around, as if she were casing the odds of finding a good brawl. I'd usually avoid eye contact and hurry away.

• • •

Half of the country was just as scared. Bella Savitsky had been born in 1920 in the Bronx. She had been a brilliant scholar, and her Hunter College friends tightened into a lifelong circle of social activists. During law school at Columbia, as one of the rare women students at the time, she edited the law review, played serious poker, and met her future husband, Martin Abzug, a stockbroker who wrote novels on the side.

Martin typed her papers and promised to support her career. They married in 1944, had two daughters, and Martin, a low-key complement to the explosive Bella, kept his word until his death forty-two years later. "I'm not politically oriented," he told *The New York Times* in 1970. "Women's Liberation? It's old hat to me. I've been living it for nearly thirty years. I wouldn't have it any other way." And a friend added: "The only times he ever blows up at Bella are at poker games. She plays a lot of hands, that, if you're a careful player, you won't go into."

During the 1950s Bella tackled McCarthyism and other controversies. Her first civil rights case was in Mississippi. A black man named Willie McGee had been accused of raping a white woman, despite the fact that they had had a long-term, consensual affair. Bella challenged the state's practice of excluding African-Americans from juries and argued that Southern judges reserved the death penalty for rape as a punishment for blacks only. She won two stays of execution. When she returned to Jackson for a third appeal, however, no hotel would accept her. Pregnant and alone, she hid from the Ku Klux Klan in the toilet stall of a bus station that night. The next day she argued before the governor for six hours, but despite her efforts McGee was executed in 1951.

Martin Abzug usually looked dour, although I'd heard that he was sweet and funny. Dad, who liked feminine women, huffed that any man would be glum with that braying fireplug for a wife. My father was seldom crude about anyone's appearance, but for Bella he made an exception. "Jack Dempsey in drag! Her butt looks like bulldogs fighting in a sack!" he snorted as we drove by one day. My mother snapped back. "Larry, she can't help her size, and she dresses very well!" Since I saw Ann grunt and gyrate into her Playtex girdle, I knew that Larry was heading for trouble.

Once I stood behind Martin at Shanvilla Grocery, everyone's spot for tomatoes and socializing. Martin and our neighbor Jack Gilford were joking about their hell-raising Bronx wives as they stood on line. The Gilfords had worked on some political projects with Bella. Mr. Abzug sounds like he loves Bella, I thought.

Years later Madeline told me a wonderful Bella story.

Bella gave me one of my most gorgeous Bank Street experiences in 1977 or so. One night after 2 a.m. I heard this loud clanging of ashcan tops. By the time I got to my front window there was a gay march, from the gay bars, probably, maybe the Stonewall Inn, turning the corner from Abingdon Square and going up Bank Street to Bella's house. That lady in Florida, Anita Bryant, had just won her anti-gay legislation in Florida. They were crying and upset, and who did they come to? They came to Bella.

They had these ashcan tops they were banging, letting the neighborhood know how upset they were. They went to where Bella lived, on Bank near West Fourth Street, and called to her. She came out on the stoop in her housecoat and consoled them and said what she would do. I think she was a Congresswoman at that time. I found it very moving that instead of going to some office and opening it up or getting on the phone or anything, they came to her. That was one of the wonderful happenings on Bank Street.

In the 1960s Bella and her friends were lobbying for nuclear test-ban treaties and protesting the Vietnam War. She was a neighbor I only saw in the news, never shopping at the A&P with her kids piled in the cart. Sometimes I saw her rushing into a waiting car as I left for school, barking instructions to an assistant who was loaded with papers, staggering to keep up. Blanche Schwartz, the principal of my junior high school, was one of Bella's Hunter College friends. They actually looked alike: well-dressed women with dark, curly hair and loud, nasal Bronx accents. Kids trembled when Ms. Schwartz got mad. And they both stomped.

• • •

My parents were politically aware, although their thinking was sometimes filtered through opera. During a discussion of women's rights, Ann swore that she had never lost a job to a man, although when I pounced, challenging her to name a male soprano, she beat a hasty retreat. They read publications like *The New York Times* and *Time* magazine and followed world events. Ironically, Dad's political opinions often seemed to echo Bella's, although I never dared point that out.

Still, it made sense. Dad was only four years younger than Bella. They'd had similar childhoods. Their immigrant parents (Italian for Dad, Russian Jewish for Bella) had come from unpopular, stereotyped groups in the decidedly un–politically correct America of the early 1900s. First-generation descendants like Dad and Bella faced raw prejudice in school and on the streets. They had to be scrappers, I thought, listening to Dad, or be squashed.

Although they met later, my parents both attended New York University in the early 1940s. It was a powerful time to be young. Like Bella, they were the children rising from the poverty of the Great Depression. All of them had front-row seats for worldwide unrest. President Roosevelt's radical new programs like Social Security, the rise of communism in Russia and China, Gandhi's resistance to British oppression in India, and the growing power of dictators such as Hitler and Mussolini lit fires here and around the globe.

"Everyone—labor rights organizers, Zionists, Catholic activists, and all—had card tables with pamphlets in Washington Square," my parents told me. "They'd follow us around, trying to get us to see things their way." Dad the college student paid careful attention. Russia's Communist government system and Italy's fascism seemed to him like too much power for too few. He decided that he preferred American democracy, lumpy and imperfect as he felt it was. Later, in the 1950s, when Stalin's atrocities to his own people in Communist Russia became news, there were fights on Bank Street and throughout the Village.

"Those poor Russian bastards, rotting in Stalin's labor camps after the way they fought fascism in World War II," Larry admonished me. "Never let anyone, left *or* right, take your freedom. Never take it for granted, either. Always stand up for yourself!"

• • •

It wasn't necessarily what Bella said but how she said it that made my father crazy. In his opinion, Bella was a dirty and disrespectful fighter. Opponents were doused in vitriol and set afire. Her lack of civil discourse drove Dad up the wall. Look who's talking, I thought to myself. The whole block knows when *he's* mad. For all of their education and drive, they really were two of a kind: tough street kids with trash mouths.

I don't remember their first tangle, but Dad threw his newspaper down one day when I was about nine. "Abzug! Calling Al D'Amato [another politician] a Nazi! He's as American as everyone who fought the Nazis for her sorry ass!"

Later that week, Dad and I were walking by Bella's house as she stepped out of a taxi. Excited because Dad and I were on our way to see *West Side Story* on Broadway, I barely noticed her. The next moment I was in the middle of a storm.

"Abzug, who the hell do you think you are? Calling an American veteran a Nazi! You know what a real Nazi would do? Throw you in a goddamned oven, that's what!"

Aghast, I tried to keep walking, but Bella pushed in front of him, bristling. Their faces were inches apart. "Yeah?" she snapped. "That guy's in bed with the milk industry. There's radiation in milk now, did you know that? *We* put it there when we nuked Japan. And he's part of a cover-up. Is it OK with you if your kid glows in the dark? Maybe she can be a light bulb when she grows up, jackass."

Martin came to the door. "Honey, are you OK?" he asked. She nodded without turning her head, keeping her eyes on Dad. Martin came over and put his arm around her, leading her inside, while Dad allowed me to grab his hand and keep walking.

Through the late 1960s there were many such neighborly parleys. Neither one moved an inch or stopped shouting until our poor dog tugged his leash to keep peeing or her car arrived. Mom sometimes managed to intervene, but if I was alone with Dad I'd run away. By then my parents embarrassed me enough by their very existence, even without Bella.

• • •

The lid blew for good at my junior-high graduation in 1969. My life was perfect that day. Ms. Schwartz had made a huge fuss over me and the other girls who'd been the first in the city to break the gender barrier and bring women's liberation into elite, previously all-male, Stuyvesant High School. It is a public school, but students are accepted only via a competitive test, and I'd taken the exam sweating bullets. When I qualified, my mother taped huge "CONGRATULA-TIONS!" signs all over the house.

I was too full of myself to breathe. It was a triple coup. I'd made my parents and principal proud and at the same time rescued myself from two horrible alternatives. One was the snooty private schools that had accepted me. Every friend I'd ever had who'd transferred to one had turned into a snob and dumped me. They made excuses, but I knew the truth. My family was ethnic and bohemian. We ate calamari at Christmas dinner. We dragged home used furniture ("It's an antique!") from the street. We didn't have a doorman.

The second awful choice, returning to Catholic school, had been less of a danger. Since I knew I'd drown myself before ever again facing the sadistic nuns who had made my early school years a horror, I'd taken the completed applications with the other outgoing mail and stuffed them down the sewer. My parents never caught on to why none of them replied.

• • •

The day of graduation, my long hair and white mini-dress looked great. "Today," I preened, "I'm a star." Parents applauded and kids giggled through the awards until Ms. Schwartz introduced the guest speaker. It was her friend Bella Abzug, who was running for Congress.

Bella stalked to the podium to great applause. A national left-wing star at our little event! What an honor! The Village crowd was excited.

Bella made a few desultory remarks about our promising lives. Then she launched into an interminable campaign speech. Issue after issue. Blah, blah, blah. We were bored and hot. Even the adults started murmuring. But Bella steamed on, flying her flags. It felt as if she were going to talk until we were old enough to vote.

Then I heard a horribly familiar bellow behind me. Larry had shot up from his seat. His face was red, and his finger shook as he pointed at her. "This is the children's graduation, not a political rally!" he screamed. "Today is about them! It's not the time or place for your campaign! You have no right to take their day!"

My lovely graduation became pandemonium. "Hear, hear!" echoed against, "Shut up, you fascist!" Kids pointed at me and their parents looked, too. Teachers whispered on the sides. Bella gripped the podium and continued grimly with her speech while Dad stood right where he was and kept shouting. It looked like a deadlock and sounded like a zoo.

I knew that I was in that room of hell made exclusively for thirteen-year-old Bank Streeters with insane fathers and equally insane neighbors. Bella glared and spoke. Dad stomped his foot and yelled. I tried to teleport myself to another planet. Why couldn't they both just shut up? Only this once. For me. I slid down in my seat, pretty dress and status high school forgotten, plotting ways to kill them both.

Bella looked at us and back at Ms. Schwartz as if to say, "What do I do?" She opened her mouth again, but no words came out. Finally, she looked across the screaming crowd, sighed, turned, and trudged to her seat. I could not believe my eyes.

The crowd got wilder, and I turned around again. My father, ignoring the boos, was bowing to his clapping admirers before he sat down. I wanted to kick him. Theatrics too? There were yells to Bella asking her to go back and continue. But after a hasty exchange with her, the principal came to the podium and thanked us for coming. No one cared. The shouts continued.

Bella and Ms. Schwartz walked off arm in arm. My beloved principal looked apologetic and humiliated. Bella patted her friend's hand as they walked. Larry glowered in his seat, arms crossed. I knew that he would defend his actions to his last breath.

• • •

Many years later, with a few principled stands under my own belt, I still don't know which one I agree with. As tempting as it may have seemed, Bella *had* taken advantage. And it was clear that others agreed with him. But of course at age thirteen, in the liberal 1960s Village, a screaming scene between my father who couldn't let it go just once for my sake and a popular left-wing celebrity in front of my entire class represented the end of my life. I fled to my favorite teacher and cried.

Bella won that election and two more. By the time she died in 1998, she was a legend. She backed the Equal Rights Amendment, wrote books, chaired national committees, hosted a television show, and piled up ten lives' worth of achievements. She opened doors for my generation, our daughters, and our granddaughters; showing us what a woman truly can do in this world. She helped shape American history.

But she never, ever won a fight with Dad.

Secret Bank Street

19 • The Jester, the Bishop, and
the Eavesdropper

Some Bank Streeters slipped into another life and walked by, not the same person who had crossed my path an hour before. Still others concealed themselves behind walls and windows. One personality was too small a skin for some of us.

In the 1950s and '60s, our block play group named one local the Silent Jester. During late afternoons we sometimes saw him in a suit, staring ahead as he walked, a dour, gray-haired man in his forties, looking like a Connecticut commuter. But in the evenings, as we played, he passed as . . . the Silent Jester. It was certainly the same man with the same glum expression. Silent Jester wore medieval motley sewn with colorful velvets and satin. He had striped leggings, a droopy, many-pointed hat, and cloth slippers with jingling bells sewn to the toes. Passersby stared.

Fresh-mouthed Xavier from 65 Bank Street once called out, "Hey, Clown Man, what time is it?" Silent Jester didn't turn a hair. He plodded on in his Arthurian Brigadoon, his eyes fixed far beyond vulgar, jeering kids. Xavier led as we tiptoed after Jester, determined to find out where he lived, even if we got in trouble for leaving the block. Silent Jester hailed a taxi, leaning forward, murmuring to the open-mouthed driver, and sped off, leaving us frustrated.

One day in the late 1960s he vanished. Years later a retired dry cleaner told me that Jester had been his customer, a Kellogg's Cereals heir who worked uptown in the family business. Perhaps days of Brooks Brothers suits and Rice Krispies were bearable, I thought, because he knew that his medieval life down in the Village was never far away.

Al, a handsome, gregarious guy in his thirties, sat on his steps at 56 Bank Street with his dogs, chatting with everyone who passed. He told me that he was a Delta Airlines pilot and described his flight assignments in great detail. He started seeing a young blonde from the neighborhood named Nina, and she eventually moved in.

Some months later, a mutual friend attending one of my parties looked out of the window and shook his head. "That guy Al, across the street, watch out for him," he said. "He's nuts. Nina's dad was in an accident while he was off, supposedly piloting a plane, and she called Delta. They'd never heard of Al. Then she looked through his papers. Nothing about Delta or any airline job at all, but she found a bankbook. The guy is seriously loaded. Maybe from his family, who the hell knows? But he kept insisting that he flies for Delta, and he refused to explain why he can't prove it. She couldn't get out of there fast enough. Who knows what kind of head case the guy is or where he goes when he says he's off flying?"

It made me think of Nathan, a character in the novel *Sophie's Choice*, leaving his Brooklyn boarding house every day for a phantom job as a scientist, telling stories about his amazing lab experiments to his fellow boarders until he is followed to the public library by the narrator and unmasked. It had never occurred to me that the author, William Styron, was describing an actual psychological disorder or that a Bank Street neighbor might have it.

Charles Kuralt, the host of *On the Road*, lived at 34 Bank Street with his wife and daughters. He wandered back roads in a camper for twenty-five years, starting in 1967, filming extraordinary lives in everyday America. I liked him, always joking and chatting with us neighbors, as gentle and unaffected off camera as on.

One day he asked my friend Ginny and me to repeat the "Miss Jenny Mack" hand slap/chant we were doing in slow motion so he could see the twisting wrist movements and hear the words. He asked us where we'd learned it, but neither of us knew. It was just a game, we said, that every Bank Street girl knew. We were scarcely raconteurs, but his respectful interest made us fluff up like parakeets.

My parents and I ran into Charles and his family at the Beatrice Inn around the corner on West Twelfth Street. Locals loved the Beatrice Inn, then a casual, family-owned place, with its soft peach walls and cozy fireplace. Charles sang "Happy Birthday" with the rest of the customers on my thirteenth birthday. When Charles died in 1997, details about his secret life of thirty years with another woman and her children emerged. I was astounded. Charles had seemed like such a regular guy.

• • •

The Episcopal Bishop Paul Moore bought 55 Bank Street in the 1980s. We exchanged pleasantries as our dogs sniffed each other. He was tall and ruggedly handsome, with the rumpled elegance of old money: wool and soft cashmeres. His low-key manner radiated breeding and an effortless courtesy that warmed me instantly. Had I known about his fame and his distinguished life story I would have been too abashed to chat, unable to imagine wasting his time. I thought Moore was an ordinary minister, albeit at uptown St. John the Divine, the world's largest cathedral, until our neighbor Tish filled me in.

Moore was a trust-fund social activist, a breed that seems to have been attracted to Bank Street's brownstones since the American Revolution. He was born to enormous wealth and status in 1919 but followed a calling to the ministry, rejecting the easy life of Palm Beach and Newport to work in destitute parishes, march with the Rev. Dr. Martin Luther King Jr., and champion the right of women to be ministers, a huge controversy at the time.

"He's rich and famous as hell, honey," said Tish, the female impersonator-performer at 51 Bank Street. Tish had lived in his ground-floor apartment next door to Moore's house since 1957. They'd chat, Tish said, while puttering in his kitchen, which looked into Moore's back yard. Moore talked about social issues and his beliefs, not himself, but Tish, as he bragged, always got the drop on someone once he was interested enough to check them out.

I was awed, as I have always been, by large, dramatic lives of vision and sacrifice. But our august neighbor carried a secret to his death in 2003. Moore's two wives and nine children never fooled Tish. "A lot of men our age never come out, but I just know he's one of us," Tish, declared, wagging his finger. "I'm never wrong." This was years before the minister's daughter, the author Honor Moore, wrote about her family's posthumous discovery of Moore's clandestine, anguished homosexuality.

• • •

A family bought the brownstone at 61 Bank Street, the building next to ours, in the early 1960s. We share an alley that has windows on our side only. My bedroom walls angle out and around, past the back of 61. I saw two daughters, older than me, grow up and move out. In 1975 a "For Sale" sign went up. One day a young man was standing on the top step of number 61 when I came out. "Donna, how are you?" he asked. He bore a strong resemblance to the daughters, but I had never seen him before.

We started to chat. He was my age, and he recounted tearful phone conversations I'd had in eighth grade. Fights with my parents. How much he liked my singing voice. The games that Irene and I played. Given the alley acoustics and the odd proximity of my bedroom to his brownstone, inches away but with windows set at disparate angles, he had been secretly listening in on my life since we were kids, as hidden as a mote of dust. I was blank, in shock, but as he kept talking, I felt violated. I backed away, stammering, as he grinned, thoroughly enjoying my discomfort. I never saw him again.

· · ·

The paintings of Edward Hopper, who lived and worked in the Village until his death in 1967, captured a diffident alienation I felt from some neighbors. Hopper painted a shadow world, a chiaroscuro between the known and unknown in both his enigmatic people and their unseen lives in silent buildings. In his famous 1942 painting *Nighthawks*, two men and a red-haired woman sit at the counter of a diner late at night, wrapped in their private thoughts, as the counterman goes about his business. I always tried to imagine who they were or what they were doing before they came in.

Years later, I was told that the actual diner, now gone, was three blocks from Bank Street. The redhead might have been my neighbor, the refined Grace Bickers in apartment 3A, who lived a gray, solitary life here for years, tended through her final illness and death by 63's residents without a single visit or letter from the life she'd lived before she came to the Village, the one she refused to discuss.

20 • Stella Crater

Some Bank Street secrets hide forever. A piece might turn up, glittering like a shard from a tomb, but dust gathers in unopened rooms.

Various neighbors shared Mom's bench in Abingdon Square Park in the late 1950s, chatting with her as I played in the sandbox. One introduced herself as Stella, but never mentioned a last name or talked about her life.

Stella's reticence was not unusual. As Mom remarked years later, people who had been leading painful lives often came to the park for respite. They talked about books and music. Stella admitted that she had "not heard enough operas to admire the form," as she tactfully phrased it, but enjoyed chamber music and symphonies. Politics came up only once, Mom recalled, and Stella was tart. "Politicians are nothing but crooks," she snapped. "All of them."

• • •

The fate of New York State Supreme Court Justice Joseph Crater is one of Bank Street's secrets. One August night in 1930 Judge Crater stepped into a taxicab and disappeared into one of the great mysteries of the twentieth century.

In 1916 the handsome, ambitious young lawyer handled the divorce of one Stella Wheeler and then married her. Joe's cronies were New York politicians, which back then meant being part of the cheerfully corrupt Tammany Hall political machine, which had ruled the city since the late 1700s. Everything from building permits to police protection to a vending license could be had if you had cash and played the game their way. Crater played and quickly rose through Tammany's ranks. By the time he was forty-one, he had a lake house in Maine and had moved Stella to a luxurious apartment at 40 Fifth Avenue, the heart of the wealthy Village.

In New York of the 1920s and '30s, the lines between respectability and the underworld disappeared behind heavy, expensive doors guarded by hulking figures in dapper suits. Affluent men like Joe, gangster Dutch Schultz, Jimmy ("The Night Mayor") Walker, the comedian Milton Berle, and the wits of the Algonquin Round Table mixed over drinks and card games in the plush, clubby parlor of madam Polly Adler's bordello, discreetly sheltered from public view. Some bought baubles at Tiffany's and Cartier's for a special showgirl and actress or set them up in plush apartments.

It was understood, at least by the men, that these diversions had nothing to do with respectable family life. If a mistress no longer amused or if another girl had caught her patron's eye, she was packed off. If she got pregnant, she was sent to one of the shady doctors or midwives who did abortions on the side. If the operation was botched and the woman bled to death or died of infection, nameless men were paid to dump her body in the river or bury it in a field.

The wives of these prominent men, with housefuls of servants and a place on the Social Register, had to either grit their teeth and look away or take shelter in delusion. Stella seemed to have gone for delusion. Although her 1961 memoir, *The Empty Robe*, was written thirty years after her husband disappeared, she swore that Joe was an honest lawyer and a faithful spouse, conveniently ignoring reams of evidence to the contrary.

But I, poking around in archives, suspect that Stella, for all of her protests, played her cards close to her chest, well aware of the costs of the good life. In April 1930, Crater withdrew $20,000 from his bank account. It was a year's salary for a State Supreme Court judge, the standard Tammany price for that position. He was promptly sworn in.

In August of 1930, Stella wrote, the newly appointed justice got a phone call at the couple's summer house in Maine. Stella didn't know who was calling or what the problem was, but she later told police that Crater was shouting. As her husband rushed to catch a train back to the city, he would tell her only that he had to "go straighten those fellows out."

When Crater got to their Village apartment, he told the maid to take the next few days off. The following day, August 6, he went to his office. His clerk testified that Crater reviewed papers, cashed $5,000 in checks, packed two briefcases behind closed doors, and dismissed the clerk for the rest of the day. The clerk said he did not see what papers Crater had reviewed or what he had put in the briefcases.

That evening, Crater went to a chophouse on West Forty-Fifth Street. Law colleagues dining there with a showgirl invited him to join them. Crater was his usual charming and witty self, they told the police. He joked and laughed through dinner, waving goodbye to the three of them on the street as a taxi pulled up. He was never seen or heard from again.

After days of unanswered calls, Stella contacted the New York police. Reporters, tipped off by informants, typed furiously, one eye on the clock. Other reporters sneaked around the Maine house, peeping in the windows while detectives turned the place upside down, looking for clues.

Crater sightings and theories poured in from around the world. He had squealed on a Tammany deal. He had had a heart attack in a brothel. He had hit his head and lost his memory. He had opened a hotel in Brazil. The story of his disappearance, a tale juicy with money, corruption, and sex, was a national story for months. Police searched for Joe's current mistress, nightclub dancer Connie Marcus, but she had disappeared, as, not surprisingly, had the showgirl from the chophouse. The police swore to reporters that they'd turned Crater's office, his summer house, and the Fifth Avenue apartment upside down, but had found nothing in the way of clues or evidence.

Stella stayed in Maine, refusing to come to New York to testify. Months later, she returned to the city. Even as her maid unpacked the luggage on Fifth Avenue, Stella claimed, she searched the apartment on her own and "found" uncashed checks, stock certificates, Crater's will, the deed to the Maine house, and life insurance policies (naming her as beneficiary) crammed into what she described as a "stuck dresser drawer." Police must have overlooked the papers, she insisted, because they were covered by lace. Hmm, I thought. Stuck drawer. Lace camouflage. How convenient.

Suicide became the leading theory for Judge Crater's disappearance, but without a body the case officially stayed open.

The good life requires cash. By 1937 Stella had been evicted from her tony flat and was living at One Bank Street, a nondescript brick apartment building. Archival photos show that she was still slim and patrician, with high cheekbones and full lips. But now she wore dowdy clothes and wire-rimmed librarian glasses. Her hair was tied in a plain bun. "The police just pretended to search for Joe," she told reporters.

"It was all a cover-up." Politicians pressured her to keep quiet, she said, fearing that her evidence would bring their own dark secrets to light. If Joe's real story came out, she said angrily, they would all have been exposed. The New York City detectives that were sent to Maine, she said, spent their time hunting and fishing. Her husband would never have true justice. "My Joe is dead," she said cryptically. "But not by suicide."

The police and most reporters played down her claims. For one thing, Crater was no longer news. Another reason was doubtless sheer self-preservation. Even if they wore custom-made suits and diamond stickpins, Stella was accusing some rough, powerful men. A zealous detective or a nosy reporter might disappear himself, maybe into the cement of that new Empire State Building rising at Fifth Avenue and Thirty-Fourth Street.

Stella took Crater's life insurance policies to court and sued the companies for payment. Her lawyer, Emil Ellis, tried to keep politics out of the trial. He contended that Crater had been making blackmail payments to a showgirl and had been killed, perhaps accidentally, by the showgirl's gangster friends. The case was dismissed because without evidence there was still no legal declaration that Crater was dead.

A distraught Stella sobbed on a 1937 radio show, telling listeners that poverty forced her to consider doing tawdry stage sketches about the search for her husband. An agent, a "promoter of cockroach and turtle derbies and of stage appearances of people brought into the news by crime," told reporters that Stella was his client. His other artistes included a teacher accused of giving cocktail parties for students.

Dramatics aside, Stella wasn't, apparently, ready for a life of turtle derbies and immoral teachers. In May of 1938, an electrical engineer from New Jersey named Carl Kunz crashed his car on the Henry Hudson Drive, killing his two passengers. Kunz admitted to drinking and was charged with vehicular homicide. Curiously, he listed One Bank Street as his address and reporters picked up a scent. Stella and Carl Kunz were newlyweds. They had eloped to Maryland the previous month.

Drunken homicide was just one aspect of this Bank Street romance. In her memoir, Stella wrote that she had been lonely and wanted a man in her life. "After months of being together almost continually," she wrote, "Carl was pressing me to marry him," adding, "this, I must admit, despite the fact that Joe had not, at this time, been declared dead legally." Also despite the fact that Carl Kunz was already married during their continual "months of being together" and that his wife, Anna, as reported in *The New York Times*, had been found dead in their New Jersey home on April 16, 1938, just days before her elopement with Carl. Stella, darling, I thought, reading her memoir, how conveniently you omit the existence of poor Anna Kunz. Another mysterious shard glittering on the floor.

Morals aside, Stella's third marriage involved murky legal waters. Anna Kunz, ruled a suicide by police, was officially and conveniently dead. But in the eyes of the law, Joseph Crater was still alive and hence still married to Stella when she wed Carl Kunz. Even Stella's devoted lawyer, Mr. Ellis, nervously remarked to reporters that he did not "care to commit myself on the legal status of the affair."

Ellis finally managed to have the courts declare Crater legally dead later in 1938. The ruling was made as Stella and Carl enjoyed an ocean cruise aboard the Normandie. Stella, crying and destitute in 1937, had splurged for passage on one of the world's most expensive luxury liners even before Crater's life insurance policies paid her $30,000. Maybe, I mused, Carl Kunz made a lot more money than the average engineer.

• • •

In July of 1955, as my parents-to-be assembled my crib in their new Bank Street apartment, *The New York Times* reported that Stella had separated from Kunz and was working as a secretary. Stella told reporters that both she and Emil Ellis, who by then had been investigating Crater's disappearance on his own for decades, remained convinced that there had been both a murder and a political cover-up.

Years later I saw a photo of Stella Crater, dated 1955, that had accompanied her 1969 obituary in the *Times*. "I'll be damned!" said my mother when I showed it to her. "If that's not Abingdon Square Park Stella, it's her twin sister."

It was indeed a find, but by now it was 1999, and Stella was inconveniently dead, just when I wanted to talk to her. My parents didn't recall seeing her after the early 1960s, which made sense. She left Bank Street in 1963 and spent the last six years of her life in a nursing home.

That, I thought, was the end of it. But more dusty rooms opened. In 2005 a widow named Mrs. Ferrucci-Good died in Queens at the age of ninety-one. Her family published a letter she had sealed, to be opened only after her death. The letter outlined secrets involving Mrs. Ferrucci-Good's late husband and his friend Charles Burn, a former New York City policeman, and it tied Ferrucci-Good, Charles Burn, and Charles's brother Frank Burn, also a police officer, to the Crater case.

Shortly after the Ferrucci-Good letter was published, the son of Stella's lawyer, Emil Ellis, released a summary of his father's private research into the Crater case. Amazingly, the two completely independent versions diverge only on a minor point at the end.

• • •

Gangs like the Dead Rabbits, the Hudson Dusters, and the Bowery Boys had run New York's streets since the 1700s. Gangs were always fighting one another to expand their turf, which meant power over gambling houses, nightclubs, bars, opium dens, and brothels. When necessary, they bribed corrupt Tammany cops, politicians, and judges to get what they wanted. Sometimes gang leaders met to negotiate on neutral ground like the back room of our local White Horse Tavern, but tough alpha crooks like Lucky Luciano and Arnold Rothstein seldom played nice together for long.

Both Frank Burn and Ferrucci-Good, the letter said, were enforcers for gangster Legs Diamond in 1930. Legs earned his name. He'd run from so many hits that one exasperated rival, Dutch Schultz, gave hell to his bungling crew. "Ain't there *nobody*," he barked, "who can shoot this guy so he don't bounce back?"

Victory in one 1930 dispute between Legs Diamond and Dutch Schultz hinged on Justice Crater's decision in a pending case. Legs tried to sway Crater by threatening his mistress, Connie Marcus, who worked in one of his nightclubs as a dancer. "Get Romeo to see things my way, girlie, or you'll be dancing on broken legs." Connie wept to Crater. He wiped her tears and slid get-out-of-town money into her hand. "Go set yourself up somewhere, Connie. Maybe start a club out West in San Francisco. Legs won't care."

Legs cared. "Get that Crater bastard in front of me," he snarled. He ordered Connie to lure Crater to one of his clubs. The cab that Crater hailed by the Forty-Fifth Street chophouse was a set-up. Frank Burn was the driver. In a few blocks Burn pulled over. More of Legs' men, including Ferrucci-Good, piled in. As Crater fought to escape they shot him by accident.

In a panic, Frank Burn called his brother Charles for help. Like many Tammany-era policemen, Charles Burn moonlighted for the opposition. He was a bodyguard for the Legs Diamond gang on the side. The Ellis findings and the Ferrucci-Good letter diverge from here. According to the letter, the men dug Crater a hasty grave on a deserted Brooklyn beach, the site of today's New York Aquarium. Several human skeletons did turn up during its 1950s construction but were interred, in those pre–DNA analysis times, in New York's cemetery for the anonymous dead on Hart Island and are now lost forever.

Ellis concluded that the men rushed Crater's body to a sympathetic undertaker for a quick cremation and dumped his ashes in the Hudson River.

The papers in Crater's briefcases were, by both accounts, connected to Legs' legal battle with Schultz. Legs' men hustled Connie to Crater's apartment with his keys, and she grabbed the briefcases. Legs was furious, but his luck had dried up anyway. Dutch Schultz's guys aimed better in 1931, and this time Legs didn't bounce back.

• • •

I am hardly the only person who still wonders what really happened. Crater aficionados visit the site of the West Forty-Fifth Street chophouse, now an apartment building, and peek into the lobby of 40 Fifth Avenue. New and recycled Crater theories abound. Connie Marcus went crazy and was locked up in Bellevue Hospital, goes one. Stella smuggled Crater's money to Switzerland, says another. Franklin D. Roosevelt, then the Governor of New York, was in on the cover-up, claims a third. Crater is buried in Yonkers, swears a clairvoyant. New books, articles, and websites are full of theories.

Government corruption, missing showgirls, gangster wars, invisible dresser drawers, convenient memoirs, drunken homicides, spousal suicides, luxury cruises, posthumous letters, Coney Island corpses . . . my thrice-married Bank Street neighbor may not have known the full story of her beloved Joe's fate, but I think that she held her own secrets to the end.

One still dark little room, at least for me, is where Stella mourned the anniversary of Joe's disappearance for thirty years. I've read that she walked to the same Village bar every August 6 and ordered two drinks. She'd pick up hers, toast, "Good luck, Joe, wherever you are," toss it down, and walk out. Joe's drink stayed on the bar.

21 • Yeffe Kimball

As Ann and Larry pushed my stroller past the couple moving into 11 Bank Street in 1957, we didn't know that we were getting art, TV scandals, the atom bomb, a real-life Hitchcock movie, and a ghost. Dr. Harvey Slatin and his wife, Yeffe Kimball, had arrived.

Harvey was a skinny man with wispy white hair. He smiled as we passed. Yeffe, a short, dumpy woman with a dark braid down her back, ignored us. This went on for years.

Jack Heineman from 15 Bank Street later told me that Harvey was a famous nuclear physicist who had been part of one of the biggest government secrets of the twentieth century, America's race to develop an atom bomb at Los Alamos during World War II. Horrified by what he helped create, he became an anti-war activist.

Roger, another artist neighbor, told me that Yeffe was a Native American artist, a member of the Osage tribe of Oklahoma, whose paintings had been exhibited at the Museum of Modern Art and the Whitney. When I looked at her work, I saw abstract symbols of motifs ranging from Native American to space exploration. Some of her paintings look like derivatives of Georgia O'Keeffe, but I like their energy and composition. Roger couldn't disguise his envy. "She's an exotic Indian so her work gets great press. I'm just a white guy from New Jersey."

Even before the Village was overrun with venture capitalists, brownstone owners usually had more money than apartment residents. Yeffe, I discovered, had rich ex-husbands too. One was a shoe mogul. As a result, Yeffe had both the money and the social clout to promote one of her biggest passions, her Native American projects. A 1951 article in *The New York Times* noted that Yeffe's "powwow" at an elegant New York hotel had raised enough money to send a "health wagon" ambulance loaded with medicines to the Navajos in New Mexico. The driver was a socialite friend. Yeffe was also prominent in Native American organizations, lobbying Congress to improve living conditions for Native Americans and creating projects to preserve their artwork and culture.

When Yeffe got into a fight with one of our other neighbors, the event made national headlines. In 1959 Charles Van Doren, a handsome Columbia University instructor from a patrician family, was working as a commentator for NBC. His television career had started in 1956 when he won $129,000 on the immensely popular NBC quiz show *Twenty-One*. Two contestants, both in soundproof booths, took turns answering increasingly difficult questions until one of them missed. The winner then took on the next challenger. Van Doren lived around the corner from us on Bleecker Street, just off Bank.

Rigging TV quiz shows had never been raised as a legal issue. But some producers, anxious to please both sponsors and the public by providing attractive, likable winners, were secretly feeding answers to crowd favorites. Van Doren, who was among those who was coached, was a popular "champion" from November of 1956 to March of 1957. His movie-star looks and illustrious pedigree gave NBC a ratings sensation.

Dotto, another show by the same producers, also pitted one contestant's knowledge against another's. Their false star in 1958 was an attractive college student named Marie. Two challengers waited backstage to take her on. One was a young actor named Ed. The other was Yeffe Kimball, outfitted in full tribal regalia.

Noticing Marie's breezy backstage familiarity with the show's staff and the way she guarded a small notebook, Ed sneaked a peek at the notebook while Marie and Yeffe were on the air. It contained the answers to the very questions Marie was answering at that moment as she bested Yeffe.

Ed showed the notebook to Yeffe when she came offstage. They ripped out the page and confronted the producers with the evidence. Hush money was offered and accepted. Ed got $1,500 but somehow discovered that Yeffe got $4,000. Ed, now doubly furious, went to the Manhattan District Attorney. The fraud investigation that resulted changed television forever. Yeffe admitted being paid off, but she wasn't prosecuted. The district attorney was after bigger game.

Van Doren lied at first, but as prosecutors pressed harder, he finally confessed. His disgrace was front-page news and got him fired from both NBC and Columbia University.

I was oblivious to this neighbor war as I played in the park sandbox around the corner. TV's *Captain Kangaroo*, a live, early-morning children's show had, like me, made its debut in 1955. I loved the portly, mutton-chopped Captain and his lanky sidekick, Mister Green Jeans. The producer's mother sat in the park with my mother. Mister Green Jeans, she whispered, was created to take over when the Captain was too plastered to go on the air, which apparently happened with cheery regularity.

· · ·

Yeffe and Harvey were already famous in art, science, and social causes before they arrived. When they bought 11 Bank Street, originally an 1880 boardinghouse, they added a whiff of the afterworld. At first, they lived in only a few ground-floor rooms in order to renovate. But it seemed as if someone was ahead of them. They told a reporter from *The New York Times* that they heard footsteps and hammering sounds echoing in the empty house. Friends and construction workers heard them, too. The couple ran upstairs with flashlights at all hours, they said, but found nothing.

But when their contractor opened the top-floor ceiling, a heavy metal canister toppled out. It was labeled as "The last remains of Elizabeth Bullock, deceased. Cremated January 21, 1931. The United States Crematory Company, Ltd., Middle Village, Borough of Queens, New York City. Number 37251."

Harvey investigated. Crematorium records stated that Bullock, age 51, of 113 Perry Street, had collapsed on Hudson Street and was carried into a nearby drugstore, where she died. There was no apparent connection to 11 Bank Street. Bullock, a mystery novel reviewer, had no discernible reason to be in their ceiling. But there she was, her own best mystery.

The Slatins' search, including a séance with a psychic, produced an explanation of sorts. According to census records, Elizabeth's widower, Edward Bullock, moved from their Perry Street apartment to the 11 Bank Street boardinghouse after her death. The psychic claimed that Elizabeth had told him that she had abandoned her family's religion to marry Edward and that her ashes were hidden during a fight between Edward and her family over her burial. She wanted to rest in a Christian cemetery, she told the psychic.

Yeffe was ecstatic. She told reporters that her Native American spiritualism had given her insights into Elizabeth's situation that had now been confirmed.

Yeffe and Harvey waited to see if any kin would claim her, but no one did. Elizabeth's remains were respectfully placed on their piano atop a piece of antique lace, and the noises ceased. Years later, a California priest who had read about Elizabeth offered a cemetery plot. Yeffe was dead by then, but Harvey threw a farewell party and mailed her off. Elizabeth's marker reads, "Died 1931—Buried 1981."

• • •

Edward may have known a fellow boarder, a young author named John Dos Passos, whose breakthrough novel, *Manhattan Transfer*, was published in 1925, when he was living at 11 Bank Street. The book, written in a radically new stream-of-consciousness style from the point of view of multiple characters, attacked America's mindless consumerism and apathy towards the poor. The novelist Sinclair Lewis called the book "the vast and blazing dawn we have awaited . . . the foundation of a whole new school of novel writing."

Dos Passos also worked at *The Masses*, the left-wing newspaper then headquartered at Greenwich Avenue and Bank Street, just steps from his home. Other contributors included the journalist John Reed, author of the incendiary book *Ten Days That Shook the World*.

And Yeffe was hardly our first famous Bank Street artist. *Masses* illustrators John Sloan and George Bellows skewered capitalist greed in cartoons as they and other local artists like Edward Hopper helped give birth to the realistic Ashcan School, one of my favorite artistic styles.

Harvey and Yeffe didn't have to seek attention. They didn't even have to leave the house. The apartment windows of the actress Mary Louise Wilson, who lived on West Twelfth Street, looked directly across the backyards and through the plate glass rear walls of 11 Bank Street. Although Mary Louise and the Slatins were never formally introduced, they had friends in common, so Mary Louise knew who they were. It was, as she wrote in a 2001 article in *The New Yorker*, a real-life version of Alfred Hitchcock's quintessentially New York movie "Rear Window." The drama with "Buffie" and "Arnold," as Mary Louise called them, started when she arrived in 1965 and continued for a quarter of a century.

From her window Mary Louise saw Eames furniture and an art studio. The lady of the house, she wrote, was short and round, with gray braids, and wore caftans and heavy silver jewelry. She fed birds and yelled at neighbors who hung laundry out their windows. The neighbors, obviously true locals, paid no attention.

With his white hair and withered arm, Harvey reminded Mary Louise of a scientist from a movie. A mutual friend told Mary Louise that he had been injured in a radiation accident. He grinned and waved to her. Yeffe ignored her, same as the rest of us.

• • •

I watched excitedly as Yeffe prepared her front garden during the early spring of 1965. I was nine, and all we had at home was a window box. City gardens were enchanted places to me, and I bombarded her with questions and offers of help. She frowned at the ground and worked doggedly while I clutched her wrought-iron fence and chattered nonstop for two days after school.

Either kindness or exasperation finally made her relent. Sighing at the sky, mopping her forehead, and finally looking at me, she demanded, "What do you want to know?"

Now that I had her attention, I tried to ask all the questions I'd been storing up at once. "What are you planting?" "Why are you planting now? Isn't it cold for the flowers? Why are you using dirt from a bag?"

I pestered her with the fervor of an acolyte as she gruffly explained soils and planting seasons. As she spoke, I sidled over to her gate and opened it. When she finally asked if I'd like to help, I rushed through, throwing my book-bag on the ground and kneeling next to her. Her mouth tightened for a moment, and then she laughed. She reached over and guided my hands, helping me place the crocus and daffodil bulbs just so. "Not too deep or they can't reach the sun," she explained. "Not too shallow or they'll freeze." I tried to be perfect, feeling like a spring goddess in training.

Yeffe kept frowning at first, but started nodding as I prattled on about school and the opera and asked more gardening questions.

"Do you know what, Donna?" she finally asked after we'd planted everything. "You discovered something you love to do today." She smiled.

Emboldened, I asked for a crocus to grow in a cup at home. Yeffe frowned again. "OK," she replied, "but don't tell your friends because I'm not giving one to every kid on Bank Street."

• • •

Mary Louise and the Slatins kept peering at each other. One night, an ex-boyfriend waved at Mary Louise from a Slatin bash. Then Mary Louise's phone rang. It was Harvey, promising her that the boyfriend was now on the wagon. Mary Louise never knew that he drank. Harvey called again during another bash, smiling and pointing to a man standing next to him and explaining that the man, a nice Jewish violinist from the Philharmonic orchestra, was looking for a girlfriend.

In 1969 I entered high school. Yeffe, I later learned, was writing a Native American cookbook. That might be why her clothes looked tight. Yeffe was still gruff, but she had softened into a sort of severe auntie-friend, even giving me advice if she was in the mood. She liked my newly long hair and swirling hippie skirts. "Show the world the person you want it to see," she said over and over. "Live any damned way you want. Don't bother with boring. Life is too short to be dull."

Harvey walked up one day as we chatted. "Donna is at Stuyvesant," Yeffe told him. Stuyvesant High, a math and science school, had been all-male until a recent court battle (and our tiny first group of brainy maidens wafted sex pheromones to hordes of panting nerds, as Stuy English teacher and author Frank McCourt quipped, watching me walk down the hall one day). Harvey the New York native and scientist politely congratulated me while Harvey the spouse watched Yeffe carefully adjusting my peasant blouse with his mouth open.

Occasionally, Mary Louise wrote, Harvey and Yeffe had wonderful fights. Objects were thrown, and furniture was shoved about. As soon as the shouting began, she and her friends doused the lights and hurried to the windows to watch the show.

In 1978, she noticed that Yeffe was losing weight. A somber group assembled in the Slatins' backyard. Yeffe was sixty-four when she died of cancer. Neighbor Jack Heineman attended the service as Mary Louise watched from her window. Native American mourners, wearing full regalia, chanted. Foods were blessed and offered to the sky. The actor-politician Will Rogers Jr. delivered the eulogy. But I was away at college and didn't realize that Yeffe was gone.

• • •

Harvey was alone and time passed. One day, Mary Louise wrote, a graceful young woman was flicking at the Eames furniture with a dust cloth. Mary Louise watched until she was sure that the visitor was growing a tummy. Jack and other neighbors returned, this time to celebrate a marriage. Jack told me that the bride was actually a daughter of Harvey's childhood sweetheart. She'd had trouble with a divorce, he said, and the new Slatins barely outran the stork. Harvey was in his sixties by then.

A baby boy pulled himself onto the Eames furniture. By then Mary Louise had lived on West Twelfth Street through marriage, divorce, and a growing stage career. Her article revealed that we had shopped at the same small family-owned stores like Heller's Liquors on Greenwich Avenue. Decades later a neighbor whispered that Mary Louise and Mr. Heller had had a fling. I hoped that wasn't true. Mrs. Heller was so nice.

The Slatins eventually moved upstate. For Mary Louise, their disappearance was yet another rip in the fabric of her special Village. I understand. I've felt the same way when neighbors moved or died. But in this case I was living abroad and never even realized that Harvey was gone until I read the article. Mary Louise finally left as well. Years later she knocked me flat in her Tony-winning role as Jacqueline Kennedy's aunt in a Broadway production of the musical *Grey Gardens*.

• • •

This might have been the end of the story, but some Bank Street secrets are hidden well. After forty years I learned just how heartfelt Yeffe's advice to create a great big sparkling life and to hell with ordinary really was. I read in *Vogue* magazine that Yeffe, the socialite, Osage artist, cookbook author, television-show contestant, and advocate for Native American rights, was actually Miss Effie Goodman, a

Missouri farm girl. Talk about dull! No wonder she took to her heels, throwing her background aside as she ran.

The arts are male-oriented and sexist and Yeffe knew it. After she married money, she had the means, and certainly the moxie, to show the art world the spectacular persona she fashioned, just as she advised me to do. Her audacious plan worked. And she tried to make her impersonation a fair exchange. However she pulled it off, she was accepted as a peer within the Native American community and used her clout for their benefit with social and cultural projects, plus extensive legal advocacy.

Harvey, now in his nineties, had known about her fake identity all along, but he never cared. "I was very much in love with that woman," he told *Vogue*, "so if she had told me she was a Martian, I would have believed her." He added, "She actually looked very Indian, but she wasn't."

Crocuses still peek up every spring behind the wrought-iron fence. Sometimes I look up as I pass and wonder what Yeffe is up to. Whatever it is, she is never a bore.

The Heart of Bank Street

22 • Billy Joyce

I learned courage and compassion from Bank Street's dancing sailor. In the early 1970s, Billy Joyce was pacing around his workplace, a luxurious double townhouse at 113–115 Bank Street. Alwin Nikolais and Louis Murray, his famous employers, were on another long tour with their dance troupe. The company, renowned for inventive, witty modern choreography and solid technique, was in demand all over the world.

As the couple's live-in butler, Billy had to stick around and guard the house. Bored and restless, he bought dog biscuits and catnip and pulled a lawn chair onto the sidewalk. Soon cats were purring around his feet and dog walkers were dragged across the cobblestones. I passed by one day. We introduced ourselves and ended up swapping stories for hours, several times a week. "He's our mayor," a dog walker called to me as he passed. "The Mayor of Bank Street."

As a toddler in 1920s Brooklyn, Billy saw a green light shining under the kitchen table. A little apple-cheeked man was under there, smiling at him, he told his mother. His Irish kin declared that he'd just been blessed with a lucky life, protected by a leprechaun. Billy's sister loved to go dancing under the stars on the Coney Island pier. Billy was her partner until he joined the navy. That was all he needed to do. The leprechaun took care of the rest.

Billy was still a World War II sailor when he saw *Finian's Rainbow*, his first Broadway show. He was amazed that the people on stage could have that much fun and actually get paid for it. In 1948, after the war, he dutifully took a desk job in export for a few months. He was bored to death by the business world, but he was good at it and got offered a promotion to the company's office in South Africa. Now what? As he walked down Broadway thinking it over, he ran into a friend who was heading for an audition at the Roxy Theater on West Fiftieth Street.

The Roxy's former dance troupe, the Roxyettes, had kicked their way to Radio City Music Hall and become the Rockettes, but the Roxy still staged extravaganza stage shows. Billy tagged along, then sneaked inside and hid in the wings. The irritated choreographer yanked him into a Spanish number. Start dancing, pal, or get lost, the choreographer ordered.

Billy had never seen flamenco in his life, but he faked it and got the job. He was cast in that production and in the next three Roxy shows. No dance lessons, no agent, and no idea what he was doing. He never moved to South Africa, and the friend never spoke to him again.

• • •

Damn Yankees, Guys and Dolls, Li'l Abner, Fiddler on the Roof, No, No, Nanette . . . Billy the chorus pony nailed their dance numbers fast. Even in his late sixties, when we met, he looked like a mischievous elf—about five-five, with light brown hair and impish blue eyes. He had always been slim and naturally flexible. Snappish directors and uppity stars didn't bother him either. His mother had been adamant that self-pity wastes a God-given life. "Don't be one of those crapped Irishmen crying in the beer," she'd said.

For years, he told me, he had the best life in the world, dancing on Broadway and touring the country. I could see how his crinkly grin and quick jokes had made him a popular escort with leading ladies. He and the comedienne Martha Raye sneaked out after shows to party in Harlem jazz clubs until breakfast. The actress Audrey Meadows once performed a matinee wearing Billy's sunglasses to hide an allergic reaction to her lobster lunch.

Although Billy was usually attracted to men, he fell for Frances Taylor, a gentle, willowy black dancer. She didn't return his feelings, but they stayed friends through and past her stormy marriage to jazz trumpeter Miles Davis. When Frances called in tears, he said, he dropped everything, day or night, and ran to her.

• • •

One Irish uncle, Billy told me, ran weapons for the anti-British Irish Republican Army. When the Brits caught on, the uncle immigrated to America, enlisted in the US Marines, and smuggled IRA guns through Brooklyn instead. A cousin, also named William Joyce, worked with the Germans during World War II. William mocked and threatened Allied soldiers during radio broadcasts, telling them that they would die in flames. He signed off the air with a mocking "Ha! Ha! Ha!" laugh and became known as "Lord Haw Haw."

England hanged Lord Haw Haw in 1946. Billy was doing *Carousel* at the time and Uncle Gun Runner sat him down for a talk. "There are eyes on you, Billy!"

Billy was, he said, the sainted Lord Haw Haw's namesake and descendant. There was cash to set him up as an IRA leader in Ireland. "It is your fate, your destiny," Uncle declared, "to lead Ireland as she breaks the chains of England. You are, never forget, kin to the great, martyred William Joyce."

Billy was incredulous. Give up show business? He was proud of his Irish background. But, for the record, he has no beef against the British or the royal family, "except for maybe that snotty Princess Anne." He took a pass on destiny and kept dancing.

Dancing eight shows a week is a great life while you can do it, but by the 1970s Billy's legs were aching and it was hard to keep up with the new kids. He had neither savings nor a proper home. When he did shows in New York, he roomed with a friend in Midtown who called horse races at Belmont. He felt trapped. He couldn't keep dancing, and he couldn't afford to retire.

Enter the glamorous avant-garde dancer-choreographer couple, Alwin (Nik) Nikolais and Murray Louis. They were international stars at the peak of their careers, performing with their troupe at Lincoln Center and through Europe. Their Bank Street home was a former glassmaking atelier, across the street from HB Studio. The troupe demanded all of their time and attention. A mutual friend told Billy that they needed a majordomo to pay bills, cook, and supervise the household staff.

Nik and Louis were charming. The three of them hit it off right away. Billy knew their theater world. Everyone loved his cooking, even the dishes he whipped up on hotel hot plates. And then there was his mother, Anna Joyce, to consider. He paid her bills, but she was feeble and he didn't want her to live alone in Brooklyn anymore. Nik and Louis offered to let Anna move in too.

Billy nervously agreed to a trial month. Being a dancer was the only life he'd known. What if he hated this job? And if something happened to him, what would become of his mother? He stayed in Midtown, commuted to Bank Street, and confided his fears to a lawyer in his apartment building. The lawyer offered to write Billy's will and arrange life insurance. Mrs. Joyce would have security if Billy died.

Billy, relieved, signed the papers and went downstairs to leave them under the lawyer's door. When he got back in the elevator, it dropped between floors and locked in place. The elevator filled with black smoke. There had been a fire in the basement and flames were shooting up the elevator shaft. He'd had no idea that wills were so instantly useful.

When a handsome fireman smashed in and gathered Billy in his arms, he thought he'd truly died and gone to heaven. Now all he wanted to do was get upstairs, have a cigarette, and pack. Destiny had spoken. He was moving to Bank Street.

• • •

The Nikolais-Murray home, with its marble floors, French antiques, and gilded mirrors, was a party every day and night. Billy never knew who would ring the bell or when. Ballet dancer Rudolph Nureyev and Jackie Kennedy's sister, Princess Lee Radziwill, giggling and holding each other up. The actress Monique van Vooren, tossing her fur stole to Billy as an Italian auto tycoon nuzzled her upstairs to a bedroom. The acrobat Philippe Petit, in town to sneak past security and walk a tightrope between the World Trade Center towers. French mime Marcel Marceau. Opera composer Gian Carlo Menotti. Choreographer Agnes de Mille. A Kuwaiti prince draped in feathers, turban, and sables, imperiously demanding breakfast at 5 a.m. after a night on the town.

Billy's first challenge was kicking the laissez-faire help into shape. "You simply must do something," Nik lamented. "We never know if we'll have socks or underwear." Billy folded his arms, watching, as Leon the housecleaner sashayed in at noon, made an espresso, and flicked a languid feather duster through the air.

"You're paid to clean from ten to two, Leon. The place is filthy, and you're never on time."

Leon's sculpted jaw dropped. He straightened his rippling torso. "Escuuse *me*? You panties tight? I know my yob. I'm Latino, honee. We don't do 'on time.' Get used to eet."

Leon looked like the movie star Victor Mature, Billy recalled, even as he snatched his last paycheck and stormed out. Billy hired his pal, Julio Rivera, brother of the dancer Chita Rivera. A few more changes, and the household ran like a hit show.

Billy's mother, Anna, had joined the Abingdon Square Park clique of seniors and bag ladies who seemed to have sunned on the rickety benches since the Earl of Abingdon rode by in the 1700s. My friend Auntie Mame, who now lived in the nursing home across from the park, sat in her wheelchair for hours, gabbling about her famous friends. "Indeed, Miss," Anna sniffed one day. "My Billy was a Broadway star. You aren't the only grand one in the land."

Billy went to the park to join her one afternoon in 1985, he told me, and found Anna, who had lost most of her sight, sharing a bench with a homeless woman, surrounded by cameras. Billy hurried over.

"Ma, we need to move. They're filming. That's Lucille Ball, the star of that *I Love Lucy* TV show you like so much, sitting next to you."

Anna leaned close to the woman, peering up and down, and then turned on her son. "William Joyce, did I raise you to mock a ragged, friendless soul? Lucille Ball! You should be ashamed!"

The friendless soul's shoulders heaved as she choked back her famous squawking laugh. Lucille Ball was filming *Stone Pillow*, a movie about a homeless woman. She was delighted, she told Billy. That was exactly what she wanted people to see.

"Well, for pity's sake, can't you comb yer hair, Lucille?" snapped Anna, getting up to move in a temper. It *was* her bench, after all.

· · ·

Mayor Billy, ensconced in his lawn chair, understood that New Yorkers can be fiercely lonesome. Illness, money troubles, heartbreak, audition jitters. . . . Neighbors stopped for a casual chat and often ended up pouring their hearts out. While I was divorcing my first husband in the early 1980s, I wept to Billy regularly. Billy just listened to us all. "When you get it off your chest," he said, "you feel better." The wall where he sat became known as the Wailing Wall.

Mayor Billy's constituents had started to play together by then. He organized sidewalk dinner parties complete with candlelit tables. I held a bottle of wine with one hand and a neighbor's child with the other as we crossed the highway to admire sunsets on the Bank

Street pier. It was rotting, but we knew the safe spots. Some of the hookers who worked the pier joined us, politely making small talk. When Budweiser, the cat from Automatic Slims, the corner bar, got hurt, Billy threw a fundraiser. Budweiser got a get-well card and full payment of his vet bill.

The crowd ranged from dancers and actors to a Wall Street CEO and his wife. Carol, an actress, swore that Bank Street was proof that dreams come true. She had met her husband, whom we called Prince Charming, when she hailed a cab as a neighborhood new-comer. Charming pulled up, with an open-mouthed passenger in the back seat, threw open the passenger door, and said, "Get in. *I'm* the one you're waiting for." Romance and friends like Billy, she told me, was the Village life she'd imagined as a kid growing up in the Mid-west. John Lennon and Yoko Ono no longer lived on Billy's block at 105 Bank Street, but they wandered back once in a while, Billy said. "John is OK for a Brit. He says hi. But Yoko never smiles. With all the women the guy could have, why does he bother with her?"

• • •

Parts of the Village had been rough ever since I could remember. It was best to stay away from the Hudson River blocks at night, for example, unless you were headed to one of the gay leather S&M clubs like the Mine Shaft or wanted to buy drugs or sex. Crime was part of everyday life. Kids snatched women's gold chains from around their neck. Subway cars and windows were opaque with graffiti. I had to run to the train doors when they opened to check for my stop.

When the city began sanitizing Midtown in the 1970s, ousted drug dealers, hookers, and their customers crowded in with our resident lowlifes. The Village went from having dicey spots to being the Wild West everywhere, day and night. A skinny addict held a switchblade to my stomach in broad daylight. A robber held Andrea at gunpoint. Billy ran from his kitchen waving a vegetable knife to chase a mugger away from a neighbor.

He decided to join the Guardian Angels, a volunteer civilian safety patrol. The macho Angels, patrolling in their signature red be-rets, were a reassuring sight as I walked home at night, although Billy was the only commando I ever saw in a mink coat, blowing kisses to passersby. When discomfited fellow Angels asked if he was "eccentric," he laughed. "No, darlings!" he replied airily. "I'm theatrical!"

. . .

We didn't know it at the time, but the 1980s marked the beginning of a far worse scourge than muggings on Bank Street, and, as it spread, throughout the world. On July 3, 1981, *The New York Times* published an article by physician Dr. Lawrence Altman, bearing the headline "Rare Cancer Seen in 41 Homosexuals."

My gay male friends began wasting away and dying for no reason that anyone could find. There was no pattern. Victims were in the closet, out and proud, conservative, flamboyant, rich, poor, healthy, feeble, young, and old, with nothing in common but their sexuality. Michael, my gregarious model friend in 1A, shriveled from moviestar gorgeous to shivering invalid to corpse in what seemed like weeks.

It felt like the end of days. Billy and I estimated that we lost some twenty friends between us in 1983 alone, and those were just the Bank Street residents. We didn't have the heart to try to count lost theater friends. There wasn't a week without a funeral in the Village. Priests, ministers, rabbis, and friends stammered through eulogies, everyone at a loss.

When I met a gay friend, I'd look at him carefully. Had he lost weight? Did he look tired? I learned to keep a fixed smile even as my heart dropped. Many doctors, who had no more idea of what was going on that we did at that point, were afraid too. Some saw AIDS cases only after hours or dropped them as patients entirely.

Sick men lay alone in their apartments, abandoned by terrified lovers, too weak to cook or clean themselves. Taxis would no longer stop for men with canes or walkers in the Village. Hospitalized patients lay unfed, food trays left on the floor outside their rooms by sullen aides who muttered that the men were being damned by God for their sinful ways. Bus drivers flinched and passengers fled to the rear exit as someone with purplish Kaposi's skin cancer, a common symptom, paid his fare.

"And be this the goddamned Middle Ages?" Billy railed. He was seldom angry, but when he was he always spoke in a brogue. "To let friends die like feckin' animals?" Ever the organizer, Billy set up a

Village help group. He made schedules for grocery runs, housecleaning, and doctor visits.

I wanted to join, but I was scared to death. In those days no one had any idea how people caught AIDS. From toilet seats? Water glasses? Maybe, I worried, I'll get it if they cough on me. Billy patted my hand. "Just do what you can," he said gently. "Even a phone call or a note. Anything helps."

I'd known Billy as a twinkle-eyed social companion, but he'd become a tireless fighter, with no fear for himself at all. He made vats of soup and lugged Ajax and bleach to apartments at all hours when friends vomited or soiled themselves, showering them and laundering dirty clothes and linens. He waved down cabs with gusto, so drivers would see a healthy person and stop. Once the door was open, he'd beckon to the sick friend hiding in a doorway. I never saw him flinch from a mess or be too tired to check up on one more friend.

My God, I thought. If Billy can manage like this, I can damn well do something too. I can't handle bathing someone or brushing their teeth, but I can make food and bring it over. I can take someone to the doctor or keep them company in the hospital.

Without Billy's compassionate example, I would never have been able to face down my fears. And I would have missed the last days of wonderful people I still remember with love, even if many of those memories are painful. I can't cook my favorite comfort food, pastina with butter and ricotta, anymore: the only dish I could coax into my gentle friend Louis at 74 Bank Street by the end. He had flown to rural New Mexico to tell his mother that he was dying and to say goodbye. He found her praying and sprinkling holy water across doors and windows, protecting her beloved only child from the AIDS demon. He kissed her and came back to New York without saying a word.

A group of us held his hands as he died. I went to Museum of Modern Art, where Louis had worked for decades as an administrative assistant, to set up a memorial service. His boss gazed out of his office window onto the sculpture garden.

"We can't hold it here," he said.

"Why? He was part of the place for years. Everyone loved Louis."

"You're right. We did love him. But please don't judge." He averted his eyes. "To be blunt, it's all over the staff. If we allow one service, we'll have to hold one for everyone, and the museum will look bad. The board just made a policy."

I bristled and leaned forward, ready to argue, but then looked at him closely, taking in the telltale hollow cheeks and pasty skin. He's right, I thought. There's nothing to judge.

But Billy was furious. "The goddamned effing cowards," he snapped. "They *should* have a service for everyone. It's a plague on humanity, and there's nothing to hide."

The arts world collapsed. Galleries, antique stores, and exhibitions closed. Mom cried almost every time I saw her as she reported another beloved colleague falling sick at the Met. Dance troupes, including Nik and Louis's company, fell apart like bodies with the bones yanked out.

Amid all of this, Nik developed cancer. Billy nursed him at home. Nik fought bravely, but he died in 1993. Louis Murray, his world in ruins, packed his bags, and left, traveling aimlessly for months at a time.

By 1996 he had decided to put the townhouse, too full of memories, on the market. Billy and Nik had been close, but Julio Rivera was Murray's favorite. "When I move to Chelsea," he told Billy, "there won't be further need of you." Billy's feelings were hurt, and he was also scared. Anna had died by then, but the job hadn't paid very well. He still had little saved. He had given up on finding a soul-mate to grow old with years before. What was he going to do?

That leprechaun was still on the job. As Billy paced and cried, the phone rang. It was an elderly friend, calling from the new Aurora Residence for retired performers on West Fifty-Seventh Street. A subsidized apartment share was available. Was Billy interested?

William Joyce: sailor, Broadway gypsy, IRA royalty, butler, Mayor of Bank Street, Guardian Angel, AIDS activist, and now dignified retiree, moved to a sleek apartment with glittering river views. We hammered his beloved show photos and autographed posters onto the walls. After working the lobby, he assembled a new party circle. Cigarette in one hand and martini in the other, he regaled guests with backstage gossip and dirty jokes. It wasn't Bank Street, but it was warm and full of life. My strong, twinkling friend Billy and his leprechaun lived in style for the rest of their days.

23 • Marty, Roz, and Marty's Harem

The Alaskan husky licked my face as I clutched his thick white fur, pulling myself upright. I was learning to walk, and King was my beloved friend. He stood patiently as I hugged him and kissed his nose. It was the start of a lifetime friendship with King and his people, Marty and Roz Braverman.

Marty and Roz lived in 75 Bank, on the corner of Bleecker Street, in Abingdon Court, a building that seemed very grand to me as a child because of its gardens and doorman. Marty was a short, wiry guy with a trim mustache and beard. His clothes were always pressed and immaculate, even on weekends. He wore a Carnaby cap. He was a bit shy and reserved, not one to smile first or initiate chats, but he was warm and dryly funny once my parents drew him out. They all had a lot of time to practice because I wouldn't let go of King until I was good and ready.

Rozzie, on the other hand, was a natural extrovert. She was maybe four-foot-nine, as wide as she was tall, but chic and adorable in her own way. Her jet-black hair rose in a 1960s beehive that towered over her head like a missile silo. Like all great budget shoppers, she ransacked the "thrifty" shops for unique clothes and jewelry, and always looked chic. "Can you believe fifty cents?" she'd brag as Mom, a kindred bargain spirit, admired her latest find. Rozzie's walk was a sort of swaying bounce, plump little hands tilted out, as if she were dancing down the street. When you saw Rozzie, you had to smile.

The couple had married in 1947, Marty told me, when he got out of the army. Roz worked in her uncle's furniture store while Marty started a window display business. The newlyweds lived with Roz's mother in the Bronx and then in Brooklyn. They decided to move to Manhattan in 1950.

Rozzie required a neighborhood with a kosher butcher, a beauty parlor, and a synagogue. The Village suited her. When she saw her perfect apartment at 75 Bank, the rental agent demanded immediate action. Apartments here were snooze-and-lose even back then. Marty was with a client in Philadelphia. Rozzie phoned, and he drove back as she chatted up the agent and treated him to lunch. "My wife wasn't letting him show anyone else this place," Marty said with a laugh, "if she had to bat her eyelashes all day."

Marty strode past the agent, sat on the toilet, and jiggled his legs around. "We'll take it!" he announced. After a lifetime of cramped tenement commodes, all he cared about was a comfortable toilet sit. If Rozzie liked the rest of the place, so did he. He signed the lease and drove back to Philly. And that was that.

Even a passing chat with Roz was like watching the Groucho Marx TV show *You Bet Your Life*. She'd morph from WASP matron to mincing salesman to gangster moll in one round of jokes. When she wanted my attention, she crooked a manicured finger as I passed. "C'mon heah, Dawnah," she'd croon in her gravelly Bronx voice. I'd always get the crook if my hair didn't suit her. "Your braids are uneven," she'd say. "Stand still." Her rings flashed as she held my hair with one hand, and pulled bobby pins from her beehive with the other, patting and shaping. I knew she was finished when I got a pat on the cheek. "OK. That's better." They had wanted children very badly, Marty said years later, but it wasn't to be.

Abingdon Court was also home to the actors Jack and Madeline Gilford and their sprawling houseful of kids. Marty and Roz became extended Gilford family: part of vacations, holidays, opening nights, and guests at Madeline's legendary parties, which were filled with theater folks. In 1972 Roz decided that she wanted to be in show business too. Marty took publicity photos and mailed them to agents. Two days later she got an Off-Broadway role in Lanford Wilson's play *The Hot L Baltimore*. After that she worked nonstop, doing films like *Tootsie*, print ads, and television. Directors loved her adorably dumpy figure and natural Bronx comedy as much as we did. "Woody [Allen] hides behind a screen during auditions," she laughed. "Maybe someday I'll sneak over and yell boo!"

• • •

Cancer was the one thing Rozzie's ebullience couldn't conquer. After a fierce struggle, Roz died in 1987. I, in my thirties by then, worried that Marty would languish on his own, and I wasn't the only one. Rozzie hadn't been gone a month before a circle of concerned women coalesced around him to provide advice, excursions, and food. If Marty wanted solitude, we decided, he could have it on his annual winter vacation in Florida. Up here, he was stuck with us.

It was a classic Village friendship family: one of the signature clans that, for all its informality and lack of legal ties, existed in this neighborhood, as tight as any blood kin. We called ourselves Marty's Harem. The harem members were Amanda, a petite Broadway singer/actress; Chloe, Marty's willowy young grandniece; Becky, a dancer/sculptress from down Bank Street in Westbeth; Madeline Gilford (Jack had died in 1990); and me.

The harem saw Marty and one another through everything from groceries to gallstones to gallery shows. We took turns hosting dinners several times a month and yakked endlessly in between. Young haremites wept about boyfriends as the older ones patted and clucked. Madeline and Becky gave Marty the fierce love and kicks of fellow Depression-era kids.

"Get dressed. The movie starts in half an hour!" Becky would bark at him. "We only get the senior rate at matinees. I don't want to hear about tired. We can be tired when we're dead." We swarmed thrift stores, waving finds at one another while Marty sat serenely in a chair reading the paper. "Chloe, this would look amazing on you." "Madeline, weren't you looking for a red scarf?" "Damn, I wish this was a size twelve!"

Amanda, Marty's surrogate daughter, took him to doctors and telephoned him daily. Chloe handled his taxes and banking. Roz, missed to this day at her synagogue on Charles Street, had been the religious one, but Marty missed their Sabbath dinner tradition, and so on Friday nights I brought his favorite takeout and set it on Roz's good china. Sometimes I drove him to Madeline's weekend house in my battered Toyota. Failing eyes had made driving hard for him, but he was petrified with Madeline behind the wheel. A performer since childhood, she saw no need to lose eye contact with her audience by watching the road in the middle of a good joke, turning around in her seat on the Thruway to deliver punch lines to passengers in the back. "Please, drive me up, Donna," Marty would beg. "I'll join Rozzie soon enough."

. . .

Marty loved to treat "my girls" to dinners and Broadway shows. "I did fine in business and in the stock market. What else is money for?" he said whenever we tried to pay. "You make me feel alive. You are family." We felt that way, too. He beamed when we were all dressed up and laughing together at Sardi's. He never even let us leave a tip.

One June evening in 2001 the harem was at Toon's, our favorite Bank Street Thai restaurant, when Dr. Richard MacKay walked in. He was moving to New York to work at Mount Sinai Hospital. We'd never met, but my college roommate, a friend of his from their native Richmond, Virginia, had asked me to help him find an apartment.

"Come join us and have a bite to eat on Thursday," I said when he called. "I'll show you around the Village. Maybe you'll want to look for a place down here." I was used to visitors and didn't think any more about it.

Until he threw dinner into chaos. Every female stopped in her tracks when he walked in. Rhett Butler was walking towards our table, bedroom blue eyes, killer smile and all. This guy was seriously gorgeous. Even Toon herself was staring. Becky and Madeline, veteran yentas with decades of experience, recovered first and closed in. "Richard! Pleased to meet you! You're a doctor? What kind? Does your wife like New York? How long are you staying?" They smiled more broadly with each answer; no kids, no wife, no girlfriend, two-year job commitment. Check, check, check, check. "New York's a great town!" they trilled. "You're going to love it!"

There was no hope of shushing them, so I desperately tried to distract my guest, hastily offering shrimp curry as Becky loudly hoped that he wasn't gay. "So many of the best-looking ones are, ya know," she said as Madeline rolled her eyes in agreement. Amanda and Chloe whispered together, nodding at him approvingly.

Marty looked at his unruly women and sighed, rolling his eyes. He passed dishes to Richard and asked about his medical career. Madeline nudged me, hard. "Don't you let this man go to waste," she ordered. "If you aren't interested, I know plenty of girls who would be thrilled." I'd known Richard for all of half an hour, and at that point the only thrill I hoped to have was rushing him off before they hog-tied him to a table and sent for the preacher. They waved us off to our tour with the cheery mien of cruise ship directors.

Richard and I did begin dating eventually, but only after my life, like everyone's, had blackened past imagination. He had moved into a studio apartment, uptown near the hospital, on September 8, 2001. No New Yorkers I've ever known were thinking of romance after 9/11. I certainly wasn't. I'd been downtown at work that day, had seen the attacks, and had had a breakdown. I stayed heavily sedated and unable to work.

Richard, meanwhile, was working long hours and finding it hard to make friends here in middle age, when most of his colleagues rushed home to families at night. I knew that he was lonesome and I would invite him to come to my place to watch a movie or, if I was feeling up to it, go to a jazz club, but the relationship was strictly platonic. The magic started to flicker, though, dimly and shyly, and only the harem knew. "He's a good person," Marty said with a smile when I confided in him. "Be happy and in love while you can. Hell, I wish *I* could find a sexy friend. Maybe I'd even get lucky!" After several secretive years of mutual hemming and hawing, we married in 2006. Just, I thought wryly, as the harem had decided we should in 10 minutes flat, back in 2001.

· · ·

Marty's health started to fail in the spring of 2002, and we grew afraid. King had steadied me, and now, nearly fifty years later, I steadied Marty, in his eighties, on slow walks down Bank Street and around the Village, reminiscing about stores and neighbors gone by. The harem begged him to cancel his annual Florida winter vacation. "It's too much flying," said Madeline. "The top doctors are here," Amanda pleaded. Throughout September and October we begged and bargained, but for once our collective force couldn't sway him.

I still wonder if quiet, loving Marty wanted to spare us. He died in his easy chair, book in hand, two days after he arrived in Florida. And then there was a posthumous surprise, just like Marty, still loving and open-handed even though he was gone. A letter came from a lawyer. Marty had left generous bequests to each of us. "He gave to all of you," his lawyer said when I called, "because he considered you family. You and the other ladies made him feel loved and alive, he told me. You were all gifts in his life." I was still crying when we hung up.

. . .

It was the gift from Marty, the Village clan kin of my heart, that kept me on Bank Street and paid my expenses during the bleak times after 9/11. His check arrived just as my savings had been used up, trying again and again to return to work but too injured to do so and too fragile to leave the city. His money helped Amanda and her husband adopt their two beautiful children. She tells them about Grandpa Marty and shows them his picture. I look at my photo of all of us, beaming together in a restaurant, every time I pass through my kitchen. It reminds me every day of who and what really matters in this world.

People live as long as we remember them, and Marty is always here. He sat with us as we held hands at Madeline's funeral and pushed Becky's wheelchair through museums. He watches as Amanda and I dish out food for her kids, still laughing together. Marty, Roz, and King gave me, their incredibly lucky neighbor, unconditional love and true family. When I pass 75 Bank Street, I close my eyes and thank them.

24 • The Many Kinds of Friendships

In 1965, after my fifth-grade friend, Mary Jacobs, went home, Mom pulled a book from her shelf. "Mary's mother is a genius," she told me. "A visionary." Jane Jacobs, Mary's smiling blonde mom from nearby 555 Hudson Street, had written a best-seller titled *The Death and Life of Great American Cities*, which was published in 1961. I paged through it, but read the book properly years later, when it made more sense to me.

The book is now considered a classic, an essential read not just for city planners but for anyone concerned about urban issues and the state of the American metropolis. Jane made compelling arguments for the vibrancy and social cohesion of communities with a wide mix of classes and ethnicities, along with small shops and residential buildings that encourage neighbors to form ties with one another. She led a revolt against the bulldozing of beautiful old American neighborhoods in order to erect sterile housing projects, helping to save much of historic Greenwich Village from the wrecking ball in the process.

Her book presented our 1950s Village as the ideal blend of races, classes, and businesses. Archeologists, movie stars, trust-fund babies, and college professors did indeed live next to secretaries and sanitation workers. In addition to brownstones and nightclubs, we had working docks, factories, and warehouses. Jane was right. The Village was mixed in every way imaginable. But Jane, born and raised in middle-class Scranton, Pennsylvania, missed some key Village nuances as far as I was concerned, especially for kids.

• • •

In a typical fifth-grade month, I played in a Fifth Avenue penthouse, a lesbian commune, an Off-Broadway theater/family home, a public housing project, and a flower shop where my friend's florist dad was a bookie on the side. Politics and accepted behaviors shifted wildly. I was an awkward, nerdy kid and had to stay on nervous alert, never sure when I might say the wrong thing. It happened. I managed to fit with some groups and was pitched headfirst from others.

Mine was a typical Village childhood, though. No matter what you were—rich, poor, black, white, Hispanic, mixed-race, Jewish, Christian, Muslim, Buddhist, atheist, left-wing, right-wing—some other kids had it out for you. Places like Washington Square Park, the Leroy Street pool, and the West Fourth Street basketball court were generally neutral, but class tensions and turf fights flared up all the same. We all navigated complicated friendships around here.

"You're My Kind of Catholic" Friendships

Location, location. . . . Jane never confronted the belligerent kids from Our Lady of Pompeii parochial school as she trespassed on their parish turf at Bleecker Street and Sixth Avenue. I went to rival St. Joseph's School on Christopher Street. Perhaps the Pompeii kids were mad at the world because their nuns were as mean as mine. Years later, when a former classmate told me that the first-grade nun who had threatened to beat me had ditched the black robes and eloped with the nun who had called me a slut in third grade, I could only manage a weak smile. At least my daily walk to school was well off the Pompeii track. The kids from private Little Red School House, right across the street, had to run for it every day.

"Old Village" Aristocracy Friendships

Arrivistes (anyone who moved here after birth) and native-borns like me are dreadful Village snobs, but the "my family has been here for generations" crowd beats us. Nancy, at 33–35 Bank, was fourth generation. Back in the 1920s her young grandfather played stickball with the Zito's Bread kids and the Garbers of Garber's Hardware Store. As parents developed social aspirations, they sent their kids to local private schools like St. Luke's. Descendants like Nancy, many interrelated by marriage, tolerated the rest of us but not by much.

"The Old Country" Friendships

The Bank Street melting pot had always been lumpy. My parents, born elsewhere, were college-educated bohemians, but as first-generation Italian speakers they were insiders with the Bleecker Street vendors. One smiling clerk at Rocco's Pastry always handed me cookies as she chatted with Dad "Si, si, è morte due anni mi' marito ma cosa fa? La vita è brutta." ("My husband has been dead for two years already but what can I do? Life is tough.") As she batted her eyes at my handsome father, it eventually dawned on me that her businesslike exchanges with Mom never scored me treats.

Mom read letters and wrote replies for a crinkled old lady she called Commare Peschaiola. Since Italians bestow descriptive nicknames, that meant that she was "Madam Fellow Italian Country-woman Fish Seller." Her fish store, around the corner from us, had been on Bleecker Street since the 1920s. Commare was illiterate and spoke broken English. Her store had sawdust floors and fresh snappers, trout, and octopus on shiny metal trays next to wood barrels filled with iced oysters, clams, and shrimp. I raced snails around their wicker basket as my mother smoothed the blue onionskin letters from Sicily and read aloud. Although her husband had died many years ago, Commare still wore nothing but black. When the correspondence was done, Commare would reach a veined hand into the lobster basket and select one, patting my head as I helped her wrap it in brown wax paper. She was grateful but nobody's fool. She only gave us lobsters with a claw missing that wouldn't sell.

In 1893 *The New York Times* reported that Conductor Campbell of the Bleecker Street Horse Car company had a "little complication" with an Italian cart driver at Bank and West Fourth Street: the carter, told to "Git af the track, yer Dago idjot!" threw a shovel at Campbell and leaped onto the horse car with a stiletto, "making forceful remarks in a loud tone" such as "Ah, maladetto, da fool Irish! Me killa you, sure!" As passengers shrieked, Campbell grabbed the stiletto and knocked "Pedro" into the street.

Things were no better by 1907, when the Bank Street dockworker/residents were mostly Irish. The *Times* reported that a steamship company with striking workers hired "Italian and negro" scab long-shoremen. When the scabs left for the day, our 1907 neighbors were waiting for them. "Like frightened deer the 300 strikebreakers . . . ran for the elevated railroad stations. The strikers, armed with cotton hooks, clubs, and paving stones ran . . . overtaking them at the corner of Bank and Greenwich Streets. There a fight occurred, about 400 men taking part in it . . . strikebreakers drew stilettos but before they had a chance to use the knives they were knocked down, kicked, and trampled. . . . The few who managed to escape were dragged into saloons where they were beaten and pounded." The police arrived, but "as the majority of the striking longshoremen live in the neighborhood, it was an easy matter for them to get away by dodging into the hallways along Bank Street."

"Hell Hath No Fury like Bank Street Mothers" Friendships

Jane Jacobs had kids, so she surely understood that when our women were protecting their families, peace departed the land. Scabs and police alike scrambled when the longshoremen's wives jumped into the fight, continued the 1907 *Times*. One missus, "armed with a poker, had knocked down three Italian men and was pounding them on the head." Another "was seated upon an Italian . . . pounding him with a baseball bat." Women threw iron pots and bottles from their windows. A flower pot cracked a cop's head.

Six decades later, when I was eight, Mom sent me to a second-hand bookstore next to Commare Peschiaola to sell some of our old books. When the bookseller told me to follow him to the back, I dutifully followed. He sat in a folding chair, pulled me between his opened legs, and pushed his tongue into my mouth. After slow heartbeats of frozen shock, I jerked away and ran home. Mom, eyes slitted, marched back and told me to wait outside. I watched through the window as my barely four-foot-ten mother, screamed, "Bastard! Pervert! I'll kill you!" toppling shelves and hurling books as the man crouched, arms around his head.

When Commare heard Mom, she ran over, shaking her fists and spitting on him. Two other Bank Street moms, passing by, asked me what was going on. When I told them, they too rushed in. "Try touching *my* kids, you fucking animal!" one yelled as she picked up the chair and brought it down on his head. Maybe he was relieved when the police showed up and arrested his tattered remains.

"We're So Cool" Friendships

When my parents transferred me from blue-collar parochial school to Public School 41 on West Eleventh Street, in 1965, my new class-mates came from other, very different worlds, and it showed. Jane's daughter Mary wore blue jeans and sandals. The rich Fifth Avenue kid wore preppie ski jackets with Aspen lift tickets. The hippie mom/jazz musician dad's girl wore tie-dyed sundresses. The daughter of the NYU professor had white go-go boots, and the wealthy social activist's girl sported Ukrainian peasant blouses. All of them had long flowing hair. I, with corny opera parents, who had only worn school uniforms, had smocked little-girl dresses, and patent leather Mary Janes, and a dismal pixie haircut. It didn't take them more than a day to figure out that I was a loser.

"Standing One's Ground" and Friendships

Politics was everywhere here, and friendships were often dictated by it. Politics and education went hand in hand, too. Miss Susanna Whitney, whose father had fought in the American Revolution, had lived at 58 Bank Street. She taught at my elementary school, Public School 41, from 1836 onward, and died in 1905, according to *The New York Times*, of "nervous prostration." The insular, reactionary New York City Board of Education has been prostrating educators, includ-ing me, ever since. But some steel-willed Bank Street educators, such as Lucy Mitchell, who was born in 1878, fought back and won.

In 1930, Mitchell, a wealthy, progressive spirit, finally gave up on trying to cooperate with the Board, bought an old factory building at 69 Bank Street, and founded a teacher training school dedicated to her own radical ideas. Her experiment became the world-famous Bank Street College of Education.

As a child I read *Goodnight Moon* by Margaret Wise Brown and *Where the Wild Things Are* by Maurice Sendak with no idea that they had been developed in Mitchell's Writer's Laboratory, just two doors away. Innovations like Project Head Start and *Sesame Street* are based on her work. Whenever anyone is excited and happy about learning in an American classroom, the odds are, in my opinion, that they owe it to my neighbor.

The educator Elisabeth Irwin moved to 23 Bank Street in 1912 with her companion, Katharine Anthony, and their two adopted daughters. Irwin wrote that mentally challenged youth are easy prey for gangs and that many discouraged learners had come from harsh home environments. Making these children sit rigid and silent all day, she claimed, just encouraged them to drop out. Her experiments included letting children learn at their own active pace and style. Not surprisingly, the Board of Ed considered her a dangerous, liberal heretic.

Irwin opened a progressive private school on Bleecker Street in 1932, with the help of her friend Lucy Mitchell. Although Irwin died in 1942, her creations, the Little Red School House and its upper school, Elisabeth Irwin High School, flourish to this day.

Elisabeth Irwin High welcomed students Michael and Robert Meeropol in 1956. They were the sons of Julius and Ethel Rosenberg, members of the American Communist Party in the 1930s, who were accused and convicted of conspiring to commit espionage, imprisoned in 1953, and later executed.

Ethel Rosenberg's brother, David Greenglass, was a technician at America's top-secret atomic bomb project during World War II. He obtained classified data that the Rosenbergs allegedly passed to Soviet Russia; he later testified against his sister and brother-in-law in exchange for his own life and a lenient prison term. After their convictions, Julius and Ethel were sent to the electric chair. Their orphaned sons were adopted by the Meeropols, a teaching couple at Elisabeth Irwin High. When Dad overheard local kids waiting outside the school to jeer at the boys one day, he talked them out of it.

"Companions in the Arts" Friendships

Village bars, coffeehouses, small theaters, and parks were full of actors, musicians, writers, dancers, painters, and sculptors. Even if you weren't in the arts yourself, you were expected to be culturally literate. Katharine Anthony, who remained at 23 Bank with her children after Elisabeth Irwin's death, expected no less of me.

When we met, in 1961, four years before her death in 1965, Katharine was an alert, blue-eyed woman reading in her front garden, looking pointedly over her wire glasses as Mom and I came from the library. I was staggering under a load of books because, as usual, I had refused to leave any prospects behind. Katharine, amused, asked Mom if I could stay and talk about books if she walked me home. Mom said yes, thus starting my friendship with this extraordinary neighbor.

Katharine nodded approvingly as I pulled out *Stuart Little* and *Charlotte's Web*. "And I make up my own stories," I bragged. "Wonderful!" she replied. "Write them down." I promised, with no idea that Katharine had written biographies of women like Queen Elizabeth and Catherine the Great. Neither of us could have imagined that her placid brownstone would house a serial killer in Caleb Carr's sinister 1994 novel, *The Alienist*.

When I asked Katharine about her family, she told me that she was a widow, with grown daughters who had moved away. I worried that I'd made her feel sad by bringing up her widowhood, but she said that she had learned to live with it. We sat on her steps for more talks before her death in 1965. She listened to my prattling social opinions with smiling patience, offering sage advice. "Don't take no for an answer," she said, patting my head. "If anyone says you can't do something, try again." I agreed, ignorant of her pitched battles for women's rights or her distant relative, the suffragist Susan B. Anthony.

"Just Because We Hit It Off" Friendships

Some people moved to Bank Street seeking like minds in journalism, politics, the arts, or social sciences. Some came because they were rejected back home for being gay or for marrying a person of a different race. Others were simply too high-spirited to fit in elsewhere and didn't care to try.

Al, my beloved artist neighbor in 2A, insisted for forty years that his friends were his true family. His Village circle, like Marty's Harem or Billy Joyce's AIDS helpers, was typically extraordinary: with the fierce warmth, companionship, and unconditional protection of a clan. If you were a rejected outsider in your native Iowa or Canada or the Bronx, you could always come to Bank Street. Whatever your dreams and whomever you loved, you found kinship with at least some folks here. For all its imperfections, at the end of the day Jane Jacobs had it right. America would be a far better country if it were more like the old Village.

Epilogue

And so it has gone and will keep going. Just as I have, people of all sorts play, weep, argue, court, and work to make a meaningful life for themselves on Bank Street. Love and dreams are eternal. Young people in their twenties and thirties who could be my grandchildren live in 63 Bank Street with me, crowding three and four to an apartment to pay the rent.

Their Bank Street, factories now apartments, grocers and bakeries now glossy boutiques, investment bankers in apartments that truck drivers once rented, would astonish the elderly neighbors of my childhood. That awful 1960s park on the corner where children broke their legs is remodeled and packed with children whose falls are now cushioned by thick rubber matting. Even shabby old Abingdon Square Park, across the street from the playground, has had a makeover; the World War I doughboy statue moved; the marble horse trough, my little concrete sandbox, and dented metal box swings gone; lovely flowerbeds now delighting the eye.

I savor the energy and enthusiasm of my young neighbors. Some want to know the stories I've collected and we talk. I've become the old local insider. I laugh when I think of what Joe the dockworker or Tom the iceman would think of these newcomers. They disapproved of anything and anyone past World War II, giving me and my friends dirty looks as we walked by with bell-bottomed jeans and long hair in the 1960s. Their jaws would drop as these kids, their great-grandchildren's age, walk down the street, eyes down, texting their friends. They'd poke their lips out as the new arrivals buy IKEA furniture and throw it away when they leave. (I don't blame them. Bedbugs are everywhere now, and I fight my lifelong reflex to cart street stuff home.)

I made snarky fun of weekend hippies in my teens. Today, the young residents laugh at the tourists who climb out of tour buses and line up for Magnolia Bakery cupcakes. They chat with Tish, now in his nineties, who has tag sales on the stoop. He does well, draping sequined dresses and feather boas from his nightclub act across the wall, plus donations like my ancient Barbie dolls. He makes a point of hand-delivering his rent check to his building's management every month. "Hi, I'm not dead yet," he announces as he sashays through the door.

My young neighbors have amazing dreams: to create socially conscious investments, to stop global warming. I poured wine for a 63 neighbor as she drooped in my living room, sure, after a divorce and a career swerve, that she would never find love or a fulfilling job. I looked at this young beauty who sparkled with life, even with tears in her eyes. "You will," I promised her. "You'll find that person and that life." She did, and I smile as we keep up our friendship.

Sometimes all I can do is listen. A young man from India in 2C, with thick black eyelashes, as beautiful as a prince, lost his Wall Street job when the economy tanked and reluctantly packed for home. I averted my eyes and hurried down the stairs as he hugged a crying girl on our landing. He had confided, one sad evening, that his high-caste parents in India were determined to arrange a suitable Hindu marriage, and he felt compelled to obey them. He would never know, he lamented, if he could have been happy with this American girl.

The celebrated twentieth-century essayist E. B. White wrote that native New Yorkers give the city grit and character and that the New Yorkers who move here seeking fame or greatness give the city energy. He was right. And everyone who arrives, whether by birth like me or under a border fence or on a jet plane, makes their own story on their own Bank Street. They are the ever-changing present, brushing the past and floating on. Time whirls around them too. Every street in America is a Bank Street in its own way. Neighbors have stories to recount and lessons to teach. Their kindness can fill the gaps left by biological family. It took me years to appreciate how all of these strong Bank Street hearts and minds have opened me to the world. All I've ever done, as anyone can do, is open my eyes and my heart and listen.

Acknowledgments

This book started out a lifetime ago as nosy fascination with the neighbors. The diverse panoramas of American history emerged as I dug into the origins of Bank Street and the forces (yellow fever epidemics, immigration, the Great Depression, Prohibition, the Industrial Revolution, the Harlem Renaissance, education reform, American communism, the Cold War, women's liberation, AIDS, among others) that have shaped the lives of Bank Streeters past and present. As I wrote, I also started to realize that in ways both dramatic and subtle, many of them had rescued me from much of the carnage (and whopping psychiatrist bills) I might have incurred as a small, unarmed combatant in my talented, sensitive, but unstable parents' bohemian battles. My neighbors could easily have looked the other way but they whisked me away and graced me in their own inimical styles. And for that, sweeping thanks and gratitude to the people in this book.

The blazing star of all thanks goes to Constance Rosenblum. It was truly my luckiest day when Connie wrote the *Times* article on my stories that kicked everything off. She went on to become an insightful editor, a How-To-Survive-Writing-A-Book mentor, and a wise friend with a wry sense of humor.

Steve Ross, agent extraordinaire, has stuck with me through thick and (all too frequently) thin with support on all levels. I thank Charles Kopelman, a Village clan friend, for introducing us.

Editor Clara Platter, Sarah Bode, Adam Bohannon, Martin Coleman, Veronica Knutson, Betsy Steve, and the staff of NYU Press have handled some serious turbulence and setbacks that often got in the way of this book with tact and professionalism.

At various points, editors Andrea Chapin and Joe Gilford wrestled reams of awkward, unstructured mess into actual stories with humor and panache. May the Story Arc Be with You, always. Joe the neighbor also gets a shout-out as my memory-jogging "Hey, Joe, do you remember . . . ?" Bank Street and theater clan brother.

Andrew Berman encouraged this project from the start. He and the staff of the Greenwich Village Society for Historic Preservation strive to support our rich history and to help us fend off the ill-advised developments that have ruined so many Bank Streets.

Neighbor Graydon Carter reached out and read an early version of the book. His kind support and encouragement made the manuscript sparkle with a bit of borrowed glamour.

Professor James Ryan of Texas A&M University shared his formidable expertise on Earl Browder, the Browder family, and the intricacies of requesting FBI files. It is completely thanks to him that Mrs. Swanson's story emerged.

Christopher Jones and the staff of the Grinnell College Libraries Special Collections & Archives shared photos and journal entries that gave texture and depth to my search for John Kemmerer.

Michael Tanner inherited his great aunt Marion's compassion and his father's lively wit—one hell of a combination. His kind praise for the Auntie Mame story came when I most needed a lift.

Irene Frydel gets the Lifetime 63 Bank Street/Opera/You Name It/Friend Award for countless blessings, including never telling me to go jump in the Hudson River no matter how richly I deserve it.

Marie McMahon Earle, the sparkling "Bank Street Girl" of apartment 5A, has gifted lucky me a lifetime of friendship as well as encouragement on this project.

Maestro Vincent LaSelva and his wife Helen put both my young parents' struggles in the 1950s opera world and their complicated characters into perspective, managing to be gentle, honest, and fair.

There is a lifetime's worth of Bank Streeters and Villagers and writing friends, some of whose stories may not have made it into the book as they deserved but who cheered my project on over wine, espresso, chocolate cake, Scrabble, and dog walks: Phyllis Andriani, Walter Casaravilla, Geraldine Claps, Nancy Cooper, Katie Dykstra, Lisa Gilford, Tami Gneissen, Eric Goss, Nancy Hoffman, Rose Iacovone, Phyllis Jenkins, Regina Kolbe, Sandra D'Alfonso Molé, Dorothy Murphy, Toon Preechathammarach, Addie Richter, Joy and Roger Smith, Becky Stein, Claire Tankel, Tish Touchette, and my raucous Los Tacos No. 1 pals in apartment 1B: Christian, Kyle, and Tyler.

Ellen Williams's Greenwich Village Grapevine group swaps memories of our intertwined lives online while her astounding collection of Village photographs prove that we really did have street peddlers and a pony farm, among other magical things. Special thanks to Anita Isola for gifting a new generation of friendship from her grandmother, my family's beloved Commare Peschiola.

The praise of the fabulous Albucher brothers, Marty and Larry, wafted Hollywood dreams, while Bob Gookin dispensed ruefully accurate advice like "If you are grumpy, overlooked, and ignored, you truly are a writer" from the west coast.

Congregation Darech Amuno on Charles Street embraced this teary shiksa who wandered in one evening and shared their Rosalyn Braverman of blessed memory with me. Kevin Walsh graciously helped a stranger. Gretchen Crary is amazing.

No one gets through this many decades without those rock-solid friends and family you can call from the police station at 4 a.m. Without these allies, there would be no book, period. Amy, Angela, Andrea and Jerry, Amanda, cugina Barb and figlie, Barb "Roomie" and family, the Carranza family, cugini Carol and Billy and figlie, Carole and Denise, Cheryl, Cindy and Steve, Dan, Edmond and Amy and Chloe, the Fogal family, Jenny and Joel and Hallie, Larry, Lilly and Alan, cugina Lola, Marines, cugini Marisa and John, Mary Ann and Brock and family, Matthew, Melissa, Michelle, Sue and Milt. My beloved famiglia in Italy. If I forgot to thank you, it is entirely my fault. Please forgive me.

I am hugging our entire Jim Thorpe, Pennsylvania posse, our ebullient hiker/kayaker/world trotting friends and neighbors who opened their hearts to two New Yorkers and a cranky dog. You should all be so lucky as to be a "Chunker By Choice."

And, first, last, middle, and forever, Richard.

Works Consulted

Books

Amato, Anthony, with Rochelle Mancini. *The Smallest Grand Opera in the World*. iUniverse, 2011.

Anthes, Bill. *Native Moderns: American Indian Painting, 1940–1960*. Durham, NC: Duke University Press, 2006.

Beard, Rich, and Leslie Cohen Berlowitz, editors. *Greenwich Village: Culture and Counterculture*. New Brunswick, NJ: Rutgers University Press, 1993.

Broyard, Anatole. *Kafka Was the Rage: A Greenwich Village Memoir*. New York: Vintage, 1997.

Carr, Caleb. *The Alienist*. New York: Random House, 1994.

Crater, Stella, and Oscar Fraley. *The Empty Robe: The Story of the Disappearance of Judge Crater*. New York: Dell, 1964.

Damaskin, Igor, with Geoffrey Elliott. *Kitty Harris: The Spy With Seventeen Names*. London: St. Ermin's Press, 2001.

Dennis, Patrick. *Auntie Mame: An Irreverent Escapade*. New York: Vanguard Press, 1955.

Ellis, Edward Robb. *The Epic of New York City: A Narrative History*. New York: Kondansha International, 1966.

Jacobs, Jane. *The Death and Life of Great American Cities*. New York: Random House, 1961.

Jordon, Richard Tyler. *But Darling, I'm Your Auntie Mame! The Amazing History of the World's Favorite Madcap Aunt*. New York: Capra Press, 1998.

Kemmerer, John. *Along the Raccoon River*. Mount Vernon: The Press of A. Colish, 1978.

Kisseloff, Jeff. *You Must Remember This: An Oral history of Manhattan From the 1890s to World War II*. New York: Schocken Books, 1989.

Kuralt, Charles. *Charles Kuralt's America*. New York: Putnam, 1995.

McDarrah, Fred W., and Patrick McDarrah. *The Greenwich Village Guide*. Chicago: A Cappella books, 1992.

McEvoy, Dermot. *Our Lady of Greenwich Village: A Novel*. New York: Skyhorse Publishing. 2008.

Meerpol, Robert, and Michael Meerpol. *We Are Your Sons: The Legacy of Ethel and Julius Rosenberg*. New York: Houghton Mifflin, 1975.

Miller, Terry. *Greenwich Village and How It Got That Way*. New York: Crown Publishing, 1990.

Moore, Honor. *The Bishop's Daughter: A Memoir*. New York: Norton, 2008.

Moscow, Henry. *The Street Book: An Encyclopedia of Manhattan's Street Names and Their Origins*. New York: Fordham University Press, 1978.

Mostel, Kate, and Madeline Gilford, with Jack Gilford and Zero Mostel. *170 Years of Show Business*. New York: Random House, 1978.

Myers, Eric. *Uncle Mame: The Life of Patrick Dennis*. New York: St. Martin's Press, 2000.

Ryan, James G. *Earl Browder: The Failure of American Communism*. Tuscaloosa: University of Alabama Press, 1997.

Stokes, Isaac Newton Phelps. *New York Past and Present: Its History and Landmarks, 1524–1939*. New York: Plantin Press, 1939.

Strausbaugh, John. *The Village: 400 Years of Beats and Bohemians, Radicals and Rogues, a History of Greenwich Village*. New York: HarperCollins, 2013.

Tofel, Richard J. *Vanishing Point: The Disappearance of Judge Crater, and the New York He Left Behind*. Lanham, MD.: Ivan R. Dee, 2004.

Valenti, Angelo, *The Bells of Bleecker Street*. New York: Viking Press. 1969.

Ware, Caroline Farrar. *Greenwich Village, 1920–1930: A Comment on American Civilization in the Post-war Years*. Berkeley: University of California Press, 1994.

Wetzsteon, Ross, *Republic of Dreams: Greenwich Village: The American Bohemia, 1910–1960*. New York: Simon & Schuster, 2002.

White, Norval. *New York: A Physical History*. New York: Atheneum, 1987.

Articles

Ryan, James G. "Socialist Triumph as a Family Value: Earl Browder and Soviet Espionage." *American Communist History* 1, no. 2 (2002).

Wilson, Mary Louise. "Village Life: Three Decades of Looking Through the Rear Window." *The New Yorker*, March 25 and April 2, 2001.

Oral Histories

Calvi, Alberto. Interview by author. Tape recording. New York City. July, 2001.

Gilford, Madeline. Interview by author. Tape recording. New York City. August 4, 2001.

Heineman, Bernard. Interview by author. Tape recording. New York City. January 23, 2002.

Joyce, William. Interview by author. Tape recording. New York City. January 10, 2004.

Murphy, Dorothy, and Marie Earle. Interview by author. Tape recording. New York City. February, 2004.

Government Reports
New York City Landmarks Preservation Commission. Greenwich Village Historic District Report, 1969. pp. 327–336. https://www.gvshp.org/_gvshp/pdf/Greenwich%20Village%20Historic%20District%20Designation%20Reports%20Vol%201%20and%202.pdf.

United States Department of Justice, Federal Bureau of Investigation. File number NY-100-25693. Subject: Earl Russell Browder.

United States Department of Justice, Federal Bureau of Investigation. No file number on cover sheet. Subject: Rose Euler Browder.

United States Department of Justice, Federal Bureau of Investigation. File number NY-100-321. Subject: William Browder.

Website
"A Native American Treat." *The Aesthete Cooks*, March 14, 2010, https://the-aesthetecooks.wordpress.com/2010/03/14/a-native-american-treat/.

Film
Scheinfeld, John, and David Leaf, dir. *The U.S. vs. John Lennon*. DVD. Santa Monica: Lionsgate, 2006.

Play
Gilford, Joe. *Finks*. New York: Dramatists Play Service, 2013.

Archival and Unpublished Material
Bendtsen, Franz. *T-CLP, Billy Rose Theatre Division, New York Public Library for the Performing Arts.

Joyce, William. "Memoir: chapters twenty-eight through thirty-two." Unpublished manuscript, 1990.

Kemmerer, John. Journals. Grinnell, Iowa. Grinnell College Libraries Special Collections & Archives.

New York City Municipal Archives, ground floor, folders, Book 73.

Index

Photo plate images are indicated by p1, p2, etc.

Abbott, George, 182
Abingdon Court, 190
Abingdon Square, 44
Abingdon Square Park, 5, 147, 148, 185
Abzug, Bella, p13, 15, 149–50; Florio, L., and, 151–54; running for Congress, 154; Vietnam War protested by, 151
Abzug, Martin, 149, 153
Addie, 95–96
Adler, Polly, 164
African Americans, 72–73
AIDS epidemic, p15, 55, 187–88, 189
alcoholism, 16, 57
Alexandria Quartet (Durrell), 111
Algonquin Hotel, 109
Algonquin Round Table, 164
Alice in Wonderland (Carroll), 40
The Alienist (Carr), 202
Along the Raccoon River (Kemmerer, J.), 111–12, 114, 118
Altman, Lawrence, 187
Amanda, p17, 192, 193, 194, 195
Amato, Annie, 20, 21
Amato, Sally, 19, 20, 22
Amato, Tony, 19, 21, 23
Amato Opera, p2, 19, 23, 30; backstage at, p3; Florio, L., directing at, p4; Florio, L., running lights at, p5; The Marriage of Figaro production

by, p6, p7; opening of, 35; orchestra at, p3; rehearsing Hansel and Gretel at, p4
American Communist Party, 3, 46, 53, 201
American Museum of Natural History, 131
American Revolution, 61
Andrea, 80, 83, 84, 85
Angela's Ashes (McCourt), 110
Animal House (1978), 96
Anne (Queen), 61
Anthony, Katharine, 7, 201, 202
Anthony, Susan B., 202
Arbus, Diane, 74, 92
Arkin, Alan, 7, 93, 97
Around the World With Auntie Mame (Dennis), 145
arson, 73
Art Forum (magazine), 40
artistic dreams, 16
art school, 70, 71
Ashcan School, 127, 173
Astor, Mary, 129
Asylum Street, 61
As You Like It (Shakespeare), 42
atom bombs, 170, 201
Auntie Mame (Dennis), 140
Austria, 100, 105
Automatic Slims, 186

Ava (daughter of Sabine), 72, 73, 75, 78–79
avant-garde theater, 54

Bacall, Lauren, 92
Bach, Johann Sebastian, 122
Backstage (magazine), 45
Baldwin, James, 111
Ball, Lucille, 111, 148, 185
Balthazar (Durrell), 111
Bancroft, Anne, 94
Bank of New York, 3
Bank Street College of Education, 11, 200
Bank Street Theater, 92
Bar Harbor, 123
Barrymore, Ethel, 142
Barrymore, John, 116
Baryshnikov, Mikhail, 81
Beatrice Inn, 160
Beauvoir, Simone de, 99
Bell, Alexander Graham, 91
Bellevue Farm, 61
Bell Telephone research laboratory, 14
Belushi, John, 96
Benchley, Robert, 131
Bendtsen, Franz, p9, 40–41, 54, 56; acting career of, 42–43; decline in behavior of, 44
Berghof, Herbert, 93
Berle, Milton, 164
Bernstein, Leonard, 23
Bickers, Grace, 56–57, 58–59, 162
Bikel, Theodore, 7–8, 93, 95
Bizet, Georges, 21, 24
blacklisting, 136
Bleecker Street, 9, 11, 12, 74, 190, 198
Bleecker Street Horse Car company, 198
Bloomingdale's, 38

La Bohème (Puccini), 19, 23, 25
Bolshoi Ballet, 81
Boston University, 66
Bowery Boys (gang), 168
Bowie, David, 81
Braverman, Marty, p16, 30, 190–91; gifts of, 195; harem of, p17, 192, 194, 202
Braverman, Roz, p16, 30, 190–92
Bridges, Jeff, 94
Broadway, 28, 30, 193; Bendtsen and, 43; directors, 99; George and Gloria on, 122; gossip, 117; Joyce, B., on, 182; Off-Broadway, 54, 196; openings on, 102
Brooklyn Academy of Music, 26
Brooklyn Dodgers, 13
Brooklyn Heights, viii
Brooklyn Navy Yard, 13
Brooks, Louise, 146
Brooks Brothers, 159
Browder, Earl, p9, 46, 47; American Communist Party and, 53; surveillance of, 48, 51
Browder, Margaret, 46
Browder, Rose, 46, 48–51, 53
Browder, William, 46, 48–51, 53
Brown, Margaret Wise, 200
Buddhism, 141, 142, 146
Bullock, Edward, 172
Bullock, Elizabeth, 172
Burn, Charles, 167–68
Burn, Frank, 168
Burrows, Abe, 182
Butler, Rhett, 193
butterflies, 28, 130, 131, 133
Bye Bye Birdie (1963), 92

Caballé, Montserrat, 27
Café La MaMa, 54
Cage, John, 94

Callas, Maria, 26
Calvi, Al, p10, 98–99, 106; Austria
    and, 100; brain damage of, 107;
    Cooper Union, 101; Corky and,
    104; ex-girlfriends of, 103; family
    of, 102, 105; Moradei and, 102–3
cancer, 39, 175, 191
Cape Cod, 72
Capote, Truman, 40
Captain Kangaroo (television show),
    172
Carmen (Bizet), 21, 24
Carousel (Hammerstein), 183
Carr, Caleb, 202
Carroll, Lewis, 40
Caruso, Enrico, 128
Casa Di Pre, 8
Catch-22 (1970), 136
Cather, Willa, 117
Catskill Mountains, 136
Cavalleria Rusticana (Monleone and
    Mascagni), 29
Cayce, Edgar, 40
CBGB, 81
Cedar Tavern, 101
Chamberlain, Alexander F., 118
Chamberlain, Ruth, 116, 118
Charles Street, 192
Chatty Cathy dolls, 24
Chelsea Market, 4
Chicago College of Performing Arts,
    42
children, 64; of Bank Street, 144;
    chorus of, 23, 24, 25, 145; in Green-
    wich Village, 10, 36; solo for, 24;
    staging complications for, 29
Chloe (daughter of Sabine), 72, 73, 75,
    76, 77, 78
chorus, 19, 26, 30; children's, 23,
    24, 25, 145; Frydel, J., joining, 36;
    makeup charts for, 25; master, 28;

    of Metropolitan Opera, 24, 36;
    women, 25
Christopher Street, 123, 135, 197
civil rights, 150
Civil Rights Act of 1964, 56
Clapton, Eric, 96
Coats & Clark, 7
cocaine, 81
Cocoon (1985), 136
Colbert, Claudette, 129
Collyer brothers, 59
Columbia University, 117, 149
Commerce Street, 35
Communist Party of America, 47,
    48
Communists, 3, 45–46, 152
Coney Island, 169, 181
Congress, 154
Connecticut, 106
Conrad, Joseph, 116
Cooper, Gary, 78, 129, 149
Cooper Union, 101
Corky (dog), 39, 104, 105
Cornbury (Lord), 61
Coward, Noel, 130
Cracker Jack candy, 134
Crater, Joseph, 163, 164–65, 167;
    aficionados of, 169; gangs and, 168;
    life insurance policies of, 166
Crater, Stella, p14, 163; *The Empty
    Robe*, 164; Kunz, C., and, 166–67;
    life insurance policies of husband,
    166; in Maine, 165; mourning loss
    of husband, 169
Crystal, Billy, 96
Cuba, 131
Cunningham, Merce, 92

Daily News (newspaper), 25, 40
The Daily Worker (newspaper), 50
Daltry, Roger, 111

Damn Yankees (Wallop and Abbott), 182
Dan (newly divorced man), 37
Dane (Thai TV celebrity), 16
Danforth, William, 128
David Copperfield (Dickens), 115
Davies, Marion, 129
Davis, Miles, 182
Dead Rabbits (gang), 168
Deane (single woman), 37
The Death and Life of Great American Cities (Jacobs, J.), 196
Defoe, Daniel, 115
deinstitutionalization, 61
Delta Airlines, 159–60
De Niro, Robert, 94
Dennis, Patrick, 140, 143, 145, 147
Desmond, Norma, 85
Diamond, Legs, 168, 169
DiBrioni, Francesca, 19
Dickens, Charles, 115
Diesel, Vin, 92
Dillard, Annie, 112
discos, 81
Divorce Italian Style (1961), 103
dockworkers, 198
Dr. K., 37
Doris, 73, 74, 77
Dos Passos, John, 3, 173
Dotto (television show), 171
Dreiser, Theodore, 117
Durrell, Lawrence, 111

Earl Browder (Ryan), 46
Elaine, 75, 78
Elisabeth Irwin High School, 134, 135, 201
Ellis, Emil, 166, 167, 168, 169
The Empty Robe (Crater, S.), 164
Erebus odora butterfly, 130

Fanny, 143–44
Farmer Green Jeans (fictional character), 172
Farrar, Geraldine, 128
Faulkner, William, 56
Federal Bureau of Investigation (FBI), 3, 4, 45, 46, 47, 53; agents, 48; files on Browder family, 49; informant from, 51; wiretaps by, 94
Feldman, Min, 8
Feldman, Saul, 8
Ferrucci-Good letter, 168–69
Fiddler on the Roof (Stein), 93, 182
Fifth Avenue, 165, 196
Finian's Rainbow (Harburg), 181
Fitzgerald, F. Scott, ix, 43
Florio, Ann, 18, 19, 20; backstage at Metropolitan Opera House, p5, p8; giving birth, 22; singing voice of, 21
Florio, Donna, p3, p4, p8, p13, p15, p17. *See also specific topics*
Florio, Larry, 18, 20, 21, 73; Abzug, B., and, 151–54; directing at Amato Opera, p4; leaving opera, 27; Metropolitan Opera and, 26; running lights at Amato Opera, p5
Forbes, Esther, 7
Frank, Melvin, 182
Freud, Sigmund, 141
Frydel, Annie, p9, 22, 30, 74; accused of Satanism, 62, 65; building management hassling, 38–39; cancer and, 39; in *The Marriage of Figaro*, p6, p7; money scarce for, 36; Sabine painting mural for, 72; sneezes of, 35
Frydel, Irene, p8, p9, 21, 26, 30, 35, 36–37, 38; accused of Satanism, 62, 65; Boston Strangler and, 108;

Lena and, 63–64, 66; living in Vermont, 67, 68

Frydel, John, p9, 21, 22, 35; accused of Satanism, 62, 65; backstage at Metropolitan Opera House, p8; building management hassling, 38–39; living in Vermont, 67, 68; Metropolitan Opera joined by, 36; money scarce for, 36

Frydel, Margie, 35

Frydel, Sally, 35

Fulton Fish Market, 109

Funny Girl (Lennart), 122

A Funny Thing Happened on the Way to the Forum (Shevelove and Gelbart), 136

Gabrielle (Maman), 143–44, 146

Gagarin, Yuri, 41

gangs, 168, 169

Garber's Hardware Store, 197

gay marriage, 7

gay men, 15, 123, 187

Gelbart, Larry, 136

General Electric, 7

Gershwin, George, 142

GI Bill, 35

Gilbert, William Schwenck, 143

Gilford, Jack, 4; HUAC and, p11, 135–36; in Metropolitan Opera, 134

Gilford, Madeline, p11; childhood of, 137; funeral of, 134; HUAC and, 134, 135–36; supportive nature of, 138

Ginny, 160

La Gioconda (Ponchielli), 27

Girl Scout cookies, 37

Giuliani, Rudi, 82

Glenn (musician friend), 57–58

Gloria, 122

"God Save the Queen" (Sex Pistols), 86

Golden Notebook (Lessing), 111

Golden Stair Press, 91

Goodman, Effie, 176

Goodnight Moon (Brown), 200

Gorham, Jane, 41

Grandma, 24, 40, 48, 55

The Grapes of Wrath (Steinbeck), 59

the Grateful Dead, 96

greasers, 12

Great Crash, ix

Great Depression, 3, 47, 142, 143, 152

Greenglass, David, 201

Greenwich Avenue, 7, 8, 9

Greenwich Village, viii, 4, 20, 35, 38, 155; AIDS epidemic in, 187; arson in, 73; bars in, 56; childhood in, 197; children in, 10, 36; gay Village hierarchy, 123; heart of, 163; mental illness and, 65; in 1950s, 196; overrun with venture capitalists, 170; Paine in, 61; puberty in, 29; Sabine and, 70; in 1798, 3; street smarts from, 13, 69; uproar of 1960s and '70s in, 37

Grey Gardens (Wright), 176

Grimes, Tammy, 95

Grinnell College, 112, 115, 116

Guardian Angels, 186

Guys and Dolls (Burrows and Swerling), 182

hallucinations, 68

Hamilton, Alexander, 3

Hamilton, George, 122

Hammerstein, Oscar, II, 183

Hansel and Gretel (Humperdinck), p4, 23, 28, 108

Harbach, Otto, 182

Harburg, Yip, 181
Harding, Warren G., 92
Hardy Boys books, 37
Harlem, 19, 20, 59, 182
Harlem Renaissance, 91
Harris, Kitty, 51–52, 52–53
Harrison, George, 94
Harrison, Rex, 95, 97
Hart Island, 169
Harvard, 112, 116
HB Studio, 13, 93–94, 183
Hearst, Patty, 84
Hearst, William Randolph, 129
The Heart Is a Lonely Hunter (Mc-
Cullers), 110
Heineman, Bernard, Sr., 130
Heineman, Bernard ("Jack") Jr., 95,
127–28, 170; American Museum of
Natural History and, 131; liberal-
ism of, 132; passions of, 130
Heineman, Ruth, 127, 131
Heller's Liquors, 8, 176
Hemingway, Ernest, 111
Hemingway, Margaux, 81
Hendrix, Jimi, 96
Hepburn, Audrey, 93
heroin addiction, 14, 80, 85, 142
High Noon (1952), 149
hippies, 10, 12, 203
Hitchcock, Alfred, 173
Hitler, Adolf, 48, 152
hoarding, 58
Hoboken, New Jersey, 18
Holden, William, 85
Holiday, Billie, 142
Hollywood, 92, 138
Hong Kong, 51
Hoover, J. Edgar, 47–48, 49, 50–52
Hopper, Edward, 92, 127, 162, 173
Horizons (magazine), 40
The Hot L Baltimore (Wilson, L.), 191

House Un-American Activities
Committee (HUAC), p11, 4, 134,
135–36
Hudson Dusters (gang), 168
Hudson River, 3, 12, 14, 71, 73, 91, 186
Hudson Street, 12
Hughes, Langston, 3, 91
Humperdinck, Engelbert, p4, 23,
108
Hurrah's, 81
hustlers, 12, 123

Iacovone, Tom, 131–32
Ibsen, Henrik, 43
"I Have a Dream" speech (King), 136
Internal Revenue Service, 147
Irish Republican Army (IRA), 182–83
Irwin, Elisabeth, 201
Irwin, May, 128
Israel, 8

Jacobs, Jane, 196, 199
Jacobs, Mary, 196
Jagger, Bianca, 81
Jagger, Mick, 96
Jakarta, 51
Jamaica, 130
Jamaica and Its Butterflies (Heine-
man Sr.), 130
Jefferson Airplane, 38, 96
Jimmy, 72–73, 77
Johnny Tremain (Forbes), 7
Johnson, Lyndon B., 56
Jones, Grace, 81
Jones Beach, 30
Jones Street, 57–58
Josh (sick child), 10–11
Joyce, Anna, 183, 184, 185
Joyce, Billy, 13, 30, 181, 189, 202; AIDS
epidemic and, 187–88; Ball and,
185; on Broadway, 182; fundraiser

for cat by, 186; moving to Bank Street, 184
Joyce, James, 54, 116
Joyce, William, 182–83
Julius Caesar (Shakespeare), 42
junior-high graduation, 153
Justine (Durrell), 111

Kahlo, Frida, 70
Kazan, Elia, 136
Kemmerer, John, p10, 3, 6, 56, 108–9; *Along the Raccoon River*, 111–12, 114, 118; critical recognition of, 120; Grinnell College and, 112, 115, 116; moving to New York, 117–18; poetry of, 120–21; private bathroom of, 119; writing style of, 113
Kemmerer, Ruth, 108–9, 119, 120
Kennedy, Jacqueline, 176, 184
Kennedy, John, 56
Kimball, Yeffe, p15, 30, 170, 171, 172; city gardens and, 174; death of, 175–76; faking Native American identity, 176–77; Native American spiritualism of, 173; writing Native American cookbook, 175
King, Martin Luther, 136, 161
Kitching, Edith, 141–42
Ku Klux Klan, 150
Kunz, Anna, 167
Kunz, Carl, 166–67
Kuralt, Charles, 8, 15, 93, 97, 160

labor organizers, 46
landlady, 62, 63, 64, 99
Lansbury, Angela, 145, 148
Lavery, John, 54
Lawrence, D. H., 142
Lee Hand Laundry, 9
Lena, 62, 64; Frydel family and, 65; mental illness and, 66–67, 69; in

old age, 67–68; police and, 66; sister of, 63, 64
Lenin School, 51
Lennart, Isobel, 122
Lennon, John, 4, 94, 97, 186
Leon, 184
Leoncavallo, Ruggero, 29
Leroy Street pool, 197
Lessing, Doris, 111
Levi, 71–72, 73, 77
Lewis, Sinclair, 117
Li'l Abner (Frank and Panama), 182
Lincoln Center, 24, 27
Lincoln Center Library for the Performing Arts, 42
liquor, 57
Little Golden Books, 138
Little Italy, 35, 107
Little Red School House, 134, 135, 197, 201
Loew's Sheridan movie house, 7
London, viii
Lord Haw Haw, 183
Louis, Murray, 13, 181, 183, 189
LSD, 96
Luciano, Lucky, 168
Lutheranism, 115
luxury housing, 133

MacKay, Richard, 193, 194
Maclean, Donald, 51, 52
Madame Butterfly, 22–23
Magnolia Bakery, 204
makeup artists, 26
Mama Bell, 35
Mandel, Frank, 182
Manhattan Transfer (Dos Passos), 3, 173
Manhattanville College, 19
Marceau, Marcel, 184
Marchese of Savoy, 104

Marcus, Connie, 165, 168, 169
Marie (game show contestant), 171
The Marriage of Figaro (Mozart),
    p6, p7
Marseilles French Bakery, 9
Marx, Groucho, 191
Marx Brothers, 27
Mascagni, Pietro, 29
The Masses (newspaper), 173
Masters, Edgar Lee, 117
Mature, Victor, 184
Max Factor makeup, 135
McCarthy, Joseph, 4, 136, 150
McCourt, Frank, 110, 175
McCullers, Carson, 110
McGee, Willie, 150
Meeropol, Michael, 201
Meeropol, Robert, 201
Menotti, Gian Carlo, 184
mental illness, 61, 65, 66–67, 69
The Merchant of Venice (Shake-
    speare), 42
Metropolitan Opera, 18, 19, 23, 27; *La
    Bohème*, 25; chorus of, 24, 36; Flo-
    rio, A., backstage at, p5, p8; Florio,
    L., and, 26; Frydel, J., backstage at,
    p8; Frydel, J., joining, 36; Gilford,
    J., in, 134
Michele (Sid Vicious girlfriend), 81–
    82, 83, 84
Midler, Bette, 81
Midtown, 183
Mille, Agnes de, 184
Miller, Ann, 148
Mimi (poodle), 65
Mine Shaft, 186
Minnelli, Liza, 81
Mrs. Ferrucci-Good, 167–68
"Miss Jenny Mack," 160
Ms. Schwartz, 153, 155
Mr. Helping Exterminator, 9

Mitchell, Joni, 96
Mitchell, Lucy, 200, 201
Monleone, Domenico, 29
Montero, Germaine, 119
Moore, Honor, 161
Moore, Paul, 161
Moradei, Rose, 40, 41–42, 44, 102–3,
    104
Mostel, Kate, 136
Mostel, Zero, 136
Mozart, Wolfgang Amadeus, p6, p7,
    122
Mudd Club, 81
Mulligan, Pat, 9
Museum of Modern Art, 30, 170,
    188
Mussolini, Benito, 152
My Fair Lady (1964), 95

Nancy (Sid Vicious girlfriend), 80,
    86
Nancy Drew books, 37
National Labor Relations Board, 141
Native Americans, 173, 175; Kimball
    faking Native American identity,
    176–77; living conditions of, 170
Natural Childbirth, 22
Navajo tribe, 170
Negri, Pola, 142
Nehru, Jawaharlal, 131
New Yorker (magazine), 103
New York Hospital, 21
New York Movie (Hopper), 92
New York Public Library, 114
New York Times (newspaper), ix, 8,
    30, 40, 91, 147, 167
New York University, 152
A Night at the Opera (1935), 27
Nighthawks (Hopper), 162
Nikolais, Alwin, 13, 181, 183, 189
9/11, 16, 114–15, 194, 195

No, No, Nanette (Mandel and Harbach), 182

Nostromo (Conrad), 116

nudism, 41

Nureyev, Rudolph, 28, 184

O'Brien, Frances, 19

Off-Broadway, 54, 196

O'Keeffe, Georgia, 70, 170

Onassis, Jackie, 81, 84

One Flew Over the Cuckoo's Nest (1975), 96

One If By Land, 123

O'Neill, Eugene, 142

Ono, Yoko, 4, 94, 186

On the Road with Charles Kuralt (television show), 8, 15, 93, 97, 160

opera, 18, 19, 26, 37, 103; backstage at, 22; children in, 23; Florio, L., leaving, 27; opening nights of, 21; solos in, 24

orchestra, p3, 27

Osage tribe, 170

Othello (Shakespeare), 27, 42

Our Lady of Pompeii parochial school, 197

Pacino, Al, 94

Pagliacci (Leoncavallo), 29

Paine, Thomas, 61

Palmer, Betsy, 104, 105

Panama, Norman, 182

Paradise Garage, 81

Paramount Theater, 3

parents' fighting, 110

The Parent Trap (1961), 92

Park, Abingdon Square, 142

Parker, Dorothy, 131

parochial schools, 38, 134, 197, 200

Pavarotti, Luciano, 97

Pelikan, Crystal, 98–99, 105

Perkins, Anthony, 93

Perry Street, 71

perverts, 64

Peschiola, Commare, p17, 198, 199

Pesci, Joe, 94

Petit, Philippe, 184

Philippines, 51

The Pirates of Penzance (Sullivan and Gilbert), 143

Plato, 109

Plummer, Christopher, 95, 97, 122

Poe, Edgar Allan, 91

police, 66, 84

Ponchielli, Amilcare, 27

poverty, 73, 152

Power, Tyrone, 129

Project Head Start, 200

prompters, 26

prostitution, 69

Psycho (1960), 93

puberty, 15, 29, 41

public address system, 92

public school, 16, 38, 135

Public School 41, 200

Puccini, Giacomo, 19, 24, 25, 28

Queens, 75, 106

radio broadcasters, 92

Radio City Music Hall, 182

Radziwill, Lee, 184

Rainbow Room, 30

Ramiro, 15, 44, 58, 59, 66, 81, 86

Rand, Ayn, 136

The Raven (Poe), 91

Raye, Martha, 182

Reagan, Ronald, 136

Rear Window (1954), 173

Red Scare, 4

Reed, John, 173

Rick, 30

Rivera, Chita, 185
Rivera, Julio, 185, 189
Robbins, Jerome, 135, 137
Robinson Crusoe (Defoe), 115
Rocco's Pastry, 198
Rockaway Beach, 36
Rockefellers, 47
Rockettes, 182
Rodgers, Richard, 129
Roger (artist), 16
Rogers, Ginger, 148
Rogers, Millicent, 130
Rogers, Will Jr., 176
Roosevelt, Franklin Delano, 48, 52, 152, 169
Rosenberg, Ethel, 201
Rosie, 25
Rothstein, Arnold, 168
Roxyettes, 182
Roxy Theater, 181–82
Royal Ballet, 28
Rudy, 64
Rukeyser, Muriel, 92
Russell, Rosalind, p12, 145, 146, 148
Russian Revolution, 47
Ruth, 95
Ryan, James G., 46, 48, 49, 52
Mrs. Ryan, 95

Sabine, 15, 65, 66; daughters of, 72, 73–74, 75, 76, 77, 78–79; death of, 77; Greenwich Village and, 70; home health aide for, 76; Jimmy and, 73, 77; Levi and, 71–72; medication for, 74
Sacks, Oliver, 96, 111
St. John the Divine, 161
St. Joseph's Church, 77
St. Joseph's School, 26, 36, 134, 197
St. Veronica's Roman Catholic Church, 72
St. Vincent's Hospital, 132–33
San Francisco, 91
Sartre, Jean-Paul, 99
Satanism, 62, 65
Savitsky, Bella, 149
Schiaparelli couture house, 72
schizophrenia, 68
The School for Scandal (Sheridan), 18
Schultz, Dutch, 164, 168, 169
Schwartz, Blanche, 151
Scottsboro Limited (Hughes), 91
Scranton, Pennsylvania, 196
Seduced and Abandoned (1964), 103
Sendak, Maurice, 200
Seoul, viii
Sesame Street (television show), 200
1776 (Stone), 122
Sex Pistols, 4, 80, 81, 86
Shakespeare, William, 27, 42, 43, 54
Shanghai, viii, 51
Shanvilla Grocery, 150
Shanvilla Market Grocer, 9
Shearer, Norma, 129
Sheepshead Bay, 30
Sheridan, Richard Brinsley, 18
Shevelove, Burt, 136
Sicily, 62, 67
Sid and Nancy (1986), 87
Silent Jester, 159
Sills, Beverly, 128
Silverman, Belle, 129
Simmons, 72, 119
skylines, viii
Slatin, Harvey, 170, 172, 173–74, 175, 176
Slick, Grace, 96
Sloan, John, 127
Smith, Patti, 82
Smith College, 141
S&M leather clubs, 123, 186
Social Register, 164

Social Security, 105
Socrates, 109
Sophie's Choice (Styron), 160
The Sound of Music (1965), 97
South Africa, 181
Soviet Union, 48, 51, 135
spies, 45, 51, 52
stagehands, 25, 27
stage managers, 26
Stalin, Joseph, 47, 48, 53, 152
Standard Oil, 130
Staten Island, 20
Stein, Joseph, 93, 182
Steinbeck, John, 59
Stone, Peter, 122
Stone Pillow (1985), 185
Stonewall Inn, 4, 77
street musicians, 5
street smarts, 13, 69
Studio 54, 80
Stuyvesant High School, 110, 153
Styron, William, 160
suicide, 136
Sullivan, Arthur, 143
Sunday crossword puzzle, 40
Sunset Boulevard (1950), 85
Swanson, Gloria, 85
Swanson family, 3, 45, 49–50
Swerling, Jo, 182

talking movie technology, 92
Tammany Hall, 163, 164, 165, 168
Tanner, Marion, p12, 3, 15, 139, 144;
    as Auntie Mame, 140; Buddhism
    and, 141, 142, 146; death of, 148;
    Dennis and, 145, 147; eviction
    of, 147; kindness of, 143; living
    arrangements with, 146–47; in
    old age, 142
Taylor, Frances, 182
Taylor, Prentiss, 91

Tebaldi, Renata, 26
Ten Days That Shook the World
    (Reed), 173
tenements, 7, 9, 11, 13, 14, 48, 191
Thailand, 131
The Thin Man (1934), 122
This Is New York (White), 112
Thomas, Dylan, 56
Thomas, Marlo, 111
Thousand Islands, 128
Time (magazine), 40, 45, 98
Times Square, 14, 45
Tom Sawyer (Twain), 115
Tootsie (1982), 191
Tosca (Puccini), 24, 28
Touchette, Tish, p14, 3, 4, 10, 132, 161
La Traviata (Verdi), 21
Tribeca, 81
Twain, Mark, 5, 111, 113, 115, 116, 120
Twenty-One (television show), 171

Ulysses (Joyce, J.), 54, 116
Upper East Side, 21

Van Doren, Carl, 117
Van Doren, Charles, 171
van Vooren, Monique, 184
Venona Documents, 51, 52
Verdi, Giuseppe, 21
Vermont, 67, 68
Vicious, Sid, p10, 4; death of, 83;
    heroin addiction of, 80, 85; Mi-
    chele and, 81–82, 83, 84; mother
    of, 85; Nancy and, 80, 86; suicide
    attempts by, 80, 87; tenants and,
    86
Vietnam War, 151
Village Nursing Home, 147
The Villager (newspaper), 18, 147
Virgin Islands, 75
Vogue (magazine), 176, 177

Wait Until Dark (1967), 93, 97
Walker, Jimmy, 164
Wallop, Douglass, 182
Walter, 86
Washington Square Park, 12, 13, 96, 197
Washington Street, 13
Waverly Inn, 8, 109
Waverly Place, 8, 141
weaving, 109
Weinstein, Harvey, 4, 133
Western Electric, 92
Western Electric Company, 91
West Fiftieth Street, 181
West Fourth Street, 5, 9, 57, 61
West Fourth Street basketball court, 197
Westinghouse Electric factory, 13
West Side Story, 28, 152
West Twelfth Street, 160
Where the Wild Things Are (Sendak), 200
White, E. B., 112, 204
White Horse Tavern, 56, 168

"White Rabbit" (Jefferson Airplane), 96
Whitman, Walt, 117
Whitney, Gertrude Vanderbilt, 71
Whitney museum, 71
The Who, 38
Williams, Tennessee, 56
Wilson, Lanford, 191
Wilson, Mary Louise, 173, 175, 176
wiretaps, 94
World Trade Center, 16, 184
World War I, 47
World War II, 35, 45, 48, 71, 181, 182, 203
Wright, Doug, 176

Xavier, 159

Yonkers, 52

Zecher, Alice, 3, 50
Zeffirelli, Franco, 29
Zito's Bread, 197

About the Author

Donna Florio is a lifelong resident of Bank Street in Greenwich Village. Nurtured by colorful, eccentric neighbors who taught her to "never wonder about life from the outside. Jump in!" Donna has, over the years, worked as an opera singer, a TV producer, a Wall Street executive, and an educator, and has backpacked around the world.

CPSIA information can be obtained
at www.ICGtesting.com
Printed in the USA
BVHW081200260321
603513BV00015B/1000/J